D1368122

Business Intelligence

The Savvy Manager's Guides
Series Editor, Douglas K. Barry

Web Services and Service-Oriented Architecture
Douglas K. Barry

Business Intelligence
David Loshin

Forthcoming

Semantics in Business Systems
Dave McComb

Business Intelligence

THE SAVVY MANAGER'S GUIDE

➤ | *Getting Onboard with Emerging IT*

David Loshin
Knowledge Integrity, Inc.

MORGAN KAUFMANN PUBLISHERS

An Imprint of Elsevier
Amsterdam   Boston   London   New York   Oxford   Paris
San Diego   San Francisco   Singapore   Sydney   Tokyo

Senior Editor	Lothlórien Homet
Editorial Assistant	Corina Derman
Publishing Services Manager	Simon Crump
Senior Project Manager	Julio Esperas
Production Services	Graphic World Publishing Services
Cover Design	Frances Baca Design
Cover Image	Getty Images
Text Design	Frances Baca Design
Technical Illustration	Graphic World Illustration Studio
Composition	SNP Best-set Typesetter Ltd., Hong Kong
Copyeditor	Elliot Simon
Proofreader	Graphic World Publishing Services
Indexer	Graphic World Publishing Services
Printer	The Maple-Vail Book Manufacturing Group

Designations used by companies to distinguish their products are often claimed as trademarks or registered trademarks. In all instances in which Morgan Kaufmann Publishers is aware of a claim, the product names appear in initial capital or all capital letters. Readers, however, should contact the appropriate companies for more complete information regarding trademarks and registration.

Morgan Kaufmann Publishers
An Imprint of Elsevier
500 Sansome St., Suite 400
San Francisco, CA 94111
www.mkp.com

07   5 4

Permissions may be sought directly from Elsevier's Science and Technology Rights Department in Oxford, UK. Phone: (44) 1865 843830, Fax: (44) 1865 853333, e-mail: permissions@elsevier.co.uk. You may also complete your request on-line via the Elsevier homepage: http://www.elsevier.com by selecting "Customer Support" and then "Obtaining Permissions".

Library of Congress Control Number: 2003104116
ISBN-13: 978-1-55860-916-7
ISBN-10: 1-55860-916-4

This book is printed on acid-free paper.

Contents

Foreword

In recent years, we have seen a comprehensive change in the way companies use data, evolving from simple operational processing to tactical decision support processing, culminating in the strategic use of information. The refinement of methods, tools, and approaches used in what is now called the business intelligence (BI) space has brought our industry to a point where the conventional wisdom is no longer defined in terms of the high costs of having a BI program, but rather in terms of the high costs of *not* having a BI program. Business intelligence has become critical to all organizations striving to succeed in this highly competitive global landscape. Properly planned, designed, and executed, a BI program ultimately will translate into substantial profits.

As publisher of *DM Review* (recognized as the premier publication for business intelligence), I am proud that our magazine has served as a pathway for our readers, educating them as they move their organizations toward effective strategic use of information. For more than a decade, we have provided thought-provoking and informative editorial covering strategic solutions for business intelligence across all major industries. I believe that we have been instrumental in fortifying the burgeoning BI industry. About one year ago when David first started writing columns for our magazine, newsletters, and Web sites, it seemed abundantly clear that his combination of passion, clarity of style, sense of humor, and ability to think outside the box would provide great value to our readers. My prediction has borne itself out, because David's columns and articles are among our most popular.

As well as being a good read, this book by David Loshin is an excellent source for forward-thinking companies that recognize the benefits of BI and need to gain enterprise-wide support for this strategic initiative. Now that BI has become a critical business initiative that has moved into the mainstream, the barriers to success are no longer merely technical. They are also directly related to organizational and political issues. In this industry, we are at the point where technical managers need to take a leadership role to bring to fruition the tremendous benefits of business intelligence. At the same time, business managers throughout the world need to understand enough about the technical issues so that they can truly plan a successful transition into the "knowledge age."

In this book, David provides more than just a clear breakdown of the technical topics that relate to a successful BI program; he provides the organizational insight that highlights not only *how* but—more importantly—*why*. In addition, he helps the reader answer critical questions such as the following:

- Why do we need a BI program?
- How do we characterize the value of knowledge?
- How do we build the right kind of team?
- What are the critical management issues involved?

As David states in the book, no BI program is going to be successful if the value cannot be articulated properly, and he provides the intellectual capital to help characterize the value of actionable knowledge. He also presents a stepwise approach for building the value vision, describing the mechanics required, and describing the value of information integration; it is the perfect manager's guide.

Business Intelligence: The Savvy Manager's Guide is destined to be a critical component of any successful BI project. If you are involved or soon will be involved in the development of a BI program, I strongly recommend that you buy two copies of this book: one for yourself and one for your manager! Enjoy the book!

Ronald J. Powell
Publisher/Editorial Director
DM Review

Preface

The boundary that divides business and technology is a fuzzy one, and this border erodes more and more as organizational managers recognize how integral knowledge and information management are to the bottom line. A natural development of this is the concept of *business intelligence* (BI), which (loosely defined) incorporates the tools, methods, and processes needed to transform data into actionable knowledge.

What I find curious about BI is that it is not just technology, nor is it just practices and methods. It is more a combination of the best of both the business world and the technical world—using advanced algorithms and data management techniques to better implement the way a business works. But what prevents BI programs from being successful is precisely what forms the dividing line between business and technology. If we are moving toward a business environment where profits are driven by the exploitation of information, then it is critical for those who run, or, more properly, improve, the business to understand what kinds of value lie within a company's information and how to unlock that value and transform it into profits.

But what is the best way to gain that understanding? I strongly believe the answer to that question lies in the ability to bridge the gap between the business side and the technical side. In other words, if we can enlighten technologists to the process of business rationalization and at the same time expose business clients to some of the workings of technology, we can encourage both sides to work together.

In August of 2002, I had a conversation with Lothlórien Homet at Morgan Kaufmann Publishers about a developing book series targeted at the "savvy manager." The goal of the series would be to introduce, at a high level, the critical aspects of particular technologies from the manager's perspective.

What better forum, I thought, to introduce the high-level concepts associated with BI.

Clearly, if you are reading this right now, either the title or the material has caught your attention. In other words: Either you are already a savvy manager (congratulations!) or you are rapidly on your way to becoming one (congratulations!).

What This Book Is

There is a logical sequence to understanding the basics of a BI program. This book will progress through that sequence, starting with the value of information, the mechanics of planning for success, data model infrastructure, and data preparation, followed by data analysis, integration, knowledge discovery, and finally the actual use of discovered knowledge. My goals for this book include:

- Providing a knowledge base for the decision maker to determine the value of integrating these kinds of technologies into the company.

- Providing a high-level description (i.e., not deep with technical jargon) of technical concepts targeted at the knowledgeable reader, followed by more in-depth descriptions.

- Providing summary information about technology concepts and their advantages and disadvantages.

- Providing leadership concepts associated with implementing or integrating these technical components.

- Acting as a multiple-use text that doubles as a detailed explanatory guide and as a quick reference.

- Providing a clear explanation of the *utility* of technology without trying to explain how to implement that technology.

As an example, there are some very good books on data mining and knowledge discovery that may cover some of the same topics at the high level, but whose authors then launch into an explanation of the algorithms and techniques to implement those algorithms. Just as someone watching a television doesn't need to know how to build one, a data analyst, IT manager, or business user does not need to know how to build an association rule discovery system to take advantage of the results of using one.

Each of the chapters in this book is meant to stand on its own, and although the sequence of the chapters relates to a typical implementation sequence, you should not feel constrained by that sequence. My intention is to provide a book that can be referred to for guidance during the entire process of building and improving a BI program.

Why You Should Be Reading This Book

You have probably picked up this book for one or more of these very good reasons.

- You are the Chief Information Officer of an organization who desires to make the best use of the enterprise information asset.
- You are a manager who has been asked to develop a new BI program.
- You are a manager who has been asked to take over a floundering BI program.
- You are a manager who has been asked to take over a successful BI program.
- You are a senior business executive who wants to explore the value that a BI program can add to your organization.
- You are a business staff member who desires more insight into the way that you do business.
- You are a database or software engineer who has been appointed a technical manager for a BI program.
- You are a software engineer who aspires to be the manager of a BI program.
- You are a database or software engineer working on a BI program who aspires to replace your current manager.
- You are a staff member who has been asked to join a BI team.
- You are a senior manager and your directly reporting managers have started talking about BI using terminology you think they expect you to understand.
- You are a middle-level manager or engineer and your manager has started talking about BI using terminology you think they expect you to understand.
- You are just interested in BI.

How do I know so much about you? Because at many times in my life, I *was* you—either working on or managing a project for which I had some knowledge gaps. And at the time, I would love to have had a straightforward book to consult for a quick lookup or a more in-depth read, without having to spend a huge amount of money on a technical book that only briefly addressed a topic of interest. Instead, I have a wall full of technical books that cost a fortune, and because they never really addressed my real needs, they just sit there gathering dust. So I have decided to take a stab at writing the book I wish I had had ten years ago to help me move forward in my career.

Organization of the Book

The transformation from data to actionable knowledge is a complex one, yet it is full of promise. Still, there are many issues that need to be addressed before an organization can expect success from a BI program. I am sure that there is a multitude of articles, white papers, and books extolling the virtues of BI, giving examples of use, and delineating scads of benefits; this book is not going to be one of those. I assume that someone in your organization has already recognized the value of BI and that you have embarked on the path toward building that practice. My goal is to discuss the essential high-level topics that are important to the successful BI program. In this section I detail the topics that will be discussed throughout the rest of this book.

In Chapter 2, The Value of Business Intelligence, we look at the modern view of the collection and integration of transactional and reference data as a valuable resource that can be used for analytical purposes. We introduce the savvy manager to the concept of "the value of information," discuss what are the aspects of information that make up its intrinsic value and what kinds of processing can be performed to add value to data. In this chapter, we will also look at the different kinds of analytical applications that are part of a BI program, a brief description of each of these applications, and the value that can be added through deploying these analytics.

In Chapter 3, Planning for Success, we'll look at some of the critical factors a savvy manager must know regarding the successful planning of a BI program. This includes the first important steps in achieving senior-level support and sponsorship for a BI program, building a value proposition, and exploring the partnership between the business user and the information technology development staff. In addition, we will look at how to establish and formally define success factors, measuring against those factors, and maintaining the partnership relationship between business and information technology (IT). Last, we look at issues associated with building the implementation team and how to leverage short-term tactics to ensure the continued development of a long-term BI strategy.

Chapter 4, The Business Intelligence Environment, will focus on the difference between the data environments for operational or transactional information and the data environments for BI applications, such as decision support processing and customer relationship management. The aim of this chapter is to provide the manager with a working vocabulary based on a high-level view of BI environments. We will discuss the differences between a transactional database and a data warehouse and look at the kinds of analytical applications that require alternate data architectures. The analytical environment is of little value if the information cannot be accessed by the business users. Also in this chapter, we look at online analytical processing (OLAP), along with the kinds of query and reporting requirements needed to access data, drill down through the information, and create reports. We'll also look at issues associated with data visualization.

The first step in the process of exploiting information is to model the way that information flows through an organization. There are two purposes for this: (1) Understanding an information flow provides logical documentation for the business process; (2) it exposes potential for adding value through the kinds of analytical processing we discuss in later chapters. In Chapter 5, Business Models and Information Flow, we will describe what the savvy manager needs to know about how to coordinate a business model information flow, why the traditional "assembly line" of data processing can make this difficult, and how to organize participants to cooperate in mapping and documenting these models.

The importance of data modeling in an analytical context, coupled with managing the metadata associated with that data, has evolved as a critical component of the BI environment. In Chapter 6, Data Warehouses, Online Analytical Processing, and Metadata, we will look at data modeling and the differences between the use of standard entity–relationship models versus the preferred dimensional models for data warehouse structure. As a consequence of looking at dimensional models, we also will look at OLAP, which relies on the ability to configure data in a multidimensional, hierarchical way. We also look at metadata management and different ways to represent information based on different operational or business requirements.

In Chapter 7, Business Rules, the focus is in abstracting the operation of a business process from the rules that govern that process. In other words, we can differentiate between the rules that drive a process and the generic machinery that implements those rules and, consequently, that process. We refer to the separation of business logic from logic implementation as *the business rules approach*. The simplest way to describe a business rules system is as a well-described set of environment states, a collection of environment variables, a set of formally defined rules that reflect business policies, preferences, guidelines, etc., indicating how the environment is affected, and as a mechanism for operationalizing those rules. In a business rules system, all knowledge about a business process is abstracted and is separated from the explicit implementation of that process. In this chapter, we will explore the use of business rule systems as a component of a BI strategy.

Part of the analysis process may require the integration of information from multiple sources. Sometimes, the data that we are given is not always in a pristine form, and frequently the data is delivered with no "manifest" at all. In Chapter 8, Data Profiling, we will discuss why different data sets may be more or less "usable" in their original states and tie the characterization of those states to their intrinsic value. We will then explore what the savvy manager must expect when faced with an integration process incorporating disparate data sets of dubious quality and how data profiling is a step toward adding value to that data.

When the quality of your data is suspect, how can you trust the results of any analysis based on that flawed data? Chapter 9, Data Quality and Information Compliance, centers on the importance of defining data quality expectations and measuring data quality against those expectations. We will also look at the general perception of data quality and what the savvy manager needs to know to distinguish between data cleansing and data quality.

Now that the manager has been introduced to the collection of raw data and its need for both profiling and quality assessment, the next step is to understand how information can be integrated, manipulated, and distributed to information consumers. In Chapter 10, Information Integration, we focus on different aspects of the integration process; extract, transform, load (ETL); the need to link information from multiple data sets; and ways to publish that information.

A successful BI strategy encompasses more than just the desired analytical functionality. It must also incorporate expectations about the timeliness of the applications. Luckily, there have been significant innovations in the area of *parallel processing* that allow us to decompose a lot of the processing that can then be "farmed out" to collections of computers. In Chapter 11, The Value of Parallelism, we explore parallel processing—the business case for incorporating parallelism into your enterprise, what conditions must be true to expose parallelism, and the different kinds of parallelism.

Sometimes it is valuable to take a step back from the traditional data collections that we see on a regular basis, such as customer data, product data, and sales transactions, to evaluate the integration of information in a completely different context. For example, by itself geographic data may not be of great interest, but merging customer transactions with rolled-up psychographic profiles associated with geographic data may provide insight into the how's and why's of your customers' behavior. In Chapter 12, Alternate

Information Contexts, we examine alternate information contexts—what kind of data is available, what its value is, and how to plan to integrate that information into your enterprise.

Data enhancement is a process by which to add value to information by accumulating additional information about a base set of entities and then merging all the sets of information to provide a focused view of the data. Through the accumulation of data from different sources, we can improve the overall quality of data, standardize it, and prepare it for further BI applications, such as data mining. In Chapter 13, Data Enhancement, we examine different ways to enhance data and provide some examples of the business process of data enhancement.

As an alternative to proactive BI operations, the knowledge discovery process is a means for finding new intelligence from collections of data. Although the methods discussed in this chapter have traditionally been referred to as *data mining*, that term has become overloaded and so we will use the more correct term *knowledge discovery*. Chapter 14, Knowledge Discovery and Data Mining, focuses on the business use of knowledge discovery techniques and the kinds of methods used. In addition, we will look at some of the management issues associated with this process as well as how to properly set expectations for the results of an iterative proactive process whose results may not be measurable right away.

In the Chapter 15, Using Publicly Available Data, we look at publicly available data sets, consider their value in terms of information integration and exploitation, and discuss the value of acquiring and managing this kind of data. In addition, we will briefly discuss the political aspects of collecting and manipulating public data in a way that poses questions regarding the perception of an invasion of privacy.

The last chapter of the book is dedicated as a quick reference guide for BI terminology. Each important topic mentioned in the book is given an entry in this section in summarized form for a quick refresher of the named topic.

Acknowledgments

I'd like to thank the following people for their help in making this book a reality. First, and most of all, for indulging my writing habit and encouraging me to make this a great piece of work, I thank my wonderful wife, Jill, and my children, Kira, Jonah, and Brianna. Next, without the entertaining and encouraging conversations I had with my acquisitions editor, Lothlórien Homet, I probably would never have jumped into this project the way that I did.

I would also like to thank the people who have contributed to making this a better work. Mary Jo Nott and Jean Schauer at *DM Review* and *datawarehouse.com* have provided me with the opportunity to validate a lot of my material through my online and print columns. A lot of the thought that went into putting this book together was inspired by conversations I have had with a number of the bright people I have met and talked with through my association with the Data Warehousing Institute, including Wayne Eckerson, Dave Wells, Larry English, Michael Scofield, and Steven Brobst, as well as the many people who have attended my sessions. Sid Adelman and Robert Seiner provided some valuable insights through their reading of the material, and Joyce Norris-Montanari also acted as a reviewer.

Contact Me

Whether you agree with what I discuss in this book or violently disagree, I would like to hear from you. I am always interested in hearing about successful (and unsuccessful) BI projects, especially if there are any suggestions that I can make to improve your program. Please feel free to contact me via e-mail at *loshin@knowledge-integrity.com* with any comments or questions or even just to let me know that you read the book. I look forward to hearing from you.

CHAPTER 1

Business Intelligence and Information Exploitation

Imagine that you are the sales manager for a large retail organization and that you were able, within some probability, to predict how much money each of your customers was going to spend and which products each was going to purchase over the next six months. Or, as the productivity manager, imagine that you could figure out which production teams within your organization build the highest quality products. Or imagine that, as the broker negotiating electricity generation and delivery contracts for a region of the country, you were able to predict with relative accuracy what the demand for electricity would be for the next 90 days.

Or imagine that you are in charge of managing your company's supply chain and that you could determine which of your vendors provides the highest-quality products the quickest. Or let's say you are the customer retention manager for a credit card company and you can identify customers about to cut up their credit card a month before they do so. I am sure you would agree that each of these people is in an enviable position, because each has special knowledge about a business situation that conveys some business advantage. These are just a few examples of the kind of knowledge that can be exposed and exploited through the use of business intelligence (BI).

In the last few years, the ability to create, collect, and store information has widely outpaced our ability to make significant use of that information. Yet there is significant hidden value locked away in corporate databases, waiting to be discovered and exploited. But to expose this hidden value, we must first gain an understanding of how to train ourselves and our colleagues to think about information in a different way. Instead of treating data as the raw material that fuels a 19th-century-style assembly line masquerading as

20th-century information processing, we must learn how to think about a company's data as a corporate information asset, one that can be manipulated in different ways to corporate benefit.

Why Business Intelligence?

What drives the desire for a BI program? We are led to believe that proper BI can lead to:

- **Increased profitability**—For example, according to financial consultants, in a typical retail bank portfolio, 20% of the accounts contribute profits equaling 200% of the overall return, whereas more than half of the accounts generate losses. Business intelligence can help business clients to evaluate customer lifetime value and short-term profitability expectations and to use this knowledge to distinguish between profitable and nonprofitable customers.

- **Decreased costs**—Whether it is improved logistics management, lowered operational costs (such as decreased warehousing and delivery costs), or a decreasing of the investments required to make sales, BI can be used to help evaluate organizational costs.

- **Improved customer relationship management (CRM)**—This is basically a BI application that applies the analysis of aggregated customer information to provide improved customer service responsiveness, to discover cross-sell and up-sell opportunities, and to increase overall customer loyalty.

- **Decreased risk**—Applying BI methods to credit data can improve credit risk analysis, whereas analyzing both supplier and consumer activity and reliability can provide insight into how to streamline the supply chain.

Of course, there are many other benefits to building a BI practice within an organization. Some of those focus on the most basic questions about how a company does business. For example, it is surprising how few senior managers within a company can answer simple questions about their business, such as:

- How many customers do you have?

- For each product, how many were sold over the last 12 months?

- Who are your 20 best customers?

- What is the value of any particular customer?
- Who are your 20 best suppliers?

What is even more interesting is that in some organizations, not only can we not *answer* these questions, there may not even be a framework in which someone can even *ask* these questions. There is a critical point I want to make here: Starting a well-conceived and comprehensive BI practice will not just provide the physical tools for answering these kinds of questions, but, more importantly, should be a catalyst for a change in the way we think about doing business and about how we can use information within that new way of thinking.

For example, before we can determine who the 20 best customers are, we must be able to articulate the difference between a "good" and a "bad" customer, as well as be able to identify a collection of metrics used to measure goodness, what data sets need to be collected for measurement, establish and integrate the methods for collecting and aggregating the data used for measuring, establish the processes required for conducting the measurement, ensure the quality of that data so as to not draw faulty conclusions, package the results into a reasonable report, and find a method to quickly and effectively disseminate the results of this process. Although a lot of this process may be automated using off-the-shelf technology, the most important part (i.e., asking the right question) needs input from individuals with expertise and a stake in the result.

The Information Asset

Although a significant amount of money has been invested in attempts at building and launching BI frameworks and applications, most of that money has been spent in infrastructure, whereas very little has been invested in managing and exploiting a valuable corporate asset—a company's data. In fact, the concept of business intelligence is so poorly defined that a manager's expectations are set based on what that manager is told by the last software tool vendor. Because of lack of focus or the absence of clear success criteria, many data warehousing implementations have been delayed or scrapped altogether because the actual BI implementations deliver far short of their expectations.

On the other hand, there are a number of organizations that have started to view their data as a corporate asset and to realize that properly collecting, aggregating, and analyzing their data opens an opportunity to discover bits of knowledge that can both improve operational processing and provide better insight into customer profiles and behavior. In these environments, there is a clear agreement on the definition of BI as a set of tools and methodologies designed to exploit actionable knowledge discovered from the company's information asset.

Exploiting Information

Anybody involved in the BI process is concerned about the ability to exploit information in a way that can improve the way a business (or any organization) operates. Yet the ultimate goal of data exploitation relies on a pyramid of abstraction (Fig. 1.1) that relates to the ways that we manage information, and the ability to provide access to that knowledge asset must first effectively manage the flow of information into an intelligence platform.

The ability to effectively exploit information is based on a hierarchical evolution of information management and knowledge management

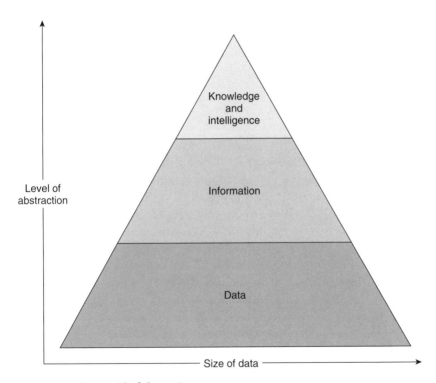

FIGURE 1.1 A pyramid of abstraction.

capabilities, each of which has its own benefits and landmines. In this book, each chapter will introduce an information management capability, including a technical description, how it is manifested in the business environment, along with some of the aspects involved in managing the technical, political, and personal issues that can pose a challenge to a successful implementation.

Business Intelligence and Program Success

Because you are reading this book, you are likely involved in the creation, management, maintenance, or development of a BI program. Probably, somewhere within your corporate senior management hierarchy, some individuals have been convinced that there is some value in starting a BI program. Unfortunately, the disparate perceptions of what BI is and how the knowledge derived through BI can be used often leads to project failure.

Looking at companies that have started data warehousing projects or have purchased large-scale data mining software suites, we see high expectations and many disappointments related to the failure in the way that data warehouse projects are conceived, designed, architected, managed, and implemented, for any, if not all, of these reasons:

- The amorphous understanding of what BI methods and products could do resulted in an absence of a proper value proposition on behalf of the business sponsor.

- The scope of the project was not fully understood, causing delays in delivering to the business sponsor.

- Insufficient technical training prevented developers from getting software products to do what the vendors said they do.

- Poor understanding of technology infrastructure led to poor planning and scheduling.

- Business users were unable to trust results due to poor data quality.

- The lack of a clear statement of success criteria, along with a lack of ways to measure program success, led to a perception of failure.

The goal of this book is to provide a high-level overview of the technical (and some political) concepts for which a savvy manager must have awareness when involved in a BI or information exploitation project in order to make that project successful. The material is intended to cast interesting technology in an operational business framework while providing the introductory technical background and highlighting important issues such as:

- Management issues
- Technical issues
- Performance issues
- Complexity

This book will describe the basic architectural components of a BI environment, beginning with traditional topics, such as business process modeling and data modeling, and moving on to more modern topics, such as business rule systems, data profiling, information compliance and data quality, data warehousing, and data mining. My hope is that this will be a valuable introduction to the technology, management issues, and terminology of the BI industry. But first, let's settle on a definition of *business intelligence.*

What Is Business Intelligence?

The Data Warehousing Institute, a provider of education and training in the data warehouse and BI industry defines *business intelligence* as:

> The processes, technologies, and tools needed to turn data into information, information into knowledge, and knowledge into plans that drive profitable business action. Business intelligence encompasses data warehousing, business analytic tools, and content/knowledge management.[1]

This is a great working definition, especially because it completely captures the idea that there is a hierarchy imposed on the different scopes of intelligence. In addition, this definition also exposes two critical notions:

- A BI practice is more than just a collection of tools. This means that without the processes and the right people, the tools are of little value.

- The value of BI is realized in the context of profitable business action. This means that if knowledge that can be used for profitable action is ignored, the practice is of little value.

Unfortunately, the words *data* and *information* are frequently used interchangeably. At the risk of clashing with any individual's understanding of the terms *data, information,* and *knowledge,* let's use these conceptual definitions:

- *Data* is a collection of raw value elements or facts used for calculating, reasoning, or measuring. Data may be collected, stored, or processed but not put into a context from which any meaning can be inferred.

---

1. The Data Warehouse Institute Faculty Newsletter, Fall 2002.

- *Information* is the result of collecting and organizing data in way that establishes relationships between data items, which thereby provides context and meaning.

- *Knowledge* is the concept of understanding information based on recognized patterns in a way that provides insight to information.

Turning Data into Information

The process of turning data into information can be summarized as the process of determining what data is to be collected and managed and in what context. A good example is the process of designing a database that models a real-world set of entities, such as *parties*, which is a frequently used term that refers to people and organizations, along with the roles taken on by those parties.

Out of context, the individual bits of data, such as names and birth dates, are of little value. Having established which bits of data are to be used to configure a description of a party, as well as creating instances and populating those instances with the related data values, we have created the context for those pieces of data and turned them into a piece of information.

We might say that this aspect of BI involves the infrastructure of managing and presenting data, which incorporates the hardware platforms, relational or other type of database systems, and associated software tools. This aspect also incorporates query and reporting tools that provide access to the data. Last, this part of the process cannot be done without experts in the area of data management integrating and coordinating this technology.

Turning Information into Knowledge

Sometimes it happens when you wake up in the middle of the night or perhaps while you are stuck in traffic or even while you're daydreaming in the shower. I am referring to that flash of insight that almost magically appears that provides you with the answer to that particularly nasty problem over which you've been agonizing. I like to compare the concept of turning information into knowledge to that flash of insight. We accumulate piles of information, which are then analyzed in many different ways until some critical bits of knowledge are created. What makes that knowledge critical is that it can be used to form a plan of action for solving some business problem.

We can say that this aspect of BI involves the analytical components, such as data warehousing, online analytical processing (OLAP), data quality, data profiling, business rule analysis, and data mining. Again, acquiring tools to perform these functions is of little value in the absence of professionals who understand how to use them and how to get the right kinds of results.

Turning Knowledge into Actionable Plans

This last aspect is probably the most important, because it is in this context that any real value is derived. If you are using BI for micromarketing, finding the right customer for your product is irrelevant if you do not have a plan to contact that customer. If you are using BI for fraud detection, finding the pattern of fraud is of little value if your organization does not do something to prevent that fraudulent behavior.

Being able to take action based on the intelligence that we have learned is the key point of any BI strategy. It is through these actions that a senior management sponsor can see the true return on investment for his or her information technology (IT) spending. A BI program provides benefits that increase business efficiency, increase sales, provide better customer targeting, reduce customer service costs, identify fraud, and generally increase profits while reducing costs. Because of this, we might say that when implemented properly, BI is one IT area that can be a profit center instead of the traditional cost center.

Actionable Knowledge

That last point is so critical that it is worth mentioning a second time: Discovered knowledge is of little value if there is no value-producing action that can be taken as a consequence of gaining that knowledge. This means that the business-technology partnership must work together not just to act on discovered intelligence but to do so in a timely fashion so as to derive the greatest benefit. This reinforces the sentiment that BI can succeed as the result of cooperation between technical developers and their business clients.

Selected Readings

There are a number of good online resources that provide a large amount of material on data warehousing and BI. Some of my favorites include:

- *www.dmreview.com*, the Web site for *DM Review* magazine
- *www.datawarehouse.com*, a community Web site with interesting forums

- *www.intelligententerprise.com*, the Web site for the magazine *Intelligent Enterprise*
- *www.dw-institute.com*, the Web site for the Data Warehousing Institute, where there are many valuable documents that discuss the meaning and the value of BI
- *www.dwinfocenter.org*, the Web site for the Data Warehousing Information Center
- *www.tdan.com*, the Web site for the Data Administration Newsletter

Understanding the percentages of profitable customers and the corresponding amount of profit attributable to them is a significant challenge, but it is discussed within the context of the banking industry in "Customer Profitability: Irrelevant for Decisions?" Peter Carroll and Madhu Tadikonda, *Banking*, Nov./Dec. 1997, *www.bai.org/bankingstrategies/1997-nov-dec/profit*.

Updates to this list will be posted at *www.knowledge-integrity.com*. Contact me *(loshin@knowledge-integrity.com)* if you are interested in learning more and cannot find what you are looking for. I am happy to help.

CHAPTER 2

The Value of Business Intelligence

According to the PricewaterhouseCoopers Global Data Management Survey of 2001, "Companies that manage their data as a strategic resource and invest in its quality are already pulling ahead in terms of reputation and profitability."[1] This statement implies a quite subtle yet radical notion: Data should be treated as a strategic resource. According to a traditional view, data is the "fuel" driving the automation of a business operation, implying that a company uses computers to help run its business. The forward-looking view of data internalizes the notion that strategic knowledge is embedded in the collection of a company's data and that extracting actionable knowledge will help a company *improve* its business.

This leads to another intriguing idea—that a company may acquire a competitive edge by viewing itself as an information business instead of taking the traditional industry—or vertical—view. Consider this: Is a supermarket chain a business that sells food, or is it a business that exploits knowledge about customer preferences, geographical biases, supply chain logistics, product lifecycle, and competitive sales information to optimize its delivery, inventory, pricing, and product placement as a way to increase margin for each item sold? The answer to that question (and its corresponding versions in any industry) may ultimately determine your company's long-term viability in the Information Age.

So how do you transform data into a strategic resource? A part of that process involves properly applying new technology to your data, but the most important part is being able to understand and subsequently build the business case for the value of information. This is partially an abstract exercise and partially a discrete one, and in this chapter we look at the difference between the traditional use of data in a transactional environment for the

---

1. Retrieved May 5, 2003 from *www.pwcglobal.com/extweb/ncsurvres.nsf/DocID/ E68F3408A463BD2980256A180064B96A.*

purpose of effecting operational side effects and the modern view of data as a valuable resource that can be used for analytical purposes. We introduce the savvy manager to the value of information, discuss what the aspects of information are that make up this value, and indicate what kinds of processing can be performed to add value to data. We also look at some examples of business intelligence (BI) applications to guide your understanding of how to build the business case for a BI program.

The Information Asset and Data Valuation

Is data an asset? Although I have never seen a company's data listed as a line item on its list of assets and liabilities, there are some reasons to consider it both ways. Certainly, if all a company does is accumulate and store data, there is some cost associated with the ongoing management of that data—the cost of storage, maintenance, office space, support staff, etc. This should show up on the balance sheet as a liability.

Alternatively, data can be viewed as an asset, because data can be used to provide benefits to the company, is controlled by the organization, and is the result of previous transactions (either as the result of data creation internally or through a data purchase). But organizations do not treat data as an asset; for example, there is no depreciation schedule for purchased data. Treating data as an asset is important, though, because it allows us to build the business case for investing in BI when we can show how the value of the data asset is improved.

That implies that we must have some way to measure the value of data, and this is where we get stuck. There are relatively few situations where we can accurately assign a discrete price for information, and this pricing structure is more frequently value based than if data were treated as a commodity. As an example, the telephone company charges you, say, $1 for each directory assistance inquiry, although that same telephone number could be acquired free through an online directory. The difference in cost is based on the convenience value of being able to pick up the receiver and get the number right away.

In most cases, though, the value of information depends on a number of contributing factors, and my discussion of these factors is adapted from research by Daniel Moody and Peter Walsh.[1] What is interesting is that as we

---

1. See "Measuring the Value of Information: An Asset Valuation Approach," Daniel Moody and Peter Walsh, European Conference on Information Systems (ECIS 99).

are made aware of these factors, we can get a lot closer to developing a model for information valuation. This is not to say that we can accurately enumerate data as an asset on the balance sheet, but it does give some parameters to understanding the value of information and, consequently, the value of BI.

The Time Value of Data

There is a timeliness or currency component to the value of information. Here's a simple example: If it is March 1st and some prophet told you today that for a certainty the March 2nd closing price of IBM stock is going to be $10 higher than the March 1st price, you can exploit that piece of information today to buy as much IBM stock as you can and sell it at the $10 profit on March 2nd. Yet if I gave you the same information on March 3rd, you could not exploit it in the same way. In this case, a large portion of the value of that piece of information is bound to its timeliness.

This example may appear to be a bit extreme, yet the concept is clear that a portion of the value of information is related to time and that value may degrade as time elapses. Because stored data represents a snapshot of a real-world state at a particular point in time, then in the absence of continuous maintenance, as the world changes our snapshot grows more out of synch with reality. For example, our direct mail database may be of high value at its initial creation, but because it is estimated that about 20% of the population changes addresses each year, then if that database is not updated with new addresses, its value declines with time. Not only that, bad data actually can be viewed as a liability: There is no reduction in the fixed costs associated with managing that bad data, and using the data as part of an integration or linkage process will yield incorrect answers, and the value of the data set as a whole declines.

Information as a Sharable Resource

As opposed to any other raw resource used in a manufacturing process, data is a raw resource that are not used up. That means that information is sharable, and the value of information increases as more people use it. An example of this is the knowledge of a process for sales professionals to alert them to the best time to contact a prospect. The knowledge of this process can streamline the process for any particular salesperson. But even if that salesperson were to share that knowledge with other members of the sales staff, there is no degradation in the value that can be achieved by any one of the individuals aware of that knowledge. This means that the value of that information is multiplied by the number of people who know it.

In the BI space, this is manifested through the data warehouse, which is used as a central repository for large amounts of shared data. If there is some economic value to be derived from a piece of information, that value can be increased through sharing.

Increasing Value through Increased Use

For most assets, as usage increases, there is some depreciation in asset value. For example, every mile a car is driven decreases the value of the car. On the other hand, the value of data does not decrease with use, because there is no degradation in information based on the number of times it is viewed. When everyone in the organization knows what information is available, how to access that information, and how to exploit that information, the value of that information rapidly increases. If data is stored, managed, and never used, there is no added value, and, as I mentioned in the introduction to this section, it actually becomes a liability.

Increasing Value through Quality

Let's look at the stock price example one more time, but let's change it a bit: This time, the prophet is a false one and tells you that the stock price will fall $10 by the close of business tomorrow, although it really will rise $10. The way you will have exploited what you believe to be true will ultimately result in a significant loss of value instead of an increase. This highlights the value of accuracy of information and the requirement for not only expecting high levels of information quality, but also having a means for defining quality metrics and measuring using those metrics. Having some understanding of the measure or quality of data being used for a decision support process lets the decision maker determine the risks associated with relying on that data.

Increasing Value through Merging

The process of combining bits of knowledge provides significant leverage when increasing the value of information. Having sales channel information is of value; having supply channel information is valuable; combining supply channel information with sales channel information provides knowledge about the movement of products from supplier to customer.

Information increases in value when it can be used to enhance and expand other pieces of information. The BI process revolves around the ability to collect, aggregate, and, most importantly, leverage the integration of different data sets together. As we will discuss many times in this book, there is a large increase in the value of information if it can be used as leverage in increasing an actionable knowledge base. In other words, if we can take two pieces of information, link them together, and infer something new that could not have been learned independently, we can exploit that inference for competitive advantage.

Value versus Volume

Contrary to the behavior of other assets, we do not necessarily gain greater value by having more information. The sheer amount of information that is produced every year is almost unbelievable; trying to integrate that with what has existed before seems like a gargantuan effort. And in fact, the more data an individual is presented with, the less likely he or she is to absorb *any* of it.

The complexity of data integration grows steeply as the number of data sources is increased. Data from alternate sources infrequently share data models, representations of the same kinds of entities, or even coded reference data. Each data set that is added to the mix must be integrated with all the other sets already extant in the repository, bringing along all the problems associated with that integration.

On the other hand, there is a perception that the more information there is, the better. So there is some fine line between having the right amount of information and having too much. Having the right amount implies that this information supports the defined business requirements and assumes that you are able to integrate that information and provide and present it within the required time.

Not only that, there is a qualitative difference between having lots of data that comes from disparate data sources and having lots of data that derives from the same source. For example, maintaining a large amount of historical transaction data (such as point-of-sale data or call detail records) may prove to be more valuable when it comes to analyzing trends over longer periods of time.

Measuring the Value of Information

One way to assess the value of information is to look at some traditional valuation models for other assets.

- **Historical cost**—In this method, we assess the value based on what had been paid to acquire or create the information or based on how much it would cost to replace the information.

- **Market value**—In this method, we assess the value based on what someone else would be willing to pay for the information. Data aggregators and packagers create products based on this model, especially when it comes to improving the quality of, improving the accessibility of, or enhancing information that is typically hard for individuals to acquire on their own.

- **Utility value**—In this method, we assess the value of information based on the expected value to be derived from the information.

Actionable Knowledge—Return on Investment

It is important to remind you at this point that an asset retains its value only if we do something with it. In the world of BI, some investment is probably required to build the environment where data can be turned into knowledge, but the real benefit occurs when that knowledge is *actionable*. That means that an organization cannot just provide for the information factory; it must also have some methods for extracting value from that knowledge.

This is *not* a technical issue—it is an organizational one. To have identified actionable knowledge is one thing, but to take the proper action requires a nimble organization with individuals empowered to take that action. Although this book is not meant as a replacement for business school, it should be clear that before embarking on building a BI program, every included BI activity should be accompanied by some return on investment (ROI) strategy.

The components of this strategy include analyzing costs, increases in revenues that are related to the activity, and other distinguishable benefits. This strategy should itemize:

- The fixed costs already incorporated into the BI infrastructure (e.g., database or query and reporting tool purchases)

- The variable costs associated with the activity (e.g., are there special software components required?)

- The ongoing costs for maintaining this activity

- The value of the benefits derived by taking actions when expected knowledge is derived from the activity

- The costs and benefits of other BI components that need to contribute to this business activity

- The value model expected from this activity

- The probabilities of successful applications of these actions to be applied to the expected value
- The determination of the time to break even as well as a profitability model

Let's look at a simple example: building a CRM data warehouse for the purpose of increasing the lifetime value of each customer within a company's customer base. The goal is to build a data warehouse that encapsulates all the data related to each individual customer. Building this data warehouse incurs costs associated with physical computational hardware, a database system, additional software tools, and integrating those components into the enterprise. Next there are the additional costs associated with the design and implementation of the warehouse model(s), as well as identifying the data sources, developing the processes for extracting data from its sources and loading it into the data warehouse, and ongoing maintenance of the data warehouse. The expected benefit of the data warehouse is a 30% increase in each customer's lifetime value by the end of the third year following the launch of the data warehouse into production. The ROI model must offset the costs just described with the overall benefit value associated with the increase in lifetime value. If there is no breakeven point, the cost to build the data warehouse is more than the value derived from it; in that case, it is probably worth looking for additional value that can be derived from the project before pitching it to senior management.

Business Intelligence Applications

It is interesting to note the different uses of data and the contexts of each use as it pertains to the exploitation of information. For the most part, we can break those into two areas. The first area is operational data use, and the other is strategic use. The predominant use of information today is operational: how data helps *run* the business, as opposed to strategic information use, which helps *improve* the business.

Clearly these both are valuable, and without the operational use of information a business could not survive. But it is up to the information consumer to determine the extent of the value to be derived from the strategic use of information as well as what strategic uses are of importance. In this section we review some of the strategic uses of information as manifested through BI analytics. Note that although many of these analytic applications may be categorized within a specific business domain, many of them depend on each other within the business context.

Customer Analytics

A common, overused term is *customer relationship management* (CRM), which has become a buzzword implying an all-encompassing magic bullet to turn all contacts into customers and all customers into great customers. The magic of CRM is actually based on a number of customer analytic functions that together help people in a company better understand who their customers are and how to maximize the value of each customer. The results of these analytics can be used to enhance the customer's experience as well.

Following are different aspects of customer analytics that benefit the sales, marketing, and service organizations as they interact with the customers.

- **Customer profiling**—The bulk of marketing traditionally casts a wide net and hopes to capture as many individuals as possible. Companies are realizing that all customers are not clones of some predefined market segment but are thinking individuals. To this end, customer analytics encompass the continuous refinement of individual customer profiles that incorporate demographic, psychographic, and behavioral data about each individual.

- **Targeted marketing**—Knowledge of a set of customer likes and dislikes can augment a marketing campaign to target small clusters of customers that share profiles. In fact, laser-style marketing is focused directly at individuals as a by-product of customer analytics.

- **Personalization**—As more business moves online, the browser acts as a proxy for the company's first interface with the customer. Personalization, which is the process of crafting a presentation to the customer based on that customer's profile, is the modern-day counterpart to the old-fashioned salesperson who remembers everything about his or her individual "accounts." Web site personalization exploits customer profiles to dynamically collect content designed for an individual, and it is meant to enhance that customer's experience.

- **Collaborative filtering**—We have all seen e-commerce Web sites that suggest alternate or additional purchases based on other people's preferences. In other words, the information on a Web page may suggest that "people who have purchased product X also have purchased product Y." These kinds of suggestions are the result of a process called *collaborative filtering*, which evaluates the similarity between the preferences of groups of customers. This kind of recommendation generation creates relatively reliable cross-sell and up-sell opportunities.

- **Customer satisfaction**—Another benefit of the customer profile is the ability to provide customer information to the customer satisfaction representatives. This can improve these representatives' ability to deal with the customer and expedite problem resolution.

- **Customer lifetime value**—How does a company determine who their best customers are? The lifetime value of a customer is a measure of a customer's profitability over the lifetime of the relationship, which incorporates the costs associated with managing that relationship and the revenues expected from that customer. Customer analytics incorporates metrics for measuring customer lifetime value.

- **Customer loyalty**—It is said that a company's best new customers are its current customers. This means that a company's best opportunities for new sales are with those customers that are already happy with that company's products or services. Customer analytics help.

Human Capital Productivity Analytics

One way to attain value internally from BI is to be able to streamline and optimize people within the organization, including:

- **Call center utilization and optimization**—If you have ever dawdled while on hold, waiting for a customer service representative to pick up the telephone, you can understand the value of analyzing call center utilization to look for ways to improve throughput and decrease customer waiting time. When a company's management realizes that inbound calls are likely to be from unsatisfied customers, making them stew on the phone is not going to improve customer satisfaction. In the more advanced cases, quick access to customer profile information may also affect the level of support provided to each customer (e.g., high level to high-value customers, minimal support to low-value customers).

- **Production effectiveness**—This includes evaluating on-time performance, labor costs, production yield, etc., all as factors of how staff members work. This information can also be integrated into an information repository and analyzed for value.

Business Productivity Analytics

Another popular analytic realm involves business productivity metrics and analysis, including:

- **Defect analysis**—While companies struggle to improve quality production, there may be specific factors that affect the number of defective items produced, such as time of day, the source of raw materials used, and even the individuals who staff a production line. These factors can be exposed through one component of business productivity analytics.

- **Capacity planning and optimization**—Understanding resource utilization for all aspects of a physical plant (i.e., all aspects of the machinery, personnel, expected throughput, raw input requirements, warehousing, just-in-time production, etc.) through a BI analytics process can assist management in resource planning and staffing.

- **Financial reporting**—Stricter industry regulatory constraints may force companies to provide documentation about their financials, especially in a time when companies are failing due to misstated or inaccurately stated results. In addition, financial reporting analytics provide the means for high-level executives to take the pulse of the company and drill down on particular areas.

- **Risk management**—Having greater accuracy or precision in tracking business processes and productivity allows a manager to make better decisions about how and when to allocate resources in a way that minimizes risk to the organization. In addition, risk analysis can be factored into business decisions regarding the kind of arrangements that are negotiated with partners and suppliers.

- **Just-in-time**—The concept of just-in-time product development revolves around the mitigation of inventory risk associated with commodity products with high price volatility. For example, the commodity desktop computer business is driven by successive generations of commodity components (disk drives, CPUs, DRAM memory chips, to name a few). Should a vendor purchase these items in large quantity and then come up against a low-sales quarter, that vendor might be stuck with components sitting on the shelf whose commodity value is rapidly declining. To alleviate this, the knowledge of how quickly the production team can assemble a product, along with sales channel information and supplier information (see Sales Channel Analytics and Supply Chain Analytics on page 21) can help in accurately delivering products built to customer order within a predictable amount of time.

- **Asset management and resource planning**—Utilization, productivity, and asset lifecycle information can be integrated through business analytics to provide insight into short- and long-term resource planning, as well as exposing optimal ways to manage corporate assets to support the resource plan.

Sales Channel Analytics

We might consider sales channel analytics a subset of business productivity analytics, yet there is enough value in segmenting this area of application.

- **Marketing**—Both the ability to fine-tune a marketing program and the ability to determine marketing effectiveness can be derived through sales channel analytics. A typical iterative process would be to identify a marketing strategy based on an analysis of a clustering of customers by profile and then to implement that strategy. The effectiveness of the strategy will ripple through the sales channel data, which can then be used to compare the actual results with expectations. The degree to which those expectations are met (or exceeded) can be fed back into the analytical processing to help determine new strategies.

- **Sales performance and pipeline**—Data associated with the sales staff can be analyzed to identify variables that affect the efficiency of the sales cycle, such as individual sales staff member, region, industry, contact people, contact times, and contact frequency.

Supply Chain Analytics

Supply channel analytics are used to characterize and benchmark a company's supply channels from its various vendors and suppliers, through internal inventory management and ultimately aspects of delivering products to its customers. Aspects of supply chain analytics involve the following:

- **Supplier and vendor management**—Many organizations are unable to identify who their vendors are or how many vendors are supplying products or services. Supply chain analytics allow a company's management to track performance and reliability by supplier, evaluating and rating the quality of the products supplied, as well as help to optimize supplier relationships with respect to spending, procurement, and risk.

- **Shipping**—There are different methods by which a company delivers its products to its customers, each with its own cost schedule. For example, it may be more expensive to ship products by air than by truck, but the products will arrive at the destination faster if shipped by air. A company can minimize its delivery costs by being able to select the most efficient delivery method for any specific business arrangement, but knowing whether the products can be available within the right time schedule is a difficult problem, especially if your production depends on external suppliers. Therefore, merging supplier and inventory information with productivity data (see Business Productivity Analytics on page 19) lets management accurately determine the best way to move product.

- **Inventory control**—As discussed earlier, maintaining an inventory of commodity products that exhibit volatile pricing *and* limited useful life creates a market risk if those products cannot be used before their obsolescence. Alternatively, we would not want to keep the shelves empty, because parts are needed to build the products that are in the order-and-fulfillment cycle. Between the sales channel information, the productivity data, and the supply chain data, it is possible to make more precise predictions about inventory requirements. It is also possible to determine the best way to quantify and mitigate risk, especially through the development of financial products (such as barrier options) to limit financial losses.

- **Distribution analysis**—Imagine that your company has a large number of retail outlets, a smaller number of regional warehouses, and a very small number of factories. The optimal distribution model would arrange for the delivery of the exact number of products from each factory to its closest warehouses so that each warehouse could deliver the exact number of products to each of the retail stores. Unfortunately for both companies and customers, this optimal distribution is pretty rare. If a company can predict demand for specific products within certain areas, though, the managers cannot only distribute the product to the right locations in the right quantities, but also minimize shipping costs by ramping up product creation at the factories most economically geographically located at a rate that matches the consumer demand.

Behavior Analysis

Most of the analytical applications we have reviewed so far deal with "drillable" data that a manager can use to optimize some kind of process, such as sales, utilization, or distribution. Another area of analytics deals with a more fluid view of activity as a way to predict trends or capitalize on identifying specific kind of behaviors. In general, any behavior pattern that presages significant business events is worth noting and then seeking. This type of analytical processing makes use of historical data to look for behavior patterns that take place before the significant event (whether or not they are causal) and then try to identify those behavior patterns as they are taking place. This allows for the following kinds of analytics:

- **Purchasing trends**—Although many product lifecycles can easily be predicted and charted, there are apparent nonlinear trends that elude predictability, the most notable cases being toy sales around winter holiday time. Yet not being able to identify a warming (or heating!) product may result in the inability to ramp up production to meet demand or the inability to move products from factory to store shelves, which can effectively dump a glass of cold water on that hot product. Behavior analytics can be used to identify purchasing patterns that indicate a growing trend that can be used to adjust a company's reaction to customer trends.

- **Web activity**—In the world of e-commerce, the ability to draw and maintain customers to a Web site and then encourage them to commit to purchasing products is not only critical to success, but also much more difficult than doing the same in a brick and mortar environment. Different kinds of content presentation may lead different kinds of consumers to behave differently. It is interesting to identify patterns that lead to committed business (e.g., product purchase)—let's call them "success patterns." Then perhaps including some personalization (see Customer Analytics on page 18), the content presentation can be crafted to direct the Web site visitor into these success patterns, which in theory should improve the probability of making a sale.

- **Fraud and abuse detection**—Fraudulent (or abusive) behavior frequently is manifested in patterns. For example, there are many popular health insurance fraud schemes involving making claims with inflated charges or practitioners prescribing expensive medications or procedures that may not be necessary. Behavior analytics can be used to seek out patterns of suspicious behavior by provider, geographical region, agent, etc.

- **Customer attrition**—Another serious problem for many businesses is customer attrition, when a company's customers decide they no longer want to remain affiliated with that company. In competitive industries, it is much easier to convince a customer to stay with the company before the decision has been made to leave rather than afterwards. For example, offering a long-distance telephone customer a better offer than can be gotten from a competitor can recapture that customer, but it is not to the company's benefit to make this offer to (higher valued) complacent customers. Therefore, it is important to recognize the signs that a customer is ready to cease being a customer. This can be done by evaluating patterns of behavior before previous attritions (such as a history of customer service complaints) and then using those patterns for ongoing customer behavior analysis.

- **Social network analysis**—Sometimes it is important to identify relationships between specific entities within a system and to analyze their behavior as a group. For example, a component of criminal intelligence is finding collections of individuals whose individual behavior may be nondescript yet who act suspiciously as a group. This kind of analytical processing is valuable to law enforcement, regulatory compliance (think of insider trading), marketing (consider *viral marketing*, which is a strategy that encourages individuals to pass your marketing message to all of their contacts), as well as sales optimization (by finding a contact path of people to find the right audience).

The Intelligence Dashboard

A key performance indicator (KPI) is some objective measurement of an aspect of a business that is critical to the success of that business. Such KPIs are a component of the conceptual scorecard for a business and can be associated with a number of different business activities, such as customer satisfaction, productivity, supply channel performance, and profitability. In fact a large number of KPIs can be defined in terms of measuring performance associated with many of the BI analytics functions that we described earlier.

Another conceptual value of BI is the ability to capture the business definitions of the key performance indicators, manage those definitions as part of the corporate knowledge base, and then provide a visualization dashboard that reflects those KPI measurements, presented in a form for management review. This intelligence dashboard displays the results of the analytics required to configure the KPIs in a succinct visual representation that can be understood instantaneously or selected for drill-down. An intelligence dashboard will not only provide real-time presentation of the selected KPIs, but will also hook directly into the BI components that allow for that drill-down.

The following are some example KPIs:

- Regional sales figures by sales location
- Personnel statistics
- Real-time supply chain reports by supplier

- Customer satisfaction measurements
- Factory productivity
- Average customer profitability

Business Intelligence Adds Value

We can confidently say that knowledge derived from a company's data can be used as an asset, as long as senior managers understand that an investment in turning data into actionable knowledge can have a significant payoff. It is important to recognize that this problem cannot be solved solely by the application of technology. In truth, the technology must augment a more serious senior-level management commitment to exploiting discovered knowledge and having a way to measure the value of those activities.

There are a number of BI analytics that provide business value. Selecting and integrating these analytic functions depends on the ability to effectively build the underlying information infrastructure to support the applications as well as the ability to configure reporting and visualization of the discovered knowledge.

For a more in-depth discussion of information valuation, I recommend "Measuring the Value of Information: An Asset Valuation Approach," Daniel Moody and Peter Walsh, ECIS 1999.

CHAPTER 3

Planning for Success

So you are going to start a business intelligence (BI) program! Whether your exposure to BI derives from the popular press, your friendly hardware or software vendor, or developers within your organization, the promise of BI is sold as a black box full of incredible technology that cranks out dollars by the cartload. Unfortunately, the reality is a bit different, and that promised benefit is often waylaid as escalating costs and limited benefits become synonymous with your comprehensive BI program.

Note that each of those folks selling BI is motivated differently. The vendors are more interested in selling product or licenses than in ensuring your success. And not only are the developers more motivated by interesting technology than the bottom line, many corporate compensation programs do not tie developer remuneration to long-term project success, because the typical annual review process is based on only the previous nine months of an employee's service.

Any manager planning for a successful BI implementation must be aware that the real driver of any internal program of this sort must be some value proposition. Whether it is a painstakingly crafted return on investment (ROI) model or just the means by which senior management can evaluate ongoing organizational performance, no BI program will succeed without being able to convince the senior management that there is value in building the program.

In this chapter we'll look at some of the critical factors a savvy manager must know regarding the successful planning of a BI program. This includes the first important steps in achieving senior-level support and sponsorship for a BI program, building a value proposition, and exploring the partnership between the business user and the information technology development staff.

In addition, we will also look at how to establish and formally define success factors and how to measure against those factors and maintain the partnership relationship between business and IT. Last, we look at issues associated with building the implementation team and how to leverage short-term tactics to ensure the continued development of a long-term BI strategy.

Initiating a Program

If you are trying to initiate a BI program, you are most likely to be doing so for one of two reasons. If you are a technical person, the driver is probably the draw of the "cool technology" or the opportunity to learn new skills and enhance a resume. Technicians are drawn to data warehousing and large-scale data-integration projects because of the technical challenge. If you are a businessperson, you are likely to believe that a BI program will magically increase profitability while drastically decreasing costs. Businesspeople are incessantly pitched the silver bullet that is going to solve all their past, current, and future business problems.

Although these drivers may have been enough in the past to guarantee a BI budget, the poor track record of these kinds of projects, coupled with increasingly focused project management and governance, has forced the reduction and even elimination of BI programs. Therefore, it is extremely important to identify the factors that are necessary for success.

- Senior-level sponsorship

- The establishment of high-level goals and expectations

- The determination of discrete success criteria

- The definition of success metrics

- Creating a partnership among the participants that provides incentives to act strategically

- Stating a value vision as an ongoing battle cry for success

Senior-Level Sponsorship

By reading the popular data warehousing, BI, or customer relationship management (CRM) literature, you would think that no single technological advance could ever have taken place without the backing of a senior business manager, although I suspect that the invention of the wheel and the discovery of fire occurred in the absence of a CEO. But seriously, when we consider the intricacies of integrating an analytical, strategic program into an operational environment, the roadblocks that appear are not technical but mostly personal and political.

Reading between the lines in the literature, what we can infer is that one of the reasons most frequently cited for the failure of a BI program is the *lack* of senior-level sponsorship. But what is *senior-level sponsorship?* This term alludes to two different concepts: the seniority of the manager(s) involved, and the financial partnership of the project.

The first concept focuses on establishing a partnership with a senior-level manager (or, better yet, managers) at a level high enough to impose governance on the program and one who is able to enforce cooperation with those entrusted with the implementation of the program. This includes defining and ensuring the organizational commitment along and across the organization structure and removing barriers to success.

The second concept focuses on the senior management's establishing a vested stake in the success of the project. Whether this involves direct profit and loss (P&L) responsibility or whether it is defined more loosely in terms of stated business expectations, having a senior manager with a personal stake in the success (and failure) of the program will project a corporate commitment to project accountability. Even more important is the financial backing (in other words: budget) needed to build the infrastructure and the right team. Also, attributing successes in the BI program to those managers with a stake provides an additional personal incentive to make sure the project succeeds.

High-Level Goals and Expectations

In the absence of well-defined goals, how can we ever determine the point of success of a project? In the past, there has been a fuzzy general expectation based on "build it and they will come"—in other words, build the data warehouse and suddenly business clients will line up to drink from an unlimited tap of business value. What happens too often is that the time to build the data warehouse exceeds the patience level of the business partners, so when the data warehouse is completed, there is either significant difficulty in extracting the right kinds of reports from it or limited trust in the information that is extracted from it.

To properly recognize success, we must have a yardstick against which to measure success. This has to be defined in terms of delivering the value that the client expects. This means that there has to be a common language with which the clients and the providers describe expectations; we will explore this in greater detail later.

Creating a Partnership/Success Stake

An old aphorism claims that you can catch more flies with honey than with vinegar. To paraphrase, it is easier to get someone to do something for you when they expect to receive some valued return in exchange. This concept must be applied across the hierarchy in a way that engages all participants by promising everyone some stake in both the short-term and the long-term success of the project.

This implies that there is some incentive for everybody associated with the project to achieve the specified goals. In a number of organizations I have observed, two environments that conflict with the notion of a stake in success seem to prevail. The first is the "What have you done for me lately?" mentality, which rewards individual achievements accomplished within short-term periods. This attitude encourages tactical steps at the expense of long-term strategy and stifles strategic thinking. The second environment is the "inequitable risk/reward" mentality, where individuals who have taken on added risk and have sacrificed short-term successes in exchange for long-term strategy are overlooked when it comes to advances in compensation or position, which in turn also discourages strategic thinking.

The success partnership should be designed so that short-term successes can be engineered into a long-term strategy, where components of a BI strategy are implemented in a sequence that provides ongoing value. In turn, all participants are to be rewarded for achieving specific goals within reasonable deadlines. This is in contrast to the "big bang" approach, where three years are spent building the all-encompassing environment and where all centralized governance and business value becomes secondary to delivering a complete, fully integrated enterprise data warehouse.

The Value Vision

What I refer to as the *value vision* is the statement that, moving forward, the organizations that best control and exploit information and knowledge will be the ones to pull forward in terms of strategy and competitive advantage. This generic expression of the concept needs to be restated for each individual instance and industry.

For example, in the financial industry, it may be expressed in terms of recognizing that the potential for increasing value lies in the most precise and fastest analysis of financial information, followed by taking some action to exploit that advantage, such as in financial arbitrage. Another example might be the retail industry, where the value vision is expressed as using information to completely understand the customer, which in turn can lead to more effective targeted marketing.

This vision embodies an agreement between the business management and the technologists that long-term corporate information-based strategy is critical to the future of a business and that synergy and cross-fertilizing technology and business expertise will result in higher profits and lower costs for the business and in personal rewards for all participants.

Business/Information Technology Partnership

One success factor in building this value vision in exploiting a company's information asset is establishing a partnership between the business users and the information technology team. Over time, the evolution of technical resources has had an interesting influence on more than the speed at which things get done. There is what we might call a psychological effect on the way people work together (or not) based on the allocation and distribution of computational resources. A clear example lies in the miniaturization of computers. Thirty-five years ago analysts shared time on huge computers housed in separate rooms; the services provided were purely operational—no BI applications at all. Twenty years ago was the beginning of the era of both the minicomputer (operating as a departmental resource) and the personal computer, along with the trend of distributed computing. With a machine on his or her desktop, a business manager could make use of local applications (including seminal personal business applications such as VisiCalc and Word-Perfect) for both operational and intelligence-oriented processing; you no longer needed to be a FORTRAN IV programmer carrying stacks of punch cards to use computers. There was a need for technical support, and the concept of the information technology department evolved into a technology development, support, and evaluation organization, investigating new hardware and applications.

Dichotomy

The way the information technology department has evolved has imposed an artificial boundary between those who require computer services and those who provide them, mostly because the ability to build user-friendly end-user applications has broken down the barrier to entry to exploiting computers. In turn, there is a greater need for both technicians to solve problems with computer use and those who can translate a business user's problems into a collection of technical issues. And although the way that these IT personnel were compensated evolved into complicated charge-backs and accounting tricks, it was clear that the division between business and IT is essentially a budgetary one: IT is usually a cost center, as opposed to the business units, which are supposed to be profit centers. But this split imposes a deeper philosophical division between information technology providers and business users because the interaction framework is built around the IT folks' asking the business folks to support the IT initiatives (i.e., with money).

Let's look at a typical exchange between developers and business users: The implementers say, "We want to make improvements, but our budget has been cut. How can we do this with no additional spending?" The users say, "We expected the data warehouse to be online already, but it is a year late and over budget and is still unusable!" The implementers say, "We want to get the project finished, but the requirements keep changing!" The users say, "The business environment continues to change, and what were requirements a year ago, when we first planned the project, are no longer the same." Clearly, the entities perceived as the "IT side" and the "business side" have aligned themselves in an adversarial relationship. Taking this interaction to its extreme, both sides are eventually dissatisfied, because reduced budgets lead to missed deadlines and unmet business-side expectations.

Partnering

Fortunately, there is a growing knowledge overlap between the IT and business sides. As the relationships between business units and IT groups grow, we find that the IT side gradually learns more and more about how the business works and that the business side has a growing understanding of the capabilities and limitations of the technology. These businesspeople now understand more about the relationship between business applications and the hardware, software, and developer resources they require, and the technologists document and learn more about business process modeling and how those processes can be encapsulated within an operational system. This is a growing knowledge management trend that reflects the need for a deeper understanding of how to exploit data and technology to gain a competitive edge.

One aspect of this trend is the abstraction of the components of the BI process. New ideas, such as business rule management, workflow analysis, classification and segmentation, and business process modeling, are being introduced as a launch pad for business/IT partnerships, effectively providing a way to formalize and document the ground rules associated with the way the BI program will work, as well as a means for planning the implementation of that program.

Business Intelligence Success Factors

Although there may be many factors that contribute to the success of any BI project, here are some critical factors for BI success.

Strong, Dedicated Management

As I have alluded to earlier in this chapter, it is important to have strong business management that can:

- Direct the business side engagement process.
- Guide the definition of success and the associated metrics.
- Manage the knowledge and technology acquisition process.
- Manage program implementation.
- Defuse any political time bombs.

Setting Appropriate Expectations

To avoid the perception that expectations are not being met, it is important to have a process for determining, articulating, and *documenting* the appropriate expectations regarding:

- **Functionality,** which refers to the kinds of BI applications and features to be provided
- **Accessibility,** which ensures that those clients who are meant to derive value from a particular BI application are able to access the application and the data underlying the application
- **Performance,** which refers to both interactive performance and scalability (see Scalability on page 38)
- **Delivery,** which refers to the timeliness and predictability of delivering functionality on a predetermined schedule
- **Quality,** in terms of data, applications, and reporting
- **Availability,** which can be dictated based on agreed-to service-level agreements
- **Business relevance,** which is of primary importance, because it relates the objectives to key business performance indicators, such as cost reduction, increased throughput or volume, and higher profits

Very often, clients define their own expectations as a by-product of a business application or service that is to be supported by a technical solution. In these cases, the perception of success or failure is (mistakenly) related to the client's ability to perform the client's jobs, which may or may not relate to the correctness of the technical solution. This is a symptom of improperly setting expectations; instead, the path to success is for the business client to articulate the business problem and then to discuss the solution process with the implementers.

Consider this example: The supplier management team for a large manufacturer wants to build a data mart to figure out how much business the company does with each of its suppliers. The team supplies its data to a data-enhancement company for the purpose of company name aggregation. Unfortunately, the enhancement company, doing what it normally does, aggregates by corporate *hierarchy*, not by company, which resolves multiple, mostly independent subsidiaries into the same grouping, which in turn is overkill for what the client wants. Not only does the supplier management team not get what it wants, but the data are made even worse, for their purposes, with the ultimate result that the entire project is viewed as a complete failure. Yet had the team properly articulated its result expectations to the enhancement company, it is likely that the data mart would have been properly constructed and then seen as a success.

Establishing Metrics for Success

The previous section explored some dimensions for setting expectations; this section talks about what is needed to determine compliance with those expectations. This boils down to the ability to identify a way to quantify compliance with an expectation and the means to measure that compliance.

Success metrics can be directly related to each of the expectation dimensions.

- **Functionality** can be broken down into an enumeration of service or product features; success can be measured by how many of those features are supported by that service or product.

- **Accessibility** is suitably represented as a collection of access policies that relate information clients to data by security constraints. Accessibility can be measured as a function of how many clients there are, what their access path is (e.g., software connectivity), and whether proper access has been granted.

- **Performance** can be distilled into individual performance components, such as timeliness (How quickly is information available?), speed of processing (How quickly are processes needed for analysis finished?), and volume/throughput (How many can I process? And at what rate?).

- **Delivery** is a function of whether what has been promised is delivered within a timely manner. Practically speaking, a program for which promises made by individuals or teams are not delivered is a program destined for failure. Even if the delivery time is not as timely as the client would like, what is more important is *predictability*, in other words, knowing when you can reliably expect a feature or access rights to be made available.

- **Quality** is very frequently talked about but seldom addressed. High quality of information in a BI program is probably the most important success factor, because if the information is of low quality, no other component of the system can be trusted. The measurement of quality is a funny thing; when we talk about manufactured objects, we can define some expected result and then impose some range of acceptable values. For example, if we are making 1-inch-long screws, perhaps we can accept screws that are 1.002 inches long. On the other hand, because it is hard to define what is right and what is wrong for data, it is very hard to objectively define data quality metrics. We treat this topic in greater detail in Chapter 9.

- **Availability** is relatively easy to measure; in fact, many systems refer to both uptime and downtime as a measure of availability. We can also incorporate a measure of those scheduled hours the systems are expected to be available. There are also concepts of the expected life-time of various components that relates to availability, such as mean time between failures (MTBF) for hardware, etc.

- **Business relevance** is easy and hard—easy because the effects of a successful program are immediately clear, hard because whether the result is attributable to the original BI may not be clearly evident. When we look at modeling the business process and then determining the importance of the pieces of the BI program within that process, we may have a better way to track bottom-line improvement to the technical program. We will explore the concept of business process modeling in greater detail in the next chapter.

Building a Strong Team

Assembling the right set of smart, motivated people to take on part of the BI program is critical to success. We discuss this in more detail in the later section on Team Building.

Understanding the Technology

In contrast to what a lot of experts say, I believe that everyone involved in BI, including the business partners, should have some understanding of the technology that comprises the BI program. There are a few reasons for this.

- Understanding the technology provides some grounding in what is possible and what is not possible.

- Awareness of the complexity of some analytical applications will help in determining the resources needed to properly service the client base.

- Many vendors dress up simplistic applications with fancy visual interfaces as a way to hide product deficiencies. Understanding the technology will help customers evaluate different products and determine which tools are of value and which are not.

Proper Data Architecture

When we build a system, we also build the representation of information within that system. This representation, which is called a *data model*, describes the different entities that exist within the system along with the relationships between those entities. But it is important to remember that it is still *just a model*, and that model, once defined and put into production, remains relatively static. On the other hand, what is being modeled is not necessarily static. This means that as things in the real world change, there must be some way to reflect those changes in the model.

A well-thought-out data architecture will account for this possibility. The data architecture reflects the needs of the business applications, including the entity relationships, as well as metadata, information sharing, and backup and recovery, among other things.

Using Quality Information

A common theme throughout this book is the importance of high-quality data to any BI program. To paraphrase what I said before in this chapter, if the input to a decision process is faulty, the decisions will be faulty. Whether the application is an operational process or an analytical process, errors in data may cause glitches in processing streams, result in incorrect analyses, or even lead to errors in judgment when carrying out the actions prescribed by the analytical process.

Different kinds of errors can wend their way into data. Some examples include data-entry errors (e.g., someone types in a last name with a different spelling than it has been entered before), data-transcription errors (e.g., the data-transformation process is flawed, creating inconsistencies in the data), or analysis errors (e.g., summarizing averages of values without considering how null values are to be treated). Integral to any BI program is a clearly defined data quality initiative; we will explore data quality and information compliance in Chapter 9.

Enterprise Integration

A successful program supplies an intelligence capability that both draws on enterprise data resources and is available as a resource across the enterprise. This implies that there must be well-defined processes for integrating information from multiple sources, whether it means merging data sets aggregated and deposited at a staging area or providing the means for integrating collections of data instances as they move through articulation points in the enterprise. Extract/transform/load (ETL) processing, enterprise application integration (EAI), and Web Services are all examples of process architectures designed for enterprise integration.

Exploiting Reuse

The concept of reuse is to leverage work that has already been done and to avoid simultaneous duplicated effort. Here are some areas of reuse to focus on.

- **Reuse of data**—Replication and duplication of data sets (especially reference data) lead to inconsistencies and errors. If there are data sets that are ultimately used in multiple information flows, it is worthwhile to manage those data sets as a shared resource and likewise share in the management responsibilities. Consistent shared data sets add significant value.

- **Reuse of metadata**—As distinct data sets are integrated into a single BI repository, there are likely to be differences in the way that similar entities are represented. Consolidating the metadata representations and creating transformations from original source into that representation will ease the data integration process.

- **Reuse of business logic**—If the same data sets are reused throughout the BI program for different aims, then it is possible that similar business rules may need to be applied to the data at different points in the information flow. Archive and manage those business rules as content, and use a methodology to make those rules actionable.

- **Reuse of business process**—If there is a human-oriented process (i.e., communications and interaction) that is successful, try to recreate the same cooperation in all aspects of the program.

Managing Scope

A malevolent notion that deviously extends the time to delivery of a project is *scope creep,* the continuous addition of deliverables into an already agreed-to scope of work. A successful manager maintains control on the scope and makes sure that additional noncritical items are relegated to a follow-on scope so as to not disturb the ability to deliver.

Scalability

Remember that as the program grows and is more successful, current client use will grow and the program will attract more clients. As the pressure on the system grows, more and larger data sets will be integrated into the repository, and the interactivity will increase. Therefore, design the program so that it can be easily scaled so as to maintain performance at the agreed-to service level.

Team Building

Because BI is not a purely technical solution, the leader must have the ability to craft the right team that can successfully implement the selection of technical components to the BI solution as well as articulate the needs and understand the results. When selecting team members, keep the following ideas in mind.

Insist on Business Participation

The team is not a team if it does not incorporate the business client. The business use of information should drive the program, and as already discussed in earlier, senior management sponsorship is a critical success factor.

Clarify Responsibilities

On both the micro and macro levels, there is a distinction between what has been enumerated in an employee's job description and "what needs to be done." Team members should be willing to take on added responsibility when it is critical to program success, and they should be rewarded accordingly.

Create Leadership Possibilities

An organizational structure can impose a hierarchy on a set of individuals, but the placement of one box on top of another set of boxes does not create a leader. Leaders arise out of opportunities to take action and responsibility for getting things done. In a strict hierarchy, fresh leadership is stifled, which only frustrates good people and leads to the turnover of critical employees. To prevent this, provide many opportunities (while, of course, mitigating risk) to let good people bubble up to their leadership role.

Create an Ego-Free Culture

One of the best experiences I have had was working on a software product implementation team where the project leader insisted that any successes experienced by the business client were attributable to the entire team. In turn, well-defined implementation standards imposed on the staff led to the development of a product that could have been easily implemented (and, subsequently, modified) by anyone on the team. The leader referred to this as *ego-free development*, which means that all individual successes and contributions were highlighted and rewarded internally but not exposed externally. This led to a seamless product that was easily maintainable and encouraged a high level of conformance to internally specified standards.

In the development of a BI program, it may be unreasonable to expect that any one team member will have *all* the skills needed for the project. But the concept of the ego-free culture implies that all team members should understand that in order for the project to be successful, all contributions are valuable.

Cultivate Believability

A major failure of BI is the "overpromise"—project managers mindlessly acceding to client requests without determining feasibility first, which raises expectations that can never be met. Before making any promises, a project manager should discuss the tasks necessary to meet that promise and have team members project how long those tasks should take to complete. Then team members should be encouraged to commit to completing their tasks within that predicted amount of time.

Maintain Diversity of Opinion

A team of yes-people will not lead to a successful program; look for those people who have different opinions and are willing to voice them.

Disagreement in a divisive manner is counterproductive, but encouraging team members to look for faults in solution paths and to voice disagreement early on will stimulate more robust and complete solutions.

Look for Diversity of Technical Skill

Some of the best data-management people I have met had their original training in other areas and came to data management as a way of achieving goals in their selected profession. Their business background prepared them for looking at information modeling and use in creative ways. Yet there is also a need for personnel trained in engineering and computer science to ensure that things are being done efficiently and in accordance with best practices.

Keep Your Eyes on the Prize

Remember that the goal is not to build the most impressive piece of technology, but to integrate the practices, software, and hardware into a system for addressing business needs. Remember the 80/20 principle: 80% of the value can be achieved with 20% of the work. Do not let your team be distracted by focusing on getting a complete solution if one is not necessary to reap most of the benefits.

Strategic versus Tactical Planning

Earlier I briefly mentioned the distinction between long-term strategic thinking and short-term tactical thinking. After having seen and heard about numerous BI program failures, I have come to the conclusion that to succeed, we must strike a balance between shooting for the long term while satisfying our clients' requirements in the short term.

Long-Term Goals

The long-term strategy of a BI program involves building an analytical information platform from which business value can be derived. The seamless enterprise BI environment essentially is a factory to collect information from multiple sources, prepare that data for use, aggregate it in a repository, provide analytical services, and supply the means for accessing and viewing the results of those analytical processes, as can be seen in Figure 3.1.

This end state is very appealing, because it provides the necessary business-oriented functions that any particular vertical area could desire. Yet the inability to deliver the entire package within a short amount of time

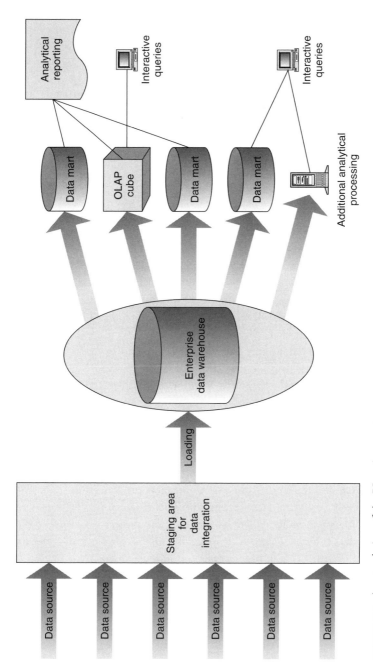

FIGURE 3.1 A general view of the BI environment.

limits the feasibility of a team's building the entire intelligence resource at one time. In fact, committing a large amount of resources to a long-term project without identifiable short-term results is the kind of risk that most senior-level managers are not likely to take.

Therefore, it is important to develop the end-state vision while keeping in mind that short-term successes are critical. And designing the implementation plan with those short-term value-adding deliverables in mind is more likely to lead to overall success than the big-bang approach.

Short-Term Success

The smart approach is to look for opportunities for short-term successes that conform to the plan for reaching the end state. For example, if a business client anticipates having a data mart populated from a data warehouse, it may not be necessary to source the mart directly from a data warehouse. Instead, it may be possible to create a data mart from the required data sources that satisfies the clients' needs, and providing the mart and the associated analytical and reporting components will yield business value while not detracting from the strategic goal. Later, when the large-scale repository is available, the data mart can be reconfigured to be sourced instead from the repository. In this case, the client may see no difference in the analytical environment, so having implemented the mart first is a short-term success that fits in with the long-term goals.

Other ways to achieve short-term successes include projects that have alternate benefits. For example, a data cleansing effort that improves a data set's quality will benefit the current users of that data and the BI clients. Being able to fund and deploy a data cleansing effort will not only provide immediate value, it will also provide a set of business processes and tools that can be leveraged for future data cleansing projects.

The decision as to which kind of smaller project to select should be directly driven by client needs. It is possible that some work may need to be done in the wrong logical order or perhaps may even need to be implemented twice. But if this must be done to satisfy the senior-level sponsor, it is important to make sure business clients are satisfied that their perceived intelligence needs are being met. And remember: Always look for an opportunity for reuse, whether it be a tool, a process, metadata, or data sets.

Summary

In building a BI program, it is important to focus on the idea that the success of the program is not always tied to whiz-bang technology. The most important factors to success are being able to partner with senior-level business sponsors, identify and articulate high-level goals and expectations, and build the right team to execute the vision. Keep these success factors in mind throughout the process:

- Maintain strong management.
- Set appropriate expectations.
- Establish metrics for conformance with those expectations.
- Understand what technology can and can't do for you.
- Create a flexible and extensible data architecture.
- Use only high-quality data.
- Reuse as much as possible.
- Deliver on your promises.

Long-term strategic compliance can be achieved through tactical short-term successes. Plan to be flexible with the long-term implementation plan if that guarantees continuation of the program. And always keep your eye on the prize!

CHAPTER 4

The Business Intelligence Environment

We have articulated the value of managing our information as an asset, we have explored the added value that can be derived through instituting business analytics in the organizations, and we have lined up the right senior-level sponsors for our business intelligence (BI) program. Now what? The time has come to discuss a high-level architecture required for implementing the BI program.

Realize that the BI process essentially revolves around the ability to flow large amounts of disparate data into a single repository and then in turn to flow restructured data for decision-support purposes out to data marts and related analytic process, as is seen in Figure 4.1.

Designing the program is the process of:

- Understanding the business requirements
- Determining what kinds of analytical applications are needed to support those requirements
- Determining the subject areas around which those analytical areas revolve
- Determining what kind of subject-oriented information framework will support those applications
- Determining what information is needed to feed the information framework
- Providing the means for integrating that data into the information framework
- Mapping those requirements onto a general BI architecture

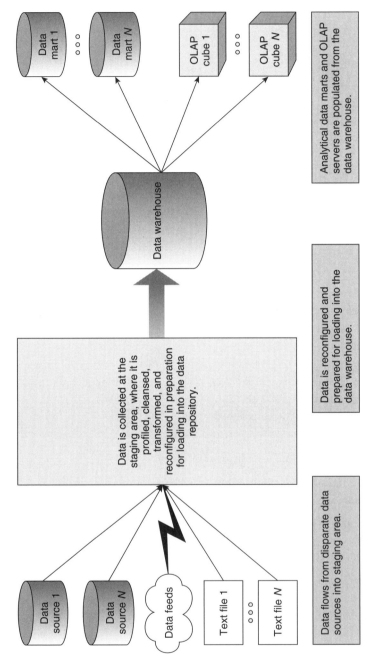

FIGURE 4.1   A high-level view of the information flow.

The focus of this chapter is to provide the manager with a working vocabulary based on a high-level view of the BI environment. Although my goal is to provide a 50,000-foot view of the entire process, there are clearly some concepts that beg for deeper discussion, and those topics are covered in later chapters. Because I do not want to minimize the importance of some of the more mundane aspects of a BI system (e.g., hardware size requirements), in this chapter I will provide a quick guide to the aspects of the entire BI system.

The Business Case

Being able to effectively plan the implementation of a BI program requires an understanding of the high-level building blocks that make up the program. Without a fundamental road map of what parts are needed, it is unlikely that your project will succeed. The business case for this chapter is to discuss the highest-level abstraction of what needs to go into a BI program and then to inspire the team leaders to identify knowledge gaps *before* actually implementing the system.

The Business Intelligence Process

The process of creating actionable knowledge is based on more than just sloshing data between different points in an organization. Most of this book is focused on discussing the procedural aspects of building the BI program, and so we will provide a quick overview here to briefly introduce those topics.

Business Process Modeling and Analytic Needs Assessment

These two topics go hand-in-hand, because it is not likely that we can analyze metrics associated with a business area if we do not understand the processes that compose that business area. Business process modeling and information flow modeling is the study of what information a business needs and how that information moves from its sources to its destination. We cover this in more depth in Chapter 5.

Information Repository Management

The keystone of a BI program is the centralized enterprise data repository. The term *data warehousing* is usually used to describe this topic, and a *data warehouse* is a centralized, nonvolatile repository of enterprise information, gathered and integrated from multiple sources and placed in a data model that is suitable for the analytical process. In Chapter 6 we discuss the star-join structure as the basic data warehouse data model, the difference between that model and the entity-relationship model, and the issue of metadata.

Business Rules

We might say that any operational or analytical process that is involved in running or improving a business is driven by a set of business rules. Whether these rules are dictated by external bodies (such as a regulatory board), by internal directives (such as an executive process leadership group), or by the way that business is done within an industry, there is a method to separate the rules that drive a process from the process itself.

Business rules expose the logical abstraction of a business process, and the collection of a process's business rules comprise part of its metadata. In Chapter 7 we will look at business rules in greater detail.

Information Integration

Information integration is the process of accumulating the data from the disparate sources that will be used to populate the main enterprise data repository. For example, a company might want to build a data warehouse that will feed a customer relationship management (CRM) application. That data warehouse will likely be populated with customer information, prospect information, sales histories, customer service histories, credit data, product data, clickstream data, along with external demographic and psychographic data enhancements, and most of this data will come from different sources.

Information integration consists of a number of components, including:

- **Data profiling,** a process to discover metadata, evaluate the statistical characteristics of columns within a data set, and document relationships between columns within a data set. We cover this topic in greater detail in Chapter 8.

- **Data quality and validation,** by which client data expectations are used as the basis for cleansing and information compliance. We cover this area in greater detail in Chapter 9.

- **Data transformation and integration,** which is the process of modifying data to conform to the target formats or applying transformation to enable the combination of data sets, as a prelude to the actual integration and binding of those data sets into a form suitable for loading into a data warehouse. We discuss this topic in greater detail in Chapter 10.

Knowledge Creation

Knowledge creation is what takes place when the data analysts review information presented in an analytical context and are able to infer or discover what we referred to in Chapter 1 as actionable knowledge. The knowledge-creation activity can be a directed one, through the use of specific business analytics (as described in Chapter 2), or an undirected one, driven by an automated knowledge discovery process. In Chapter 12 we will look at some of the directed processes; in Chapter 13 we look at the data-enhancement process; and in Chapter 14 we look at data mining and knowledge discovery.

System Infrastructure

There are three logical system platforms that are required for a BI program; these correspond to the three aspects of provisioning information from source to ultimate destination (Fig. 4.1). Those systems are:

- The **data staging area,** the target area where data from the different sources are collected and integrated in preparation for loading into the data warehouse
- The **data warehouse,** the centralized nonvolatile data repository
- The **analytical environment,** consisting of data marts, which are subject-oriented subsets of the data warehouse (and which source data from the data warehouse), along with the analytical interfaces and tools that provide the interface to the user

Although it is likely that there is only one staging area and warehouse, there may be many instances of the analytical systems, each possibly requiring its own physical system. In this section we look at some of the issues associated with the components of the infrastructure needed to support these activities.

Hardware

The hardware requirements for the three virtual components differ based on the activity that is to be performed. The goal is to concentrate on the performance of that activity and to size the hardware to meet the clients' agreed-to service levels. For the staging area, the most significant activities are (temporarily) collecting and storing data and the applications needed to integrate that data, as a prelude to loading it into the data warehouse. The basic requirements, therefore, are high-connectivity bandwidth (for moving data into and out of the staging area), lots of storage space, and high performance capability for the integration process. We will explore the benefits of high-performance parallel systems in Chapter 11.

The data warehouse manages the centralized repository and is mostly characterized as a system for managing a very large database. There are two aspects to this: (1) the need for storage to maintain the data tables that compose the warehouse; (2) the kinds of interactions that are performed on the front end. If the warehouse is directly accessible to a large number of data clients and analytic applications simultaneously, again the client base and the implementers must agree to performance levels to which the system must adhere, and the system would be sized accordingly. If the warehouse is used solely as a source for alternate data management and analysis platforms, some of those performance requirements may be pushed to the analytical system.

Depending on the kind of analytical system, there may be different requirements. For example, an OLAP server (see Chapter 6) may need to store data in a multidimensional form along with aggregated summary data, perform the aggregations, and support a number of simultaneous data analysts with interactive queries. On the other hand, a different analytical platform might just provide a visual interface to a query tool used for speculative analysis, and that system may not need either the computational or storage power of the OLAP system.

Relational Database Management System

Whether it is used as a temporary holding place for staging data or as the database platform in which the data warehouse data is stored, the BI environment relies on the use of a relational database management system (RDBMS) for information management. Even as data is stored in the star-join structure (see Chapter 6), the linkage between the tables is enabled through a relational database framework. Separate OLAP servers may manage their own copies of data in a dimensional database that is separate from the data warehouse.

Data Management/Storage Management

When large amounts of data are being manipulated, there must be an underlying data storage management platform that can support the kinds of activities performed in a BI environment. The implication is that a separate data storage subsystem can be a major component of the BI environment. It is worthwhile to incorporate a sharable, networked storage system that provides efficient data access from any point while allowing for simple extensibility.

Application Servers

Business intelligence analytics are likely to have been built using a three-tier architecture, in which the base data server acts as the first tier, the data consumer's desktop acts as the third tier, and separate application servers act as the middle tier. No matter what the analytical application, there is a need for separate computational resources unbound to the client location that can interact with the data warehouse.

The choice of the type, size, and number of application servers depends on the kinds of analytics. OLAP servers that manage their own copy of data will need more storage and computational power, whereas simple query engines may only need to manage connections to the database and the ability to stream data.

System/Network Management

As in any multitiered hardware and software architecture, the more mundane aspects of network and system management are not to be ignored. Typically, your data consumers will expect the BI team to guarantee certain levels of service, with respect to content delivery as well as timeliness of data warehouse population, propagation of data to the data marts and OLAP servers, and especially system response times and the delivery of reports. After the process has been refined, these service levels may depend on operating a healthy system, which in turn requires staff and tools for system and network management.

The system administration effort incorporates the following topics:

- **Performance management,** which evaluates system performance and highlights bottlenecks within the environment

- **Capacity planning,** which is the task of determining how to size the components within the environment

- **Backup and recovery management,** for backing up data resources and restoring the data after a data loss

- **Configuration management,** for mapping and designing the network and system layout, managing changes throughout the systems (such as upgrading client software at a large number of client desktop machines), and versioning (such as managing multiple generations of metadata or system configurations)

- **Continual monitoring,** which incorporates tools to keep track of how the system is performing and to generate alerts when performance or correctness issues arise

Information Access, Delivery, and Analysis

We have already looked at the physical nature of the overall system, but a BI program cannot succeed without providing easy but secure access to the data required for analysis. In this section we look at the aspects of information access and analysis.

Information Delivery

This area includes the ability to manage the creation and dissemination of information and knowledge throughout the enterprise. This includes:

- **Query and report management** from the content-based side (i.e., being able to create the queries for reports and manage those queries so that they can either be exploited in raw form or exported to individuals for customization).

- **General content management,** such as the ability to describe templates for the assembly of reports from the results of queries coupled with other supporting documents, such as text or images.

- **Document management,** which provides a searchable and accessible repository for all kinds of documents in alternate forms (e.g., plain text, html, pdf, multimedia files). A document management system may also support workflow and version control associated with evolving documents.

- **Publish/subscribe mechanics,** which enable data clients to provide general access to their own work products or to request information (such as daily reports). This is accommodated through various means of broadcasting, such as periodic e-mails, or even more sophisticated alerting mechanisms, such as paging, wireless broadcasting to laptop computers or personal digital assistants (PDAs).

- **Information packaging and delivery,** which provides for assembling reports and documents in the best format for the business client and the means for delivering all the information packages to their destinations in a timely manner. An example might be capturing the results of a financial analysis through a series of data mart queries, but then assembling the report in spreadsheet form that can be automatically delivered to a business client's desktop.

Security

Many of your data clients will not be physically located at the site of the data warehouse or even in the same building. Also, there may be sensitive data that is now to be seen by all data consumers. Last, even data that is visible to all internal clients should not be readable by malicious people external to the organization. There is a requirement to integrate a security framework as part of the BI architecture.

A security framework incorporates:

- Hardware and software firewalls for managing network traffic.

- Encryption of information, both on the server side and on the client side.

- Intrusion protection, to prevent outsiders from breaking into the system; these applications may include rule-based and behavior-based monitoring to look for suspicious network behavior.

- Policies for managing or restricting client access to specific data sets within the RDBMS, whether on the table, column, or row level.

- Policies for controlling access to data and security for analytical and interface tools.

Portals

A portal usually refers to a configurable Web-based interface that allows a data client to personalize the presentation of reports, results, and automatically generated trigger-based alerts. A portal will also provide an interactive interface for ad hoc queries. As an example, the customization of a portal can be driven by the creation of an *executive dashboard* (similar to the intelligence dashboard covered in Chapter 2) that highlights key performance indicators (KPIs) that are fed from the data warehouse and BI analytics engines. This kind of portal should also allow for drilling-down through any visual representation of a KPI.

Visualization

The term *visualization* can refer to the different ways that information can be represented for the purposes of quick analysis. *Visualization* can refer to the ability to create two- and three-dimensional views of numeric data, which can ease the process of looking for unusual data or outliers within a data set, or perhaps summarize a business event or situation that is difficult to express in a text report.

Visualization can also refer to more creative ways of exploring information, such as connectivity relationships between entities, widgets (i.e., components) for building dashboards, displaying attribute intensity (such as how "hot" a product is based on the acceleration of demand in particular regions), and geographical plotting. Visualization tools often accompany other analysis end-user tools, such as OLAP environments.

Query and Reporting

Although we have addressed different kinds of data delivery and formulation in other sections in this chapter, it is useful to distinguish the packaging and delivery of information from the information that is expected to be inside these delivered reports. Typically, the kinds of reporting that would be expected in a BI environment include the following:

- **Standard reporting,** which are reports meant to convey the status of the business in operation, such as P&L reports, budget versus actual spending, expense reports, and production reports.

- **Structured queries,** which result in exposing specific routine queries such as sales per region. These can be parameterized to allow different clients to modify aspects of the queries for their own personalized use.

- **Ad hoc query systems,** which allow the client to formulate his or her own queries directly into the data. Some systems will provide query builders to help those unfamiliar with the query language syntax to assemble proper ad hoc queries.

- **Exception-based reporting,** which alerts individuals to events that have taken place within the environment.

A query and reporting tool is a visual interface that allows the data client to formulate the queries required for a particular business report and then to assemble the report presentation. The tool will mask out the technical details of the data access and configuration and can be used to manage and reuse canned queries or sequences of ad hoc queries.

Online Analytical Processing

Online analytical processing (OLAP) is both a process of viewing comparative metrics via a multidimensional analysis of data and the infrastructure to support that process. OLAP can support aggregation of cumulative data (e.g., sums, averages, minimums, maximums) or numeric data (such as sales, number of employees, number of products produced, inventories) presented in a way that allows for interactive "drill-down," or successive detail analysis and exposition. OLAP is both a process and representative of infrastructure; we discuss this in greater detail in Chapter 6.

Text Analysis

Data that lives in a database is called *structured* data; information that is incorporated into a document (or framework) that has some basic structure and taxonomy (such as certain kinds of Web pages, wedding notices, catalog descriptions) are said to be *semistructured*, in that they exhibit some structure that is looser than the standard ⟨attribute, value⟩ pairing of data within a database table. Free-form text is said to be *unstructured* data.

It is relatively easy to look at structured data and figure out what to do with it, because effort has already been invested in binding values to named column values within a record. It is more difficult to make sense out of less structured data, and we rely on more complicated text analysis tools to scan through that kind of information to extract any usefulness. The most recognizable form of text analysis tool is an indexing application that then allows for indexed searching, such as those Web sites that provide search capability through other Web sites.

More complex text analysis tools are used to try to transform the data embedded within the text into a structured form. For example, a recruiter might fancy a system that can transform a candidate's resume into a structured representation of that candidate's skills and training, with some value judgment of that candidate's skill level with each skill area. Because resumes are semistructured, this kind of text miner or analyzer would need to understand the structure of a resume as well as the key words that are of relevance in the business context. We will look at this kind of analysis in greater detail in Chapter 13.

Services

It is probable that the expertise required to assemble and run the BI program is not available within your organization. It is also probable that many stages of building the BI infrastructure require expertise no longer needed once the system has been put into production. For these and assorted other reasons, it is probable that you will need to augment your staff with external service providers to help move the BI program along. In this section we look at some of the services external suppliers can provide.

Architecture and Integration

When assembling a data warehouse and BI architecture, it may be beneficial to bring in consultants who have worked on previous successful BI projects to help architect the overall solution. Frequently the concept of "not invented here" (NIH) cannot only slow down the construction of the environment but also lead to its demise. Remember that the ultimate client is the business partner and that making that business partner satisfied with the program is the ultimate project goal. If that means hiring external consultants to help make it happen—do it!

In terms of data integration services, the numerous data integration and ETL software providers are likely to have supplied software to many similar organizations building similar systems. They may also offer consultative help in assembling the data integration process and making sure that it works.

At the end of the spectrum are service providers willing to import your data and your integration parameters, perform the integration, and then return the reformatted data to you. This may be a viable option when the provider has numerous tools and hardware at its disposal, for which you can eliminate your company's capital investment requirements.

Migration

Some organizations are interested in instituting a BI program, but their data resources are not in a state that can be properly integrated into a BI environment, either because their environment is in disarray or because their information is embedded in proprietary legacy systems from which it is hard to extract. As a preface to building a BI program, and in conjunction with a business process improvement program, it is useful to migrate older systems into more modern systems that are more amenable to data extraction and manipulation. Because this system or data migration is a one-time deal, bringing in a service provider to assist in the migration process is a reasonable choice.

Analytical Service Providers

If the cost of building the infrastructure is too much for your organization, though you still want to exploit a BI environment, then the answer might be an analytical service provider. This is a company that can provide any or all of the components of the BI process, ranging from data cleansing and integration services all the way to completely hosted data warehouse and analytical solutions.

Training

There are organizations (most notably, the Data Warehousing Institute) that are dedicated to providing training and education in the BI and data warehousing areas. It is worthwhile to make sure that your staff members are properly trained and that the organizations doing the training are recognized as providing the best knowledge when it comes to the techniques, design, and strategies to build successful BI programs. Training should focus on all aspects of the BI program, including data warehouse architecture, data integration, data marts, operational data stores, as well as the tools that are used, such as data extraction and transformation, OLAP systems, and front-end data consumer analysis tools.

Strategic Management

Last, sometimes neither the technical staff nor the business clients are completely aware of the capabilities that exist within the marketplace for providing business analytics. Again, it may be beneficial to engage external consultants familiar with your industry and with the analytical applications that have been built to support your industry.

Management Issues

The most critical management issue to be aware of at this point is that although the conceptual structure of a BI program is relatively straightforward, there are a lot of pieces that need to properly fall into place for the program to be successful. Realize that neither you nor those on your staff can possibly be experts in all of the areas necessary to successfully build the program. Also: At any time implementation starts to be driven by technology (i.e., "what's cool") rather than by business client needs is a serious red flag signaling that clients' needs are not being addressed at the necessary level. Make sure that the business partners are incorporated into the high-level architecture process as a way of vetting that design for their specific needs.

Seek to Learn More

The BI process is a combination of infrastructure and methodology. In this chapter we have tried to enumerate the high-level overview of both infrastructure and process. In the coming chapters we will peel away some layers of the onion to provide insight into those areas that require the most detailed management focus and understanding. But don't let this detract from the importance of the infrastructure details. Use this as an opportunity to explore those other books that treat it in much greater detail.

CHAPTER 5

Business Models and Information Flow

In any business application, there is (or at least, there *should* be) a distinct understanding of what business problem the application is meant to solve. For example, the side effect of a customer billing application is the generation of bills to be sent to customers. Other side effects may include registering accounting details and the calculation of a monthly usage report, but overall the application is meant to create bills.

Unfortunately in practice, as applications are modified, merged, and expanded, the high-level understanding of the business problem gives way to dependence on implementation details and decisions that impose artificial constraints on the system. By virtue of the structured algorithm design in which most implementers are trained, we impose a control structure on the way that information flows through the processing. But this control structure does not always reflect the true dependencies inherent within the original application, because, for instance, we may have decided to break up a single subprocess into two stages that could truly have been executed in parallel, but an implementation decision may force one stage to precede another.

And as the system evolves, technical employee turnover leads to a loss of knowledge about how that application really models the original business problem. Interim decisions have imposed a strict flow of processing control, which may no longer reflect the true data dependence of the application. So when they attempt to dissect the way information is being used within the system, most analysts might throw up their hands in frustration.

As a case in point, I remember a particularly difficult analysis project meant to identify performance optimization opportunities within a processing environment in which 40,000 programs were being run. Our goal was to look for ways to streamline the processing by finding programs that could be run in parallel. In theory it should have been simple to figure this out, because the environment in which these programs were run required manual scheduling. Yet the imposed execution schedule did not reflect the true control and data dependencies among the programs; instead, the schedule was based on the historical clock times at which the critical programs had finished! In the absence of a proper business model describing the control and data flow, this proved to be an exercise in futility.

In this chapter, we will describe what the savvy manager needs to know about how to coordinate a business model information flow, why the traditional assembly line of data processing can make this difficult, and how to organize participants to cooperate in mapping and documenting these models.

The Business Case

Consider this scenario: You have been tasked with building a data mart for the purpose of analyzing a customer value portfolio based on all customer interactions, ranging from telephone inquiries to purchases, returns, customer service calls, payment history, etc. On the one hand, you must determine what organizations are going to be supplying data, how and when the data sets are to be supplied, and how the data is to be organized and modified for integration into the data mart. In addition, you must be able to manage the quick integration of new data sets when it is determined that they are to be included in the data mart. Alternatively, you must be able to manage the provision of information services to the business analysts, each of which may be logically or physically situated in a different location.

It would be difficult, if not impossible, to build this system without having a clear understanding of where the data is coming from, how it needs to be manipulated before it enters a data warehouse, what data is to be propagated along the data mart, and what kinds of applications are using that data. More importantly, after the system is built it is critical to have a blueprint of the way that information flows into and out of the system to provide a tracking mechanism to back up any conclusions that are drawn through data analysis. To get a handle on how to manage this environment, it would be useful to have a high-level model of the processes associated with populating and using this data mart.

The Information Factory

Most systems can be viewed as a sequence of processing stages fed by directed information channels in a manner that conjures up the image of an Industrial Age factory. In fact, there are many practitioners who have taken to describing information systems in terms of an information factory (most notably Bill Inmon, Claudia Imhoff, and Ryan Sousa in *The Corporate Information Factory*). Although this view may actually constrain our perspective of the use and value of information, it is a useful paradigm for how a business process can be modeled.

The Value of Modeling Information Flow

At this point you may be wondering: "This is a book on business intelligence. Why should I care about nonanalytical processing?" The answer is that business intelligence (BI) is not limited to a company's interaction with customers, but instead includes knowledge accumulated from any collection of data consumers, such as internal (i.e., within the organization) and external (i.e., cross-company) business applications. As an example, consider a supply-chain interaction between your company and a collection of product suppliers. There is embedded business knowledge that can be derived from examining all details of those interactions, including measuring vendor sensitivity to your requests, response time, methods of delivery, compliance with contractual agreements, and conformance to just-in-time delivery issues. To extract this intelligence we must understand how we have implemented our business applications and determine what data we need to collect and where that information needs to be collected. The information flow model will assist in this determination.

Design versus Implementation

Traditionally, implementers are trained in algorithm design to break down each application into a collection of discrete processing stages that can be essentially implemented in isolation. When all the stages are finished, they are combined to form the complete application. But this process of discretizing the construction of applications leads to an assembly line model of information processing in the way that data and partial results are forwarded from one processing stage to another. These processes take data (e.g., a transaction stream or extracted records from multiple data sets) as input and provide some product as output. That can be a physical product (such as invoices to be sent out to customers), a side effect (such as the settlement of a sequence of transactions), or an information product (such as a BI report).

To remedy the eventual effects of this development process, an important part of the methodology of designing and implementing a business application is modeling the business process as a way of guiding the algorithmic implementation. In fact, building this model is the first step in the process of exploiting information. This business process modeling incorporates descriptions of the business objects that interact within the system as well as the interactions between users and those business objects. The same concept holds true for analytical and intelligence applications, where the eventual product is described in terms of analytical use and benefit.

Benefits of the Business Process Model

There are some major benefits for building this model. One is that understanding an information flow provides logical documentation for the business process. Another is that it exposes potential for adding value through the kinds of analytical processing we discuss in later chapters. A third benefit of this business modeling process is in communicating user requirements to the implementation team. When a formal framework is used to describe a process, not only does it ease the translation of user needs into system requirements, but it also provides the manager with a high-level view of how control migrates throughout the system and how information flows through the system, both of which in turn help guide the dissection of the problem into implementable components.

More generally, an information flow, as embodied as part of a business process model, provides the following benefits.

- **Development road map:** Identifying how information is used and diffused helps direct the development of interfacing between the discretized execution components as well as tracking development against the original requirements.

- **Operational road map:** When the application is in production, the model provides a description of how any analytical data sets are populated as well as a launch point for isolating problems in operation. It can also be used to track and isolate data quality problems, map workflow and control back to information use, and expose opportunities for optimization.

- **Management control:** This model provides a way to see how information propagates across the organization, to identify gaps in information use (or reuse), and to expose the processes involved in information integration.

- **Calculation of return on investment (ROI):** This allows the manager to track the use of information, the amount of value-adding processing required, and the amount of error prevention and correction required to add value and to relate the eventual business value back to the costs associated with generating that business value.

Information Processing and Information Flow

In this section we look at a number of different kinds of processing paradigms and how we can view a business application.

Transaction Processing

Operations in a transaction processing system are interactions between a user and a computer system where there is the perception of an immediate response from the system to the user's requests. A commonly encountered example of transaction processing is the use of an automated teller machine (ATM).

Although there is an appearance of a monolithic system that responds to user requests, behind the scenes each interaction may involve a large number of interdependent systems. The concept of a transaction actually incorporates this reality: A transaction is really a set of operations grouped together as a unit of work, where no individual operation takes its long-term effect unless all of the operations can take effect. So, using the ATM example, before the bank allows the ATM to disburse cash, the user's account balance must be queried to see if there are sufficient funds, the ATM must be checked to see if it has enough cash to satisfy the request, the user's account must then be debited, and the cash can be disbursed. Yet if the result of any of these subsidiary operations indicates that servicing the request is infeasible, all of the operations must be rolled back—you wouldn't want the bank to debit your account without giving you the cash, nor would the bank want the cash to be disbursed without debiting your account.

In this case the information flow follows the thread of control as it passes through the individual interaction associated with each transaction. A rough view of this information flow can be seen in Figure 5.1.

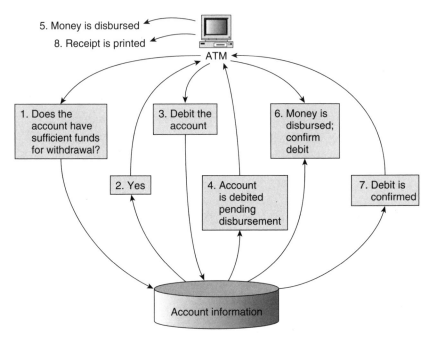

FIGURE 5.1 A transaction-based information flow.

Operational Processing

We will use the term *operational processing* to refer to a system that makes use of computers to control a process. An automated manufacturing line may have multiple machine components, each requiring system control instructions based on its internal operational requirements as well as depending on information inputs from other interconnected machine components within the entire system. For example, a potato chip manufacturing process contains a series of machines, such as a washer, a slicer, a fryer, a sorter, a flavor enhancer, and a packaging machine, each of which helps transform a potato into a collection of potato chips.

In this example, there is a lot of information required at multiple processing locations throughout the system to guarantee continuous, managed control of the system. Data about the individual interactions between sequential stages as well as systemic data need to be propagated to multiple controllers. To continue our potato chip factory example, each processing stage requires information about the flow of (unfinished) product from the previous stages. In addition, certain events will trigger auxiliary control operations (e.g., the seasoning hopper volume falls below the required amount, triggering an alert and a pause in the assembly line). And global events can also trigger actions (e.g., the cooking temperature exceeds a safe limit, triggering a complete line shutdown).

Operational process information flows are likely to connect heavy sequential operational processing augmented by lightweight interconnections for exchanging control information.

Batch Processing

In contrast with transaction processing, batch processing takes collections of sequences of similar operations that are to be executed in *batches* (hence the name). Although both transaction processing and batch processing execute a series of operations, batch processing differs from transaction processing in terms of information flow in the granularity of application of each processing stage. A batch processing application is more likely to apply each processing stage to a set of data instances as a whole and then push the result to the next processing stage.

As an example, a company might accumulate transaction-based sales orders during the day but process those orders and prepare order fulfillment as a batch process at night. The fulfillment processing aggregates order line items by customer, determines packaging requirements, generates pick lists that instruct the warehouse workers what items are to be selected for each shipment, generates shipping labels with appropriate shipping vendor data, updates inventory totals, and generates orders to restock inventory, among other operations.

Batch processing information flows typically convey heavy data payloads between multiple processing stages, each of which performs a single component of the overall unit of work for the data collection. A rough view of a batch processing information flow can be seen in Figure 5.2.

Analytical Processing

Analytical processing involves the interaction between analysts and collections of aggregated data that may have been reformulated into alternate representational forms as a means for improved analytical performance. In this case, the information flow model most likely will take on two aspects: the flow of information into the analytical processing environment from its suppliers and the flow of information from the analytical processing system to its users. The first flow is likely to be more of an operational flow, in which data sets may

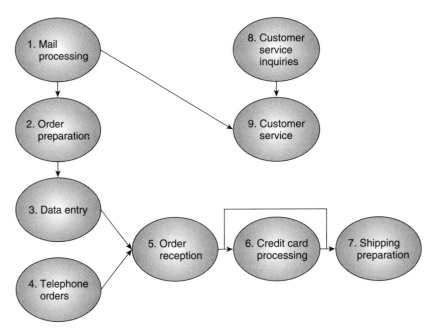

FIGURE 5.2 A batch processing information flow for order fulfillment.

be extracted and moved in large chunks to a staging area where those data sets move through different processing stages. And despite the BI aspect of the users' interactions, the information flow between the data mart clients may resemble a transactional information flow, with multiple analysts executing sequences of queries, although here there is less likely to be true transactions. A sketch of the information flow for analytical processing can be seen in Figure 5.3.

The Information Flow Model

The business process model reflects how a business process works; when we peer under the top layer of that model, what is exposed is the model for how both information and control are propagated through the business application. It is useful to have a formal way to describe the way data propagates through a system; in this section we will introduce a high-level information flow model.

An information flow model distinguishes the discrete processing stages within the process, describes how information flows through that system,

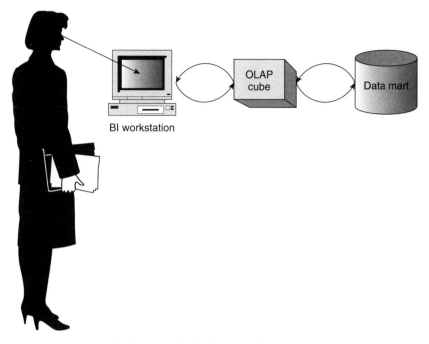

FIGURE 5.3 An analytical processing information flow.

and characterizes the kinds of data items that flow through the process. This model is valuable because it provides a basis for distinguishing between data dependencies, control dependencies, and artificially imposed implementation dependencies, which in turn can lead toward flow optimization, identification of bottlenecks, finding locations for insertion of data validation monitors, inserting data collection points for later analysis, and opportunities for increased business analysis points.

Information Flow: Processing Stages

In an information flow model, we distinguish discrete processing stages. Although the following list is by no means complete, we can characterize each processing stage as one of these classes.

1. **Supply**—the stage from which external suppliers provide data
2. **Acquire**—the internal stage where external data is acquired
3. **Transform**—a stage where information is modified to conform to another processing stage's input format

4. **Create**—an internal stage where new data instances are created

5. **Process**—any stage that accepts input and generates output (as well as generating side effects)

6. **Package**—any point at which information is collated, aggregated, and/or summarized

7. **Switch/route**—a stage that determines, based on some discrete set of rules, how to route data instances

8. **Decide**—a stage where some interactive (real or automated) agent's choice is captured

9. **Portal**—the delivery point for data that is meant to be consumed

10. **Consume**—the exit stage of the system

Information Flow: Directed Channels

Data moves between stages through *directed information channels*. A directed information channel is a pipeline indicating the flow of information from one processing stage to another, indicating the direction in which data flows. Our model is represented by the combination of the processing stages connected by directed information channels. Once we have constructed the flow model, we assign names to each of the stages and the channels.

Data Payload Characteristics

The last aspect of an information flow model is the description of the data items that are propagated between any pair of processing stages. The characteristics include the description of the information structure (i.e., columnar attribution), the size of the data instances, and the cardinality of the data set (i.e., the number of records communicated). More sophisticated models may be attributed with business rules governing aspects such as directional flow, validation, and enhancement as well as processing directives.

Usage in Practice

This section provides a few examples where value can be derived from modeling business process and information flow.

Information Valuation

In Chapter 2 we discussed the concept of the value of information; we can make use of a business process model to guide the determination of metrics appropriate for measuring the value of data as well as identifying the locations for the insertion of monitors to collect those measurements. For example, if we want to measure how much a certain data set is used, we may want to tag the data at its insertion point into the information flow and to insert monitors at delivery points to check for the tagged item to tally usage statistics.

Root Cause Analysis

One example of the use of an information flow model is in identifying the source of a data quality problem. The effects of a data quality problem might manifest themselves at different stages within an information flow, perhaps at different data consumption stages. But what appear to be multiple problems may all be related to a single point of failure from earlier in the processing. By identifying a set of data quality expectations and creating validation rules that can be imposed at the entry and exit from each processing stage, we can trace back through the information flow model to the stage at which the data quality problem occurred. At that point we can follow forward through the information flow to find all processing stages that might be affected by this problem. Fixing the problem at the source will have a beneficial affect across the board, because all subsequent manifestations should be eliminated.

Operational Performance Improvement

Another use of an information flow model is to gauge both the strict control and data dependencies within the system, and the performance behavior for transferring data between processing stages as well as processing at each stage. An information flow model will show the true dependencies, which can then expose opportunities for exploiting task parallelism at the processing stage level. In other words, if there are two processing stages that are control independent (i.e., neither stage requires the completion of the other in order for it to begin) and data independent (i.e., neither stage's input is directly or indirectly derived from the other), then those two stages can be executed at the same time.

Large data set transfers also form bottlenecks, as do computationally intensive processing stages. If there are no data dependencies associated with the data flow or associated with each processing stage, then the business and information flow model can be used to explore opportunities for exploiting data parallelism. For example, if there is a large data transfer between two processing stages, it may be of value to break up the transferred data set into chunks that can each be transferred over multiple physical input/output (I/O) channels.

Modeling Frameworks

Conceptual business process and information flow modeling can be actualized in different ways. In this section we'll explore some formal frameworks used for information and activity modeling, although these are just a sampling of the many frameworks available.

Use Case Analysis

Use case analysis, a process described by Ivar Jacobson in his book *Object-Oriented Software Engineering*, was designed to understand the nature of interaction between users of a system and the internal requirements of that system. A use case model specifies the function of a system and describes what the system should offer from the user's perspective, using three components.

- **Actors,** representing the roles that users play
- **Use cases,** representing what the users do with the system
- **Triggers,** representing events that initiate use cases

Whereas a use case describes a specific way of using the system by performing part of the function, a use case also represents a course of events that takes place when an actor interacts with the system. In the use case model, a trigger (which may occur as a result of an input data structure or an actor requesting an action, such as a report, but providing no input data, time, or some internal database or system event) is an event that initiates a use case. The collection of use cases constitutes a specification of the system. Embedded in the use case model is the conceptual business process model, although because the model is meant to help drive the requirements gathering for implementation, it may not be sufficient to represent the actual information flow model we discussed earlier.

Unified Modeling Language

As a successor to use cases, the Unified Modeling Language (UML) was developed as part of the Object Management Group's (OMG's) model-driven architecture. UML is a very rich descriptive framework that allows analysts to describe many aspects of system architecture. UML integrates some of the best notions of previous formalisms, including use cases.

UML can be used to develop business process and information flow models, especially because it has a facility for describing system behavior. In particular, state machines and activity graphs can be used to model process stage interaction. In a **state machine**, each state represents a situation where some condition is true. When a condition changes, the system is represented by another state; this behavior is modeled as a transition from one state to another within the state machine, which ultimately summarizes the entire system behavior as transitions between multiple states within the system.

An *activity graph* is a special kind of state machine that models a computational process in terms of how control flow and object flow affect transitions between states. It is the activity graph that could be best used for modeling information flow.

Integrated Definition Language

Integrated Definition language (IDEF) is a modeling language designed to describe functional processing and information flows. It comprises two descriptive standards: IDEF0, which is used to describe activity models, and IDEF1X for describing data models. Although IDEF is mostly used for system requirement analysis and workflow modeling, the IDEF language can be used for modeling information flow.

The basic IDEF0 activity modeling object in an IDEF model is referred to as an ICOM, an acronym for "input, control, output, and mechanism." A general ICOM object can be seen in Figure 5.4. For modeling information flow, each ICOM object would represent a processing stage, with the input(s) and output(s) representing information channels and the control and mechanism describing the gating factors controlling the activity as well as the activity that takes place within the processing stage. The data that is being propagated along the inputs and outputs within the model is characterized using IDEF1X; each IDEF1X object describes an entity being modeled as well as relationships to other entities.

A complete system model, which embeds the information flow, is constructed as the outputs of one ICOM are connected to the inputs to other ICOMs. This sequential ordering of ICOMs exposes the operational dependencies inherent in the process and highlights the data dependencies. In addition, we can represent a processing stage at a high level and then decompose that stage into multiple ICOMS at a lower level, providing a hierarchical view through which the system may be drilled-down.

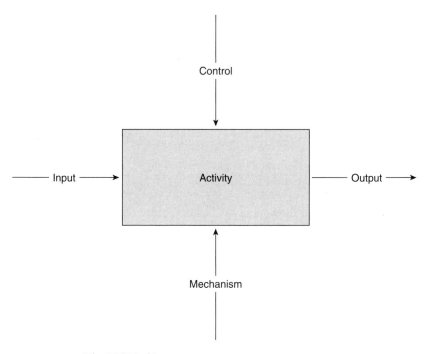

FIGURE 5.4   The ICOM object.

Management Issues

Probably the most critical management issue associated with business process and information flow modeling is the disconnect between the representation of the model and the actual implementation. There are a number of proposed standards for business process modeling, although the UML probably integrates the most popular methods.

The real issue is that despite the availability of CASE tools using UML or use cases, the output of these tools most likely will not be in a form that is easily integrated with legacy systems without a lot of external effort. In addition, even if these tools are used to generate code for actual use, there is little support for what could be referred to as the *roundtrip*, where generated code is modified or retooled for some reason but where that modification cannot be recaptured in the original modeling framework.

These issues imply that without a lot of investment in software infrastructure and management, the utility of a business process flow model is limited to management purposes, and positive input must be made by the savvy manager to relate application development and operation back to the model. This means that there must be frequent synchronization between the documented model and the actual system itself.

Another issue is the sheer size of these modeling frameworks. Because of the attempt at converging on one modeling framework, attempts at standards include so much material that it is unlikely that you would ever be proficient in all aspects of the modeling language, which adds to the risk of using any particular choice. Also, the learning curve for these modeling languages may be quite steep, requiring an investment of time and money in training staff.

Learning More

The modeling of how information flows through the different implemented business processes in an organization can provide detailed information about how the business is run. In turn, this information can be captured as virtual metadata that can be fed into later analytical contexts. This information flow information can help in the determination of what data sets are to be incorporated into the enterprise data warehouse that will eventually feed the analytical applications. It also identifies the best locations within the information flow from which the data should be extracted.

The use of CASE tools to augment the documentation of information flow (and general workflow) is a good idea, although it is preferable to use tools that do not rely on proprietary formats and that can export their representations to other knowledge management tools.

For information on use case modeling, consider the following books.

* *Object-Oriented Software Engineering: A Use Case Driven Approach*, Ivar Jacobson et al., Reading, MA, Addison-Wesley, 1992.
* *Writing Effective Use Cases*, Alistair Cockburn, Reading, MA, Addison-Wesley, 2000.

For information on UML, see the following.

* *The Unified Modeling Language Reference Manual (UML)*, James Rumbaugh et al., Reading, MA, Addison-Wesley, 1998.
* *www.omg.org/gettingstarted/what_is_uml.htm*
* *UML Distilled: A Brief Guide to the Standard Object Modeling Language*, ed 2, Martin Fowler and Kendall Scott, Reading, MA, Addison-Wesley, 1999.

CHAPTER 6

Data Warehouses, Online Analytical Processing, and Metadata

The hub of the business intelligence (BI) environment is the data warehouse, which is a centralized repository of data that has been compiled from a number of disparate data sources and is in turn used to power the analytical processing from which business value is derived. For the savvy manager to get the high-level view of the data warehouse, he or she must first be aware of the differences between traditional entity-relationship models and dimensional modeling, which is more suitable to the data warehouse environment.

The importance of data modeling in an analytical context, coupled with managing the metadata associated with that data, has evolved as a critical component to the BI environment. In this chapter we will look at data modeling, online analytical processing (OLAP), and metadata management, all of which incorporate ways to represent information for the purposes of BI.

The Business Case

There is a significant difference between the traditional use of databases for business purposes and the use of databases for analytical purposes. The traditional use revolves around transaction processing as the means by which a business's operation is modeled. The processes that surround the translation of a business operation into an operational system concentrate on two ideas: (1) Business requirements reflect interactions and relationships between modeled entities; (2) each discernable business activity can be described as a sequence of transactions grouped together as a single virtual operation to capture the effects of that activity in the model.

The evolution of relational database systems to accommodate the transactional flavor of the entity-relationship model was driven by the need to streamline this kind of business activity. On the other hand, the representation of information in this framework is not suitable for analytical purposes. First of all, the data model is optimized for the transaction process, but analytical performance would severely suffer, and secondly, the contortions through which database analysts put their models result in a data layout that is likely to be confusing to a business analyst.

To this end, the BI community has developed a different kind of data model that more efficiently represents data that is to drive analytic applications and decision support, called a *dimensional model*. By creating a centralized data repository using this kind of data model and aggregating data sets from all areas of the corporate enterprise in this repository, a data warehouse can be created that can then supply data to the individual analytic applications.

The business case justification here is simple: There is no BI program without the ability to separate and formulate data for analysis, whether through the construction of a data warehouse or through individual data marts. And a data warehouse cannot be built without understanding all aspects of what is in the data.

Data Models

A data model is a discrete structured data representation of a real-world set of entities related to one another. Over time, our understanding of the best way to represent our perceived model has changed to reflect the ways that we understand information along with the ways that we want to process that information. There is a significant difference between how we use data in an operational/tactical manner (i.e., to "run the business") and the ways we use data in a strategic manner (i.e., to "improve the business").

The traditional modeling technique for operational systems revolves around the entity-relationship model. Unfortunately, analytical applications that are relevant to BI are less able to take advantage of data when it is structured in the entity-relational form; alternatively, casting the same information into a dimensional structure greatly simplifies the ability to use data for strategic purposes.

Entity-Relationship Models

In the early days of databases, all the aspects of a data object or transaction (such as a bank account or a store purchase) would have been likely stored in a single entry in a database table, with all the aspects of the data instance embedded within that single record. For example, a sales record might log the buyer's name, address, the time of the transaction, and then a list (perhaps separated by commas) of the items and quantities of each product that was purchased. In terms of managing the business, this may have been sufficient, but it was difficult to manage; application code was written to handle any data manipulation necessary to extract any kind of information from these systems (Fig. 6.1). Additionally, because the buyer information was collected for each transaction, there was a significant amount of repeated and redundant data being unnecessarily stored, with the possibility of many errors creeping into the system.

In the early 1980s, a number of practitioners and researchers (most notably, E. F. Codd and Chris Date) explored the concept of a relational database, in which the way that information was modeled was viewed in the context of representing entities within separate tables and relating those entities within a business process context between tables using some form of cross-table linkage. In our (simplified) relational view of our sales database, we would have broken up our table into a customer table, a product table, a sales table, and a sales detail table, where each record in the sales table would represent a purchase transaction by a related customer and each item and quantity purchased would be in a related record in the sales detail (Fig. 6.2).

One essential goal of the entity-relationship model is the ability to ease the development of transaction processing by providing a reasonable scheme for mapping a business process to a grouped sequence of table operations to be executed as a single unit of work. The result of executing the group of operations is to reflect the effects of the business transaction inside the data model. Another essential goal of the relational model is the identification and elimination of redundancy within a database. This process, called *normalization*, analyzes tables to find instances of replicated data within one table (such as the names and addresses in our old sales table in Figure 6.1) that can be extracted into a separate table that can be linked relationally through a foreign key.

Although the entity-relationship model significantly helps in the design of operational systems, the diffraction of the information into the relational entities is, to some extent, confusing (consider the hallway-length entity-relationship diagrams that decorate the Database Administration [DBA] department's walls). In addition, the kinds of analytical extractions that are useful for BI applications are constrained by the representation of data in the pure relational model, turning what one might think would be an intuitive extraction into a set of poorly performing queries.

Name	AccountNum	Address	City	State	Order
David Loshin	018776	123 Main Street	Springfield Heights	NY	1 sprocket 10-X12, 3 widgets 10-Y39, 1 Vertical Wedge 11-8773, 2 Monc. 12-Y6554
James Banding	021745	84 Causington Way	Springfield	NY	4 5/8 widgets 10-Y33, 1 Horizontal Splunge 11-H6473, 1 cantiv. 19-K754, 2 sprocket 10-X12
SprockCorp	014145	10244 Washington Hwy	Springfield	NY	42 sprocket 10-X12, 42 sprocket holder 10-X12a
Shelbyville Engineering, Inc.	013189	1477 Shelbyville Tpk.	Shelbyville	NY	13 7/8 widgets 10-Y34, 1 Diag. Corker 17-D1273, 11 cantiv. 19-K754, 2 sprocket holder 10-X12a
Roger Simmons	016290	1022 Elm St.	Springfield Hghts	NY	12 Widget chains 10-Y72, 4 3/4 glod. 17-G511, 10 widget 10-Y39
ooo					
Dave Lotion	018777	123 Main Street	Springfield Hghts	NY	2 sprocket 10-X12, 1 widget 10-Y39, 5 Vertical Wedge 11-8773, 2 3/4 glod. 17-G511

FIGURE 6.1 A simple fat-record sales table.

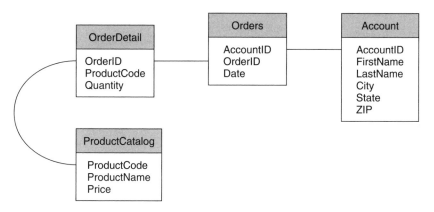

FIGURE 6.2 An entity-relationship model for sales.

Dimensional Models

The apparent failure of the relational model to efficiently provide data to knowledge workers is mostly due to the complexity of the data models and the difficulty in reconstructing a natural view of information that can be used in an analytical context. In contrast, an alternate technique to model data has evolved that allows for information to be represented in a way that is more suitable to high-performance access. This technique, called *dimensional modeling*, captures the basic unit of representation as a single multikeyed entry in a slender *fact* table, with each key exploiting the relational model to refer to the different *dimensions* associated with those facts. A maintained table of facts, each of which is related to a set of dimensions, is a much more efficient representation for data in a data warehouse. This is due to the ability to efficiently create aggregations and extractions of data specific to particular dimensional constraints quickly while being able to aggregate information.

Fact Tables and Star Schemas

The representation of a dimensional model is straightforward. A fact table contains records that refer to observable objects, usually within a business context. A straightforward example, seen in Figure 6.3, has a fact table that contains a key whose components are keys to individual dimension tables, along with some specific pieces of information relevant to the fact. This data is typically numeric so that it is amenable to aggregate functions (sum, max,

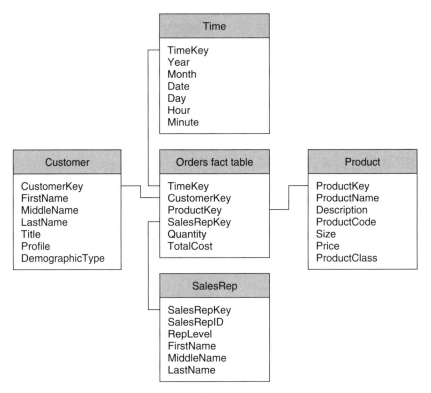

FIGURE 6.3 A dimensional sales model.

min, etc.). Each fact represents the total quantity of a product sold to a specific customer at a particular point-of-sales location at a particular point in time.

This model contains four dimensions: product, customer, point-of-sales location, and time. When you look at the picture of the model in Figure 6.3, you can see that the relationships between the fact table and the dimensions resemble a star, which is why this model layout is referred to as a *star join layout* or a *star schema*. Looking at this model, it is easy to see how straightforward drillable aggregates can be formed by collecting information by scanning through the fact table. For example, to derive information about the sales of any particular product by sales location, you would group the fact table records by sales location and then by product.

The fact table is related to dimensions in a star schema. Each entry in a dimension represents a description of the individual entities within that dimension. For example, in our sales example, the product dimension contains information associated with products, with text descriptions that accurately describe each product, such as product category, description, SKU number, package type, and package size.

Benefits of the Dimensional Model for Business Intelligence

Using a dimensional model for managing data in a data warehouse has a number of benefits.

- The framework is simple and predictable, which simplifies the process of extracting data, whether through client query tools, user interfaces, or general reporting tools. In fact, there is a generic process for extracting information that relies on the star schema: Create a join between the fact table and the desired dimensions and then group by dimension. By virtue of the key relationship between the fact table and the dimensions, this join is basically a single pass through the fact table.

- No matter what the dimensional breakdown, there is no inherent bias lent to any individual dimension, which means that as data consumers change their activity or behavior associated with the kinds of analyses or reports they desire, no specific action need be taken to rebalance the data to improve performance. In other words, the performance characteristics are not related to the data layout.

- Because the dimensional model is easily extensible, changes to the model can be handled gracefully without disrupting the operation of the data warehouse. For example, adding new values to a dimension involves simply adding new rows to that dimension; adding a new dimension is done by creating the new dimension table and modifying the key values in the fact table to incorporate the references back to the new dimension. Adding new attributes to dimension values is done by altering the tables and adding the new attribute values.

There are variations on the star schema that involve breaking out additional dimension information associated with a preexisting dimension (called *snowflaking*), but the general star schema is a powerful representational abstraction that is ubiquitous in building data warehouses. Dimensional modeling is not limited to a sales data repository; it is easy to imagine the same approach used to represent different kinds of business activities, such as supply chain models, insurance claims, medical records, and telephone call details.

The Data Warehouse

OK, so what is a data warehouse? Basically, a data warehouse is the primary source of information that feeds the analytical processing within an organization. In Chapter 2 we discussed a number of different analytic applications that are driven by business needs, yet most, if not all of these applications are driven by the data that has been migrated into a data warehouse.

It is interesting that there is a general consensus as to what constitutes a data warehouse. If you ask a number of experts, you will probably get a variety of answers, but they will focus on the following concepts.

- A data warehouse is a centralized repository of information.
- A data warehouse is arranged around the relevant subject areas important to the corporation as a whole.
- A data warehouse is a queryable source of data for an enterprise.
- A data warehouse is used for analysis and not for transaction processing.
- The data in a data warehouse is nonvolatile.
- A data warehouse is the target location for integrating data from multiple sources, both internal and external to an enterprise.

A data warehouse is usually constructed using a dimensional model. Information is loaded into the data warehouse after a number of preprocessing steps that include extracting data from the various data sources, data profiling (see Chapter 8), data cleansing (see Chapter 9), and a series of transformations (see Chapter 10), which may incorporate the application of business rules (see Chapter 7). That data is subsequently reformulated into dimensional form and loaded into the target warehouse. These processes compose what is referred to as the data warehouse's *back end*.

Once the data is in the warehouse, it may be extracted for canned reporting purposes, be subject to ad hoc querying, or be subject to subsetting for the construction of data marts, (or conversely, could be virtually constructed as the union of a set of data marts). Certain OLAP tools may draw their input directly from the data warehouse or from the extracted data marts.

The Data Mart

A data mart is a subject-oriented data repository, similar in structure to the enterprise data warehouse, but it holds the data necessary for the decision support and BI needs of a specific department or group within the organization. A data mart could be constructed solely for the analytical purposes of the specific group or could be derived from an existing data warehouse. Data marts are also built using the star join structure.

There are differences between a data mart and a data warehouse, mostly due to the different natures of the desired results. There is a school of thought that believes that data warehouses are meant for more loosely structured, exploratory analysis, whereas data marts are for more formalized reporting and for directed drill-down. Because data marts are centered on the specific goals and decision support needs of a specific department within the company, the amount of data is much smaller, but the concentration is focused on data relevant to that department's operation. This implies that different departments with different analytical or reporting needs may need different kinds of data mart structure (which may account for the diverse set of data mart products on the market).

Online Analytical Processing

Online analytical processing is different from the operational online transaction processing (OLTP). I have seen many definitions of OLAP, most of which describe what OLAP is used for. But the most frequently used terms are "multidimensional" and "slice and dice." Online analytical processing tools provide a means for presenting data sourced from a data warehouse or data mart in a way that allows the data consumer to view comparative metrics across multiple dimensions. In addition, these metrics are summarized in a way that allows the data consumer to *drill-down* (which means to expose greater detail) on any particular value or dimension.

The dimensions of data to be analyzed in an OLAP environment are arranged in a cube structure (actually, a hypercube), where summaries of any dimension can be seen in the context of other dimensions. Typically, values are aggregated up and down each dimension's natural hierarchy. For example, consider a database of sales information that records every sales transaction, including date, time, location, customer, product, quantity, price per product, and total sales. We might configure an OLAP cube with these dimensions:

- Customer
- Sales Location
- Product
- Time

Within these dimensions is a hierarchical structure, such as time periods (hour, day, week, month, quarter, year), sales locations (point of sale, store, city, county, state, region), and product classes (including specialized products such as shampoo, which is contained within the hair-care product class, which is contained within the beauty aids product class). The OLAP environment provides an aggregate view of data variables across the dimensions across each dimension's hierarchy. This might mean an aggregate function applied to any individual column across all the data related to each dimension (such as "total dollar sales by time period" or "average price by region"). For example, the data analyst can explore the total sales of beauty aid products within the Western region and then drill down across another dimension, such as the product dimension (total sales of hair-care products within the Western region) or the region dimension (total sales of beauty aids in California).

Because of the cube structure, there is an ability to rotate the perception of the data to provide different views into the data using alternate base dimensions. This conceptual ability to pivot or rotate the data provides the "slice" part; the ability to drill down on any particular aggregation provides the "dice" part.

The value of an OLAP tool is derived from the ability to quickly analyze the data from multiple points of view, and so OLAP tools are designed to precalculate the aggregations and store them directly in the OLAP databases. Although this design enables fast access, it means that there must be a significant amount of preparation of the data for the OLAP presentation as well as a potentially large storage space, because the number of cells within the cube is determined by both the number of dimensions and the size of each dimension.

For example, an OLAP cube with two dimensions, customer (1000 values) and sales locations (100 entries) would need 100,000 cells. Add a third dimension, product (with 200 entries), and you suddenly need 20 million cells. Add that fourth dimension, time (52 weeks), and your space requirement jumps to 1.04 trillion! Not only that, computational requirements grow in this same manner, because those aggregations need to be calculated and stored. No wonder many vendors rely on large-scale parallel machine architectures to support the OLAP data environment.

Metadata

The standard definition of *metadata* is "data about the data," which unfortunately is not a particularly enlightening description. It is useful to think of metadata as a catalog of the intellectual capital that surrounds the creation, management, and use of a collection of information. That can range from simple observations about the number of columns in a database table to complex descriptions about the way that data flowed from multiple sources into the target database.

From relatively humble beginnings as the data dictionary associated with mainframe database tables, the concept of metadata has evolved over time to become a major component of a BI program. Essentially, metadata is a sharable master key to all the information that is feeding the business analytics, from the extraction and population of the central repository to the provisioning of data out of the warehouse and onto the screens of the business clients.

The Importance of Metadata

The management of metadata is probably one of the most critical tasks associated with a successful BI program, for a number of reasons.

- Metadata encapsulates both the logical and physical business knowledge required to transform disparate data sets into a coherent warehouse.

- Metadata captures the structure and meaning of the data that is being fed into the warehouse.

- The recording of operational metadata provides a road map for deriving an information audit trail.

- One can capture differences associated with how data is manipulated over time (as well as the corresponding business rules), which is critical with data warehouses whose historical data spans large periods of time.

- Metadata provides the means for tracing the evolution of information as a way to validate and verify results derived from an analytical process.

Metadata is divided into two areas: technical metadata, which describes the data mechanics, and business metadata, which describes the business perception of that same information.

Technical Metadata

Technical metadata describes the structure of information, whether it is the data that is sourcing the warehouse or the data in the warehouse. Technical metadata characterizes the structure of data, the way that data move, and how it is transformed as it moves from one location to another. This may incorporate some or all of the following.

- **Connectivity metadata,** which describes the ways that data consumers interact with the database system, including the names used to establish connections, database names, data source names, whether connections can be shared, and the connection timeout

- **Table information,** including table names; the description of what is modeled by each table; in which database the table is stored; the physical location, size, and growth rate of the table; the data sources that feed each table; update histories (including the date of last update and of last refresh); the results of the last update; candidate keys; foreign keys; the degrees of the foreign key cardinality (e.g., 1:1 versus 1:many); referential integrity constraints; functional dependencies; and indexes

- **Record structure information,** which describes the structure of the record; overall record size; whether the record is a variable or static length; all column names, types, descriptions, and sizes; source of values that populate each column; whether a column is an automatically generated unique key; null status; domain restrictions; and validity constraints

- **Record manipulation metadata,** which includes record creation time, time of last update, the last person to modify the record, and the results of the last modification

- **Index metadata,** which describes what indexes exist, on which tables those indexes are made, the columns that are used to perform the indexing, whether nulls are allowed, and whether the index is automatically or manually updated

- **Data practitioners,** which enumerates the staff members who work with data, their contact information (e.g., telephone number, e-mail address), and the objects to which they access

- **Security and access metadata,** which identifies the owner of the data, the ownership paradigm, who may access the data and with which permissions (e.g., read-only versus modify)

- **Data model metadata,** which captures entity-relationship diagrams, dimensional layouts and star join structures, logical data models, and physical data models

- **Physical features metadata,** such as the size of tables, the number of records in each table, and the maximum and minimum record sizes if the records are of variable length

- **Reference metadata,** such as defined enumerated data domains, value ranges, likely values (for reasonableness tests), and mappings between data domains

- **Management metadata,** such as the history of a data table or database, stewardship information, and responsibility matrices
- **Transformation metadata,** which describes the data sources that feed into the data warehouse, the ultimate data destination, and, for each destination data value, the set of transformations used to materialize the datum and a description of the transformation
- **Process metadata,** which describes the information flow and sequence of extraction and transformation processing, including data profiling, data cleansing, standardization, and integration
- **Supplied data metadata,** which, for all supplied data sets, gives the name of the data set, the name of the supplier, the names of individuals responsible for data delivery, the delivery mechanism (including time, location, and method), the expected size of the supplied data, the data sets that are sourced using each supplied data set, and any transformations to be applied upon receiving the data

This list is by no means inclusive—it is up to the implementation to determine what information about the data is important. It is also important to maintain metadata for all the different data sets that are relevant to the BI process, which spans the sets of data that source a data warehouse, including legacy or mainframe systems, externally supplied data, vendor application data (such as the data stored in proprietary enterprise resource planning [ERP] systems), the data representation at the any preprocessing staging area, the data warehouse, any data marts, and all business analytics applications.

Realize that despite the length of this list, there are few organizations that capture all of this metadata. In addition, even those organizations that do capture a lot of metadata still have ample opportunity to make use of it.

Business Metadata

Business metadata incorporates much of the same information as technical metadata, as well as:

- Metadata that describes the structure of data as perceived by business clients
- Descriptions of the methods for accessing data for client analytical applications
- Business meanings for tables and their attributes
- Data ownership characteristics and responsibilities
- Data domains and mappings between those domains, for validation

- Aggregation and summarization directives
- Reporting directives
- Security and access policies
- Business rules that describe constraints or directives associated with data within a record or between records as joined through a join condition

The Metadata Repository

Metadata is data, which means that it can be modeled and managed the same way other data is managed. As the primary source of knowledge about the inner workings of the BI environment, it is important to build and maintain a metadata repository that is available to all knowledge workers involved in the BI program. Whether the metadata repository is physically centralized or distributed across multiple systems and however it is accessed, it is important to provide a mechanism for publishing metadata. The existence of disparate data systems that contribute information to the BI environment complicates this process, because each system may have its own methods for managing its own metadata.

Management Issues

As a manager, it is important to know that the area of data warehousing is not just about building BI frameworks. As is typical with any loosely structured technology, the amount of buzz surrounding data warehousing seems to be inversely proportional to the number of truly successful implementations, and my guess is that the number of available experts on data warehousing is probably equal to the number of failed data warehousing projects. The significant management issues associated with the topics in this chapter deal with aspects of this.

Dueling Opinions

There are basically two different schools of thought about how to build a data warehouse and a BI program, and for some reason there seems to be an almost religious adherence by practitioners of these different schools. One approach believes that a data warehouse is essentially the union of a number of data marts and that a warehouse can evolve over time from individual data marts. The other approach focuses on defining the centralized repository first, which then is used for sourcing the individual data marts.

The first approach provides the ability to deliver some value on a regular basis, whereas the second approach is more of a delayed big bang from which value can be achieved quickly after the initial implementation. In reality, there are advantages to both approaches, and perhaps there is some common ground that might apply to both approaches, in an iterative sense, to achieve intermediate results while conforming to the concept of an information factory driven by an enterprise warehouse.

The Technology Trap

One major plague of the data warehouse industry is that it is very easy to lose sight of the ultimate goal, which is to provide an environment from which business data clients can analyze and explore data that can help to improve their business. I have sat in interminable meetings associated with a particular project where data warehouse and metadata management architectures were discussed for hours on end without a single mention of why one choice was better than another for the ultimate business clients. Needless to say, not only was that project cancelled, but also within a year almost none of the meeting participants still worked at that company.

There are many interesting technologies associated with data warehousing, but too often technologists drive these projects. It is important to keep in mind that the *coolest* way to do something is not necessarily the *best* way to do it.

The Vendor Trap

Be aware that there are many vendors producing canned solutions and products under the guise of data warehouse, data mart, metadata repositories, and OLAP environments. Many of these are good products and can provide significant value to the process, but bear in mind that vendors are less concerned about ultimate client success than about making their numbers for the current quarter. There are many examples of high-cost software products that are too complicated for the customer to use without additional investment in training and consulting, and these ultimately end up as "shelfware."

Summary

The centerpiece of the BI environment is the data warehouse, which is a repository of data aggregated from different sources and reconfigured for analytical efficiency. Data marts are more concentrated departmental repositories that are designed for goal-directed analysis and that can be used to populate OLAP databases. Online analytical processing tools enable the data analyst to view comparative aggregated metrics across multiple dimensions while allowing for further exploration by drilling down a dimensional hierarchy.

For more information, consider these books:

Building the Data Warehouse, ed 3, W. H. Inmon, New York, John Wiley & Sons, 2002.

The Data Warehouse Lifecycle Toolkit, Ralph Kimball et al., New York, John Wiley & Sons, 1998.

Metadata Solutions: Using Metamodels, Repositories, XML, and Enterprise Portals to Generate Information on Demand, Adrienne Tannenbaum, Boston, Addison Wesley Professional, 2001.

CHAPTER 7

Business Rules

Within any industry, companies are basically guided by the same business directives and governed by the same laws and regulations. In either case, there are typical scenarios that drive any competitor's processes guiding both tactical (i.e., operational) and strategic decisions. Yet despite the assumption that all competitors are likely to respond to any event or situation in similar ways, numerous businesses are still able to enter and compete within the same industry, with different levels of success. For example, there is no significant difference between the way that various insurance companies operate, and they are all subject to the same industry-imposed rules (e.g., standardization of health care claim information) and government-imposed rules (e.g., government-imposed fees, taxes, regulations). But clearly, some insurance companies are much more successful than others.

In the past, success has been attributed to good management techniques, efficiency in running the business, and the ability to capitalize on opportunities quickly and efficiently. This last point implies the ability to recognize standard business operation as well as the ability to distinguish between normal operations, deviation from normal operation, and when deviation presents a profit opportunity. As the amounts of data pile up, though, the ability to absorb and, more importantly, react to opportunities exposed through data analysis decreases. Therefore, if we can articulate business behavior in a way that not only eases normal operations but also helps expose opportunities, then we can enhance our ability to succeed.

From our perspective, we are interested in the technologies associated with success, and we can paraphrase the previous paragraph by saying that business operation and behavior is driven by a set of rules, laws, regulations, guidelines, and policies. The ways that a company executes within those defined boundaries can affect that company's degree of success. From the business intelligence (BI) perspective, we might say that all business processes are governed by a set of *business rules*. What is also interesting is that in the myriad queries and reports generated within any organization, there are processes that apply different embedded business rules to data as it moves along the information flow.

In this chapter, the focus is on abstracting the operation of a business process from the rules that govern that process. In other words, we can differentiate between the rules that drive a process and the generic machinery that implements those rules and, consequently, that process. We refer to the separation of business logic from logic implementation as the *business rules approach*. The simplest way to describe a business rules system is as a well-described set of environment states, a collection of environment variables, a set of formally defined rules that reflect business policies, preferences, guidelines, etc. indicating how the environment is affected, and a mechanism for operationalizing those rules. In a business rules system, all knowledge about a business process is abstracted and is separated from the explicit implementation of that process. In this chapter, we will explore the use of business rule systems as a component of a BI strategy.

The Business Case

What we have in the past referred to as business rules are those rules applied by an industry expert when presented with a business problem and a description of the current state. Sometimes business rules are applied by a data analyst sitting in front of a database front end, and sometimes rules have been documented as program logic. Unfortunately, because programmers are frequently unknowledgeable in business details and lax in documenting their implementations, along with the high degree of IT employee turnover, business logic embedded in application software is at high risk of quickly growing stale or, worse yet, completely invalid.

Fortunately, therein lies an opportunity to capture business logic and turn it into a company asset. The area of business rules is an evolving technology that derives its value specifically from the separation of business logic from logic implementation. A business rules system is designed to capture the knowledge of all the assertions, constraints, guidelines, policies, regulations, etc. that drive a business process and manage that knowledge as a corporate asset. What follows are some of the major advantages of implementing business processes using a business rules system.

Encapsulation of Successful Business Logic

Presuming that we have successfully isolated the right queries or program logic used to identify a business opportunity as part of our BI program, it is worthwhile to attempt to automate that logic to free analyst resources for exploring new opportunities. For example, if our BI process has exposed a sequence of events that take place before a customer closes a bank account, it would be worthwhile to embed the knowledge of that sequence in an operational framework that can identify the sequence at an early stage and alert the proper agent within that workflow to contact the customer before the undesired event takes place. Implementing this *sequence watch* as part of a business rules system is much more efficient than having individuals continually querying a system looking for that specific transaction sequence.

Componentized Development

Large business processes can be decomposed into smaller subprocesses, each of which can be addressed using a set of business rules. Therefore, a team can implement an intelligence system that relies on business rules by selecting individual components of the BI process and incrementally developing and deploying a rule set for each component process.

Speed of Implementation

In the past, traditional business system development relied on multiperson coordination and communication that spans the gap between the business clients and applications programmers, filtered through a sequence of business liaisons and technical managers. The last link of this chain, the programmer, is unlikely to understand much of the modeled business process, and this communications chain can resemble the children's game of "telephone," where the message is incrementally eroded as it passes from the source to its intended target. The result: a flawed implementation requiring additional resources to coordinate and execute these communications.

Recall that the focus of BI development is not in the programming of code per se, but rather in the transformation of the business process into an executable application. Therefore, instead of spending time translating a business requirement into a specific hard-coded implementation, that time can be used in properly understanding and documenting the business rules to be implemented, which in turn separates the implementation of complex business logic from nonexperts. This narrows the time needed to complete an application. In addition, given the set of business rule inputs and expected outputs, many possible states of the system can be enumerated based on the rules set, and test cases can be automatically generated, subsequently reducing the time needed to test.

Ease of Modification and Rapid Response to Change

By extracting business logic from implementation, then when the business environment changes it is easier to update the rule base (instead of digging through undocumented code) to speed up policy implementation. Because a business rules system is built as a collection of rules, the system is easily changed by adding, removing, or modifying a single rule at a time. Changes to the rule base, as long as they do not create inconsistencies, can be integrated quickly into execution. Changes in policies, laws, and regulations effect changes in business processes, and rules systems make it easy to isolate those rules relevant to a specific process and adapt them to a changing environment, and because the application integration mechanics are handled by a runtime-based rules engine, the amount of coding is decreased. In addition, managing business rules as content makes business process reengineering easier. Having all the policies situated in one location enables analysts to understand what the application under investigation was meant to do.

Reuse

We have discussed the concept of reuse many times in this book, and the use of business rules is another instance where we can apply this idea. In any large environment, there are many situations where the same business rules affect more than one area of operations. Frequently the same business logic must be applied in different operational environments or departments. When different departments implement their own sets of business rules, each department will probably have implemented those rules in a different way, leading to dichotomies in understanding (at best) and to enterprise-wide inconsistencies or even contradictions, at worst.

The idea that each group relies on similar business logic allows us to try to capture similarly defined rules and reference data throughout the enterprise into a coordinated, centralized repository. We can start out by aggregating metadata (as discussed in Chapter 6) and then use this as the basis to build second-order business logic metadata based on higher-level business rules. Once the repository of rules is centralized, the actual processing and execution of these rules can be replicated and distributed across multiple servers located across an enterprise network. Therefore, a business rules system exposes an opportunity for enterprise-wide reuse through an organizationally shared business rule repository.

Persistence of Encapsulation of Business Knowledge

An expanding rule base is the basis for documenting and archiving the blueprints of its intellectual expertise, leading to a persistent knowledge base. The first benefit of this is that business processes that have been archived as rule sets can survive the departure of those subject matter experts (SMEs) that manage the process. This is in contrast to the past, when system knowledge was almost always embedded within the minds of individuals, although that knowledge could be considered corporate intellectual capital. Although the use of business rules cannot remove this knowledge from an individual's mind, it can encapsulate that knowledge as content that can be managed by the company, in a format that allows an easy transition during personnel turnover. The second benefit is reaped when business knowledge expressed in a format can be analyzed automatically, yielding an opportunity to infer additional BI embedded within the set of rules.

Augmented Capabilities

Rules engines operate in stages: Evaluate the environment, check for triggered conditions, and execute corresponding actions. Only those rules that are affected by inputs or triggers at each execution stage are going to be executed. In procedural languages, rule sequence execution is predetermined by the programmer. This not only forces many "rules" (as embedded in "if-then" statements) to be unnecessarily executed, it opens up the possibility for incorrect execution if the nesting of rules is not appropriate.

The Business Rules Approach

The business rules approach takes into consideration the encapsulation of business logic for the purpose of identifying or highlighting entities or events within a system. In essence, a business rules approach is meant to capture and subsequently automate the repetitive operations that have been properly vetted in terms of business value so that analyst resources can be engaged in discovering new opportunities for improvement or adding value. A business rules approach integrates the following:

- **Technology,** which includes the actual machinery that represents the different operational states of the business environment as well as the mechanics for describing and implementing the rules. This involves evaluating and selecting componentry and tools to use business rules and coordinating the integration with other aspects of the system.

- **Workflow,** which includes exploring the different entities involved in the business process, whether human or automated, the business scenarios in which these entities interact, and how these entities interact. The analysis for this involves describing the scenario, enumerating the entities, looking at the different business events that can take place within the environment, and evaluating how each entity reacts to each business event. In our vocabulary, the workflow aspect describes the changes in state that take place when a data input appears and a rule is applied.

- **Information,** which concerns the actual data that is used within the business process. Evaluating the data requirements of the business process eventually drives the parameters for using business rules as part of a BI program.

- **Rules,** which define the analysis of the assertional system that describes the interactions between the entities within the system. These also incorporate the description of what events trigger which responses and how those interactions relate to the business process.

What Is a Business Rule?

According to the Business Rule Group (an independent organization comprising practitioners in the field of systems and business analysis methodology, focusing on the nature and structure of business rules and the relationship of rules to systems' architectures), a business rule is a directive intended to command and influence or guide business behavior, in support of business policy that is formulated in response to an opportunity or threat. From the information system perspective, a business rule is a statement that defines or constrains some aspect of the business. It is intended to assert business structure or to control or influence the behavior of the business.[1]

From a practical standpoint, a business rule asserts a statement about the state of a business process or a directive describing changes in the state of a

---

1. Retrieved May 5, 2003 from *www.businessrulesgroup.org/brgdefn.htm*

business process. More simply, a business rule dictates what happens when a sequence of inputs is applied to one or more well-described scenarios.

There is strategic value to an organization that can consolidate its business rules and automate the implementation of those rules. Consolidation of business rules captures and controls strategic knowledge; in executable systems, this knowledge is most frequently incorporated into program logic, which is hard both to access and to control. Capturing and controlling the embedded knowledge requires that it be moved from the opaque representation of the computer program and restated abstractly using a formal definition framework.

One must realize that although there are many benefits to using a business rules system, this kind of technology cannot be introduced without overcoming some philosophical hurdles, which are discussed in the next two sections.

Rule Basics

When contemplating the use of business rules, you must first understand the lingo for describing such rules. In business systems, rules form the programmed representation of business policies and practices. Here are some examples.

- If the purchase costs more than $5000, it requires senior manager approval.

- If the customer's total of withdrawals today is less than $500, dispense the requested cash.

- If a reservation cannot be found for this customer, attempt to place the customer at another local hotel.

- Do not authorize a purchase that exceeds the cardholder's credit limit.

A rule is a statement that asserts some truth about the system, along with optional actions to be performed, depending on the assertion's truth value. Note that the examples just given meet this definition; in fact, all those rules can be restated in these simple forms. Rules stated either way can be transformed to the other form. For convenience we will make use of the "condition followed by action" form. Actions may consist of modifying the environment (which then may turn on other conditions or assertion violations) or restricting some modification to the environment, such as disallowing a transaction. Conditions are evaluated when some trigger event occurs; when a condition is evaluated, followed by taking of some action, we say that rule has been *fired*. For simplicity, we can describe different classes of business rules, and we will look at six kinds of rules, along with some examples.

Definitions and Specifications

In any system of rules, there must be a well-defined, agreed-upon "vocabulary" for rule specification; we can then enumerate the participants within the system along with the descriptive "nouns" and "verbs" that are used in describing the business process. For example, in a telecommunications application, we might define the different kinds of customers (e.g., business versus residential), the billing plans, and the different services and products that may be provided. This encapsulates a lot of the terminology that requires SMEs, and it also provides the first cut at accumulating business knowledge from the implementation of a business process. For example, when we begin to identify and name data domains, such as "United States Postal Service state abbreviations," or "International currency codes," we begin to assign some business meaning to sets of data whose previous identity revolves solely around its strict type structure.

Assertions

Assertions are statements about entities within the system that express sensible observations about the business. Assertions describe relationships between entities and activities within the framework. Together, the definitions and assertions drive the construction of the logical data model within which the business rules operate. Assertions incorporate business knowledge, connecting noun terms with verb phrases to describe facts about the system, such as:

- An *account holder* may *make a deposit* into an *account.*
- Any *order* must reference a *product code* and a *quantity.*
- *Delivery* may be executed via *air, rail,* or *truck.*
- An *option* must have an *underlier, expiration date,* and *strike price.*

Constraints

Constraints express unconditional conformance to a business statement; compared to a constraint, a data instance either conforms to that constraint or violates it. An event that violates a constraint will be rejected by the system, and therefore by definition no action can be taken that will violate a constraint. As a corollary, this implies a set of triggers and actions to indicate a violation in conformance. Here are some examples of constraints:

- A customer cannot order less than three items.
- A customer's debit total cannot exceed his account balance.
- No payment will be issued for any invoice missing a PO number.
- The kiln temperature may not exceed 2000°F.

Guidelines

A guideline expresses a desire about the state of the system or a warning about a potential change in the system. A violation of a guideline may indicate a change in the business process that requires attention. Here are some examples:

- If the total amount of all monthly loan payments exceeds 35% of an individual's monthly gross income, the loan request is subject to senior-level review.
- The payment is due within 10 days of receiving the invoice.
- The transaction should clear within the same 24-hour period in which it was initiated.
- If the customer has not initiated a transaction within the past 60 days, the account may be in danger of closure.

When guidelines are violated, the system is still in a valid state but may be progressing to an undesirable state in which some action is needed to prevent the system from reaching that state. Because violations of constraints do not constitute a system violation, events that violate a guideline are not rejected, but a notification should be generated to indicate the violation. Guidelines fit nicely into the BI program, because we may represent trends or predictability in this format.

Actions

An action is any operation that changes the system state, typically as a result of the violation of some constraint or guideline. Actions may include the following:

- Computations involving the determination of the value to assign to a named variable based on system state
- Initiating communication, such as packaging up a message and sending it to a specific user, or turning on a siren
- Initiating a workflow or a sequence of actions

Triggers

A trigger specifies a collection of conditions and the initiation of an action contingent upon the conditions' value. Triggers may combine constraints or guidelines with actions. For example:

- If the patient's temperature exceeds 104°F, alert a doctor.

- If a customer's shopping cart total exceeds her credit limit, notify the customer and restore the contents of the shopping cart to a state where the limit is not exceeded.

- If the transaction is not completed within 60 seconds, remove the transaction from the queue, increase its priority, and resubmit.

Inference

An inference specifies a collection of conditions establishing a fact that becomes true as a by-product of changes within the states of the system. An inference is essentially a new piece of information derived from the system state; when an inference rule is executed, that new piece of information must be integrated into the system state. Therefore, the application of an inference rule may result in the initiation of new transactions to log the new data within the logical rule model. For example:

- If the customer is delinquent in payment three times, the customer's alert status is raised one level.

- If the number of long-distance minutes used by the customer exceeds 500 four months in a row, the customer is a "high-volume" user.

What Is a Business Rule System?

A business rules system encapsulates sets of environment states, environment variables, and formally defined rules that reflect business policies, preferences, guidelines, triggers, etc. and how the environment is affected based on those rules. All knowledge about a business process is abstracted and is separated from the explicit implementation of that process; in operation, rules are coupled with a generic rules engine to form an application to implement the business process. A business rules system incorporates the following components.

- A *rule definition framework* that should present a methodology and environment for defining (and managing) a set of rules that are relevant to a particular business process.

- A *persistent rule base* enabling the storing, browsing, editing, and forwarding of defined rule sets throughout the rules system. Expect to have some globally shared repository and a publish/subscribe interface.
- A *rules engine* that can read a set of rules, connect to the requisite data sources and targets, and manage the state of the rules environment.
- An *execution framework* in which the rules engine will execute, whether it refers to a message stream, a database system, a workflow environment, or the like.

We can think of a business rules system as an abstract machine with a finite number of system "states," each of which represents some aspect of a business process (Fig. 7.1). Events and data act as triggers to change a state within the system, and business rules essentially describe the current state of the

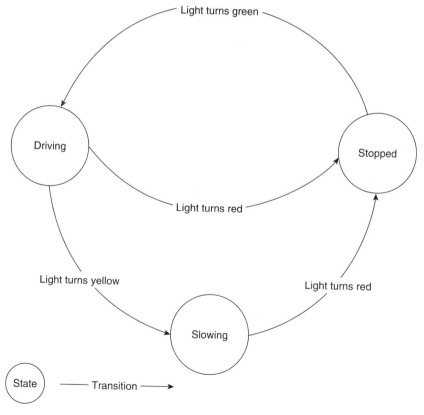

FIGURE 7.1 The abstract machine is governed by transition directives that indicate how the system changes state based on different inputs and events.

system, events or data elements that triggers state transitions, and the new state of the system. This system should include all state changes related to each input, as a matter of completeness. Because rules are declarative (i.e., they describe the system) instead of procedural (i.e., a description of a sequence of operations), at any point a number of rules may be applied without any predeclared constraint as to order of execution, thereby injecting a possibility of nondeterministic behavior.

For example, a traffic light can be described as a simple business rules system implementing a travel safety policy. A traffic light may exist in one of three states:

1. Green
2. Yellow
3. Red

Consider a single traveler within the system. When the system is in state 1, the light is green and the traveler may cross the intersection. If the light changes to yellow, the system moves into state 2 and any travelers that have not yet approached the intersection must slow down in preparation for the transition to state 3. When the light changes to red, the system is in state 3 and all traffic must stop. The final transition is when the light changes back to green, reentering state 1.

Rules Definition

All rules-based systems employ some kind of rules language as a descriptive formalism for describing all the aspects of the business process, including the system states, the actors, the inputs and events, the triggers, and the transitions between states.

A rules language is a framework for describing sets of rules. Because our description of a rule includes both a condition and an action, any standard programming language, such as C or C++, that contains IF-THEN-ELSE constructs can be used as a rules language. But the standard procedural programming languages impose a sequential order of execution, so their use as rules languages are limited.

This is because nondeterminism is associated with events and assertions in the modeled world. A procedural language will impose an artificial dependence on the sequence of events and can lead to unexpected results if those events take place in different orders. Instead, rules languages, by virtue of their declarative syntax, provide a way to express a set of rules without imparting any order of execution.

More frequently, rules definition is being embodied within a visual interface. The benefit of the graphical user interface (GUI) is the inclusion of syntax-directed editing that prevents the user from entering ill-formed rules.

Rules Engines

A rules engine is an application that takes as input a set of rules, creates a framework for executing those rules, and acts as a monitor to a system that must behave in conjunction with those rules. Rules engines work together with a rules language. A rules engine always acts abstractly, in that its operation is the same no matter what rules are being used; this reflects the separation of business logic from its implementation.

Complex rules engines allow for multiple concurrent evaluations of rules as well as parallel triggered execution. Other kinds of rules engines perform complex mathematical reductions to verify the continued truth values of the system. Simpler rules engines will (perhaps in a nondeterministic way) select a rule for evaluation and possibly execute an action if the condition evaluates to true.

Sources of Business Rules

There are many sources for rules, such as conversations with people, design documents, laws, regulations, and program codes, to name a few. Each of these sources may be rich in business rules, but because of the peculiarities of each source, the extraction of rules from each requires different skills.

People

Conversations with SMEs are likely to yield a treasure trove of business rules, especially when these conversations are prompted as a result of previous iterations of analysis. For example, I recently performed some data profiling on a data set that revealed some questionable data values lurking within some of the columns. The mere mention of this to the SME immediately provoked a response from which I was able to derive a business rule. This process can be quite fruitful as long as the focus is on adding BI value.

Documentation

Another interesting experience I had in business rule analysis was in identifying a pile of rules embedded within a data dictionary stored in a popular spreadsheet format. The description of valid values for data elements as well as relationships between different elements within the same table and across other tables were all hidden within text fields as part of the spreadsheet. Documentation is a rich source of business rules, although you must be careful, because documentation frequently does not remain synchronized with what is being documented. Descriptive text is rich with rules, and you must gain a lot of experience in translating text into rules (see Turning Language into Rules below).

Regulations

Organizations that are bound by a governing board's set of regulations may find that regulations are an excellent source of business rules. Clearly, laws and regulations, directives, and even suggestions by governing organizations or industry consortia are good sources for business rules. Reading through regulations requires the finely tuned eye of an SME who can reasonably extract the rule from the text.

Program Code

One stickier problem in rule discovery is extracting business rules from existing application programs. Because all application code logic is likely to be related to some business directive, the amount of time it would take to collect and analyze an entire software system might prove to be a resource sink. Alternatively there have been some suggested tools to perform what could be called "code mining," which would:

- Analyze program control structure.
- Look for code locations where conditions are being tested.
- Extract those conditions.
- Look for actions being taken based on the truth of conditions.
- Extract those actions.

The extracted conditions and actions could then be presented to an analyst to determine whether business rules are encapsulated within that program logic.

Turning Language into Rules

A major benefit of the business rules approach is that analyzing a business process provides a mechanism for extracting BI from program logic and allowing it to be treated as content. The rule analysis process leads toward the ability not just to isolate intelligence rules, but also to identify terms, facts, and assertions about the business entities that are typically modeled in a database. By accumulating business rules, routing them into sets, naming those sets, and managing those as actionable content, we gain some control over our business processes that was missing when the all of the logic was buried in the implementation.

The Value of Subject Matter Experts

The interesting (read: difficult) part of this process is learning enough of the lingo in the selected sources of rules (people, documentation, legislation, etc.) and figuring out how to translate it into rule syntax. This is particularly valuable in an environment where knowledge needs to be published to a number of players throughout an organization, especially where context or subject matter expertise is required. This is a good example of a process that takes advantage of the BI team's technical and business knowledge diversity. Having business-savvy staff or SMEs on the team will ease that process.

Consider this excerpt from an extension to Securities Exchange Commission (SEC) rule 17a-25, of the Securities Exchange Act of 1934.

> For a proprietary transaction, the broker-dealer must include the following information: (1) clearing house number or alpha symbol used by the broker-dealer submitting the information; (2) clearing house number(s) or alpha symbol(s) of the broker-dealer(s) on the opposite side to the trade; (3) security identifier; (4) execution date; (5) quantity executed; (6) transaction price; (7) account number; and (8) identity of the exchange or market where each transaction was executed. Under the proposed rule, if a transaction was effected for a customer account (as opposed to a proprietary account), the broker-dealer would have been required to also include the customer's name, customer's address, name of the customer's employer, the customer's tax identification number, and other related account information.[2]

From this example, an expert in understanding SEC regulations would be able to describe what goes into an electronic submission; the BI professional must prompt that SME to define those components, such as alpha symbol, clearing house number, security identifier, account numbers, and tax identification number (which we then add to our knowledge base), as well as the relationships between those components before any advantage can be gained through rule translation.

---

2. This material is taken from a proposed rule 17–25a of the Securities Exchange Act of 1934, the text of which can be found at *www.sec.gov/rules/proposed/34-42741.htm*.

Management Issues

When deciding to develop a system using the business rules approach, we have to invert our thinking process by imagining what the state of the universe is when we have arrived at the end state. In other words, consider what the system should look like after it is built, and enumerate all the rules that specify our expectations about how that system works. These expectations are the seeds of our business rules.

What this means is that we have to envision our business process in operation and enumerate all animate and inanimate participants (people, events, data sources, etc.) in that process. Having done so, we then articulate all of our expectations of that business process and how those expectations are affected by inputs, people, and changes in state. Last, we look at ways to specify those expectations within the rule definition framework, as well as evaluating our system to ensure that we can handle all potential business events within the system.

Political Issues

Similar to other components of a BI program, a big roadblock to a successful business rule implementation is a social issue, not technical one, for a number of reasons.

1. **Risk assessment**—When migrating to a new technology, there is always a measure of risk. Although rule-based systems have been available for a long time, their use in production systems is limited, and this will naturally lead to suspicion about the technology's effectiveness.

2. **Turf concerns**—Trying to extract business logic from programmer code for the sake of automatically building applicationware is likely to stir concerns among the people working on the original code. They are likely to be resistant to the introduction of a technology that will render their positions obsolete.

3. **High expectations**—Because the use of a rules system dictates that a system will be built employing rules, instead of traditional procedural programming languages, this might imply a decrease in the need for programmers. In reality, business rule analysts are as specialized as programmers, and care must be taken not to set unrealistic expectations.

Limitations of the Approach

There are of course limitations to the use of business rules.

- **Detail management**—Associated with any set of rules is the specter of a rule base gone wild, filled with meaningless trivialities and stale rules that only clog up the system. When using a rules system, one must be detail oriented to the extent that the rules engineer is willing to commit to understanding the rule definition system and the rule management system. The rules approach requires a dedication to detail, because all objects operating in the business process as well as all attributes of each object must be specified. This requires a dedication to detail as well as an understanding of business process analysis.

- **Inflated expectations**—Enthusiastic adopters of rules-based technology may have expectations that a converted set of complex business policies into a rules-based system will always be faster to implement, easier to maintain, and efficient in execution. Although this may be true for some applications, the fact is that business policies themselves frequently are poorly specified, and the business process of converting a policy statement into a rules base can be very complicated.

- **Programmers are not eliminated**—Because of the nice "natural language" qualities of rule descriptions, there is a general impression that a business process application can be built by nonprogrammers and that the IT resources and association can be eliminated. This is a naïve impression, because rule specification itself is dominated by strict syntactical structure; even if it is not called "programming," the skill and experience required match those of a programmer.

To Learn More

Business rules provide a nice mechanism for encapsulating discovered BI to be integrated into an ongoing operational framework. Some examples of this kind of application include ongoing fraud detection, customer behavior analysis and alerting, and customer attrition. In addition, business rules can be used as the basis for the data preparation process, such as information compliance, data cleansing, data profiling, and data integration.

To learn more about business rules, see *Business Rules Applied: Building Better Systems Using the Business Rules Approach*, Barbara Von Halle, New York, John Wiley & Sons, 2001.

CHAPTER 8

Data Profiling

Finally we are going to talk about data. Most of the book so far has basically centered on planning and infrastructure—what goes into the project before you actually start. At this point, it is time to get our hands dirty—and I really mean it! No matter what any external consultant tells you about the status of what is in your data, there is no excuse not to settle down for a good hard look at your data sets just to see whether they really display the characteristics you think they do. This process, a large part of which can be automated, is referred to as *data profiling*.

The goal of profiling data is to discover metadata when it is not available and to validate metadata when it is available. Data profiling is a process of analyzing raw data for the purpose of characterizing the information embedded within a data set. Data profiling incorporates column analysis, data type determination, and intercolumn association discovery. The result is a constructive process of information inference to prepare a data set for later integration. This chapter discusses these issues and describes the data profiling process.

The Business Case

No business intelligence (BI) program can be built without information, and that information may be coming from many different sources and providers, each of which may have little or no stake in the success of the outcome of your BI program. There is an oft-quoted statistic claiming that 70% of the effort associated with a data warehousing project is spent on data preparation. The bulk of this effort involves trying to shoehorn collections of disparate data sets into a single repository. To this end, those responsible for collecting and aggregating data for installation within a data repository must understand what is really represented in the data that is being aggregated, and this is more than just trusting what is apparent in any supplied documentation or data models.

Anyone who has gone through the drill of preparing data for an analytic process understands this. Sometimes the data that we are given is not always in a pristine form, and frequently the data is delivered with no manifest at all. Different data sets may be more or less usable in their original states, and the value of that data may differ based on how much positive energy needs to be supplied to make that data integratable. When faced with an integration process incorporating disparate data sets of dubious quality, data profiling is the first step toward adding value to that data. Data profiling automates the initial processes of what we might call *inferred metadata resolution*: discovering what the data items really look like and providing a characterization of that data for the next steps of integration.

The business argument for data profiling falls into the cost-savings realm: If, by providing a reasonable characterization of the metadata associated with a data set, we can reduce the amount of effort required to automate the preparation of data for integration into a data warehouse, then there is a significant reduction in the cost of building that data warehouse. According to a Standish Group report, using a data profiling tool can yield a savings of 35% of the cost of a data warehouse project. A $100K investment that provides this kind of savings for a $2 million data warehouse corresponds to an overall reduction of data warehouse cost of more than half a million dollars. Such an argument is hard to refute.

Data Profiling Activities

Data profiling is a hierarchical process that attempts to build an assessment of the metadata associated with a collection of data sets. The bottom level of the hierarchy characterizes the values associated with individual attributes. At the next level, the assessment looks at relationships between multiple columns within a single table. At the highest level, the profile describes relationships that exist between data attributes across different tables.

The complexity of the computation for these assessments grows at each level of the hierarchy. The attribute-level analysis is the least burdensome, whereas cross-column analysis can actually be costly in terms of computational resources. This provides one aspect of evaluation of data profiling tools: performance.

Another important evaluation criterion is ease of use of the results. Because there is so much information that can be inferred from the data values that make up a data set, it is easy to get lost in reams of statistics and enumerations. Remember the goal of reducing the effort required to integrate data, and keep this in mind when reviewing a profile assessment.

One other item to keep in mind while profiling data is that the most significant value is derived from discovering business knowledge that has been embedded in the data itself. Old-fashioned (and currently frowned-upon) database administration (DBA) tricks, such as overloading data attributes (in lieu of adding new columns to production databases) with encoded information, carry embedded business knowledge that can be shaken out and lost during an automated data cleansing process. As an example, in one of my client's employee identifier fields, most of the values were all digits, but a large number of records had a value that was all digits except for the character "I" appended to the end of the number. Appearances of asterisks as the last character in a name field and combination codes in a single column (i.e., a single string that comprises three distinct coded values, such as "89-NY/USA") are other kinds of examples of business knowledge embedded in the data.

The existence of a reason for a rule shows one of the subtle differences between a data quality rule and a business rule. Declaring that all values assigned to a field in a database record must conform to a pattern gives us a way to validate data within a record but gives us no insight into why the value must be in that form. When we associate meaning with a data quality rule, we suddenly have a context that allows us to understand why values must conform to that format and what deviations from that format mean.

Data Model Inference

When presented with a set of data tables of questionable origin, (or sometimes even with a pedigreed data set), a data consumer may want to verify or discover the data model that is embedded within that set. This is a hierarchical process that first focuses on exposing information about the individual columns within each table, then looks at any relationships that can be derived between columns within a single table, and then resolves relationships between different tables to generate a proposed data model for a data set. We look at some of the more complicated details in the upcoming sections on Attribute Analysis and Relationship Analysis, but here we'll look at some high level ideas regarding type inferencing and relational model inferencing.

Simple Type Inference

When we structure information within a logical framework, we impose some semantic support beams that both provide guidance to the application programmer as to how to deal with manipulating data and clue the information consumer into what kinds of data values are expected. A column's data type provides this guidance by constraining the kinds of values that should appear within that column. For example, if we have a column called "sales_quantity," we might expect the values populating this column to be in whole units (e.g., we don't sell fractions of a shirt), and therefore all the values in that field should be integers. All structured data sets are typically described using some kind of data typing system.

Yet when a data set is first introduced into a data environment, even if the set is accompanied by a corresponding data definition, the analyst may choose to verify the corresponding types through the profiling process. This is done through simple type inference, which is a process of resolving the view of each column's data type to its most closely matched system data type.

Every structured data set conforms to some data type assignment, so we can always assume that there is some data type definition assigned to each column, even if that type is an extremely broad type, such as "variable-length character string," and assign its maximum length to the length of the longest character string within the column. Data type inference is an iterative analysis of a value set to refine the perceived data type. For example, a column that contains strings consisting solely of digits could have its type refined from a *varchar* type to a proposed *integer* type. A column all of whose values strings were 10 characters or less could be resolved to varchar(10).

Simple type inference centers only on assigning system data types (such as integer, decimal, date) to columns. I distinguish this from the more valuable abstract type inferencing (see Abstract Type Analysis on page 119), which involves more complicated algorithms but yields more interesting semantic business knowledge about the column.

Table Model Inference and Relational Model Inference

Given a collection of data tables, an important piece of information is whether and how any of the tables are related in a data model. There are two approaches to resolving a relational model from a collection of data tables. The first is a brute-force approach that uses the results of overlap analysis to determine whether any pair of columns exhibits a key relationship. The second approach is more of a semantic approach that evaluates column names to see if there is any implied relation. For example, two tables from the same data set may each have a column called "party_addr_id," which might lead us to conjecture that these columns refer to the same object identifier.

Attribute Analysis

Attribute analysis is a process of looking at all of the values populating a particular column as a way to characterize that set of values. Attribute analysis is the first step in profiling because it yields a significant amount of metadata relating to the data set. The result of any of these analyses provides greater insight into the business logic that is applied (either on purpose or as a by-product of some other constraints) to each column. The end product should be a list of questions about each column that can be used to determine data quality or validation constraints or even information from which some BI can be inferred.

Typically this evaluation revolves around the following aspects of a data set.

- **Range analysis,** which is used to determine if the values fit within a well-defined range
- **Sparseness,** which evaluates the percentage of the elements populated
- **Format evaluation,** which tries to resolve unrecognized data into defined formats
- **Cardinality and uniqueness,** which analyzes the number of distinct values assigned to the attribute and indicates whether the values assigned to the attribute are unique
- **Frequency distribution,** which shows the relative frequency of the assignment of distinct values
- **Value absence,** which identifies the appearance and number of occurrences of null values
- **Abstract type recognition,** which refines the semantic data type association with a specific attribute
- **Overloading,** which attempts to determine if an attribute is being used for multiple purposes

Range Analysis

Relating a value set to a simple type already restricts the set of values that a column can take; most data types still allow for an infinite number of possible choices. During range analysis a set of values is tested to see if the values fall within a well-defined range. If so, depending on the data type, some inferences may be made. For example, if the data type is a date, the range may signify some time period for which the corresponding data is relevant. Another example might distinguish a small range of integer values that correspond to some enumerated encoding (i.e., a hook into some other reference data set).

More complex range analysis algorithms may be able to identify nonintersecting ranges within a data set as well. Consider an integer column that contains values between 0 and 9 as well as the value 99 as an error code condition. A naïve range analyzer might propose 0 through 99 as this attribute range, whereas the more sophisticated analyzer could bisect the values into two ranges, 0 through 9 and the single-valued range of 99. The more refined the distinct extant value ranges are, the easier it is for the business analyst or domain expert to recognize a meaning in those ranges, which then can be documented as attribute metadata.

Range analysis can be used in an intelligence application to explore minimum and maximum values of interest, perhaps related to customer activity and monthly sales or to prices customers are being charged for the same products at different retail locations. Another example might look for evidence of insurance fraud based on the existence of a wide range of practitioner charges for the same procedure.

Sparseness

The degree of sparseness may indicate some business meaning regarding the importance of that attribute. Depending on the value set, it probably means one of two things. Either the attribute is extremely important and needs to be available so that in the rare cases there is a need for the value, it can be populated, or the attribute is effectively meaningless because so few records have a value for it. Of course, this is most likely determined by the data analyst reviewing the profile reports.

Format Evaluation

It is useful to look for the existence of patterns that might characterize the values assigned to a column. For example, if we determine that each value has ten characters, where the first character is always "A" and the remainder are digits, we are thereby presented with a syntax rule that can be posited as a domain definition. We can use the discovered definition as a validation rule, which we would then add to a metadata database of domain patterns. Simple examples of rule-based data domains include telephone numbers, zip codes, and social security numbers. What is interesting is that frequently the pattern rules that define domains have deeper business significance.

As a more detailed example, consider a customer accounts database containing a data field called ACCOUNT_NUMBER, which always turned out to be composed of a two-character prefix followed by a nine-digit number. There was existing code that automatically generated a new account number when a new customer was added. It turned out that embedded in the data and the code were rules indicating how an account number was generated. Evidently, the two-character code represented a sales region, determined by the customer's address, whereas the numeric value was assigned as an increasing number per customer in each sales region. Because this attribute's value carried multiple pieces of information, it was a classic example of an overloaded attribute. The discovery of a pattern pointed to a more complicated business rule, which also paved the way for the cleaving of the overloaded information into two separate data attributes.

One method for pattern analysis is through the superimposition of small, discrete "meaning" properties to each symbol in a string, slowly building up more interesting patterns as more symbol components have their meanings assigned. Consider the following symbol classifications.

- Letter
- Digit
- Punctuation
- White space

Symbol pattern assignment is the first pass at pattern analysis. In each string, we assign one of the foregoing classifications to each character appearing in a data value. When all the characters in a string have been classified, the string will have an associated pattern string as well. For each value string, we prepare and record its pattern string. When all value strings have been analyzed, there is a column of associated pattern strings ready to be collated and counted.

At this point, there are two tasks to be accomplished. The first is to look for recurring patterns within the set of generated pattern strings; the second is to check the generated pattern strings against the known sets of patterns. Either way, the goal is to present candidate patterns representing rule-based domains to the user.

If no candidates reveal themselves through simple symbol pattern assignment, then there may be additional embedded information in the patterns themselves that should be investigated. Our next method for pattern analysis takes a more macro view of the data by categorizing strings instead of symbols. At this point, all strings can be classified as:

- Alphabetic
- Alphanumeric
- Numeric
- First name
- Last name
- Business word
- Address words
- Or one of any other categorized word class

In each attribute value, we now assign to each white space–separated string one of the word categories, forming a new pattern string. After all the strings have had patterns assigned, again, these patterns can be collated and counted, and we check both for recurring patterns and for matches to previously known patterns (Fig. 8.1).

In either the symbol or whole word analysis, if we find common patterns that have not yet been registered, it is possible that we have discovered a new pattern, which then should be documented. At this point, it is worthwhile to perform a little detective work to see if there is some implicit business rule embedded in this pattern. It may turn out that there is some historical reason for the pattern, which may reflect some business condition that currently exists and must be maintained or one that existed at some point but is no longer valid, thereby allowing the rule to be changed.

Cardinality and Uniqueness

The *cardinality* of a value set is the number of distinct values that exists within a column. Cardinality is interesting because it relates to different aspects of the correctness of the value set and because how it relates exposes business knowledge. For example, in some contexts there is an expected cardinality, such as a SEX field, where only "M" and "F" might be anticipated. In one of my client's data tables, we found a SEX field with three values: "M," "F," and "U." The "M" and "F" were expected, and it turned out that the "U" indicated that the person's sex was unknown.

In other contexts, the cardinality of a value set should equal the number of records contributing to that data set. An example of this is an expected key field: If the cardinality is less than the number of records, there is at least one

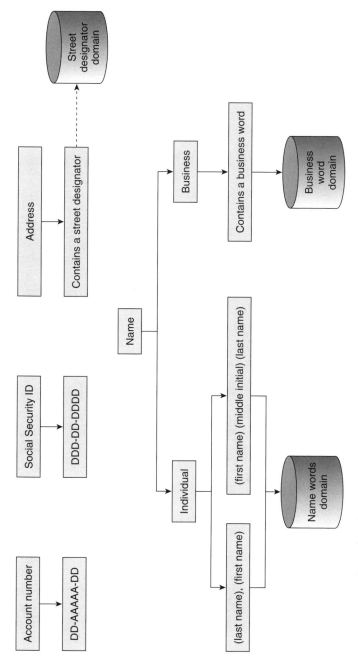

FIGURE 8.1 Examples of pattern analysis.

duplicate value, which in turn indicates that that field does not contain a true key. Alternatively, cardinality analysis can be used to find columns whose values are unique, from which candidate keys can be inferred.

Frequency Distribution

The frequency distribution of values yields the number of times each of the distinct values appears in a value set. This gives the data consumer some insight into whether certain values have more significance than others based on a high (or low) frequency, and it highlights potential nonconforming values that appear as outliers in the distribution report.

Frequency distribution is also useful when looking for variations from the norm that might indicate something suspicious. Consider a column whose values should be randomly distributed; if a frequency analysis showcases a handful of values whose frequency is unusually high, this might trigger some deeper investigation to determine whether those values are correct or whether they indicate some kind of fraudulent behavior.

Value Absence

There are actually two problems associated with the absence of values that can be explored through data profiling. The first involves looking for values that are not there, and the second is to look for nonvalues that are there.

The first issue, truly missing values (which in modern relational database systems are represented using a true system null), are of significance because the data analyst may be interested in determining whether these values really should be null, under what circumstances they should be null, or perhaps why the value is missing. Of further interest may be attempting to figure out a way to fill in the missing value.

The second issue refers to those cases where some distinct value (or, more likely, values) represents one or more kinds of nulls. As we discuss in greater detail in Chapter 9, there are different reasons why we might want to use different explicit strings as representations of correspondingly different kinds of nulls. There is a distinction between a value that is missing because the data entry analyst did not know the value and leaving the attribute null because there really is no value. Making this distinction explicit can cause problems when trying to perform further analysis. The problem is even more acute when there is no standardization of the explicit nulls.

To illustrate this, I suggest looking at any database that carries an attribute for Social Security number and see how many values look like

"000-00-0000" and how many like "999-99-9999." I would gamble that both forms are meant to convey some kind of missing value, probably the result of a business process that requires filling in a value (even if there is no valid one), but I might hesitate to claim that they have identical meanings or that they are both the same as the system null.

Abstract Type Analysis

An abstract type is a more semantically descriptive qualification of a type definition that conveys business meaning. For example, "people names" "telephone numbers," and "ZIP codes" are all abstract data types that qualify as character strings. The difference between type recognition, as discussed earlier, and abstract type analysis is the degree of complexity involved. Abstract data types are by definition more complicated, because the business meaning is captured through some set of assertions that constrain the set of values belonging to that type.

Typically abstract data types are represented by some kind of semantic definition, including:

- *Constructive assertion* (e.g., all product codes consist of two uppercase characters followed by a hyphen followed by a six-digit number, whose leftmost digit represents the factory at which the product is manufactured)

- *Value enumeration* (e.g., the set of USPS state codes via an enumeration of the valid two uppercase character values)

- *Pattern conformance* (e.g., the string matches one or more of a set of defined patterns similar to those inferred via the approach described in the earlier section about Format Evaluation).

The goal of abstract type analysis is to propose an abstract data type for a specific column based on a suggestive statistical conformance to one defined abstract type. For example, once a column has been identified as a varchar(30) data type, all the values can be tested to determine if they represent, say, a telephone number (by matching each to telephone number patterns) or colors of the rainbow (by checking for enumerated domain membership). If an overwhelming number of values match to a known type, this not only provides more business knowledge about the data model, but also provides insight into distinguishing those values that do not conform to the discovered type.

Overloading Analysis

Presuming that we have already identified some value sets that represent reference data domains with business value, we can attempt to resolve domain membership by checking the values in an attribute against those known enumerated domains. Yet it is possible that as an attribute's data values are checked against known domains the profiling process will see significant matches against more than one domain. This might indicate that two attributes' worth of information is in one column, where the same column is being used to represent more than one actual attribute (Fig. 8.2).

Alternatively, the use of more than one domain by a single attribute might indicate that more complex business rules are in effect, such as the existence of a *split attribute*, which is characterized by the use of different domains based on other data quality or business rules. As a simple example, consider a banking application that registers customer account activity. When a customer makes a deposit, a credit is made to the customer's account in the form of a positive amount of money; when the customer withdraws money, a debit is made to the account in the form of a negative amount of money. In this case, the same column is used, but in fact there are two domains used for this attribute—positive decimal values (when the action is a credit) and negative decimal values (when the action is a debit).

Overloading can appear in other ways as well, such as the compaction of multiple pieces of data into a single character string. Sometimes this is intentional, such as the example we saw earlier where a product code carried sales region information, or perhaps less so, such as the example we saw in the section about Data Profiling Activities.

Relationship Analysis

What is frequently referred to in the data profiling space as *cross-column analysis* focuses on establishing relationships between sets of data; I believe it is more accurate to refer to this activity as *relationship analysis*. The goal of these processing stages is to identify relationships between value sets and known reference data, to identify dependencies between columns (either in the same table or across different tables), and to identify key relationships between columns across multiple tables.

Domain Analysis

Domain analysis covers two tasks: identifying data domains and identifying references to data domains. We have already discussed one virtual process of

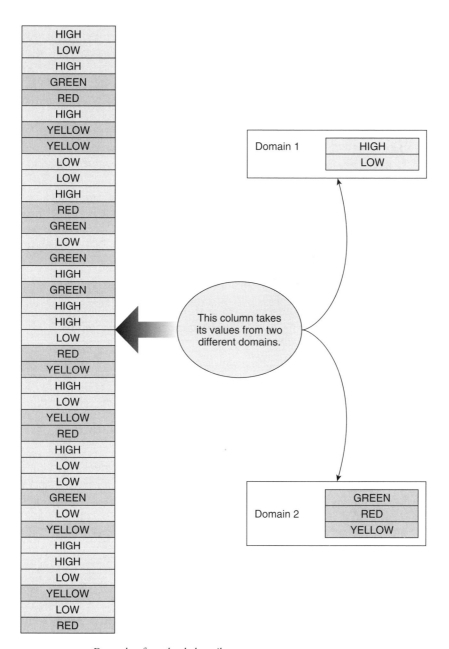

FIGURE 8.2 Example of overloaded attributes.

domain identification in the earlier section about Format Evaluation; discovered format specifications can represent data domains. Enumerated domains may be inferred and proposed from a value set when:

- The number of values is relatively small as compared to the context in which it is used (i.e., the number of possible values that an attribute might take is limited to a small set).

- The values are what we could call *intuitively distributed.* This means that the distribution, although not always even, will take on characteristics specific to the context. In some cases there is a relatively even distribution; in other cases there may be more weighting given to a small subset of those values.

- Other domains exist that may be derived from this domain.

- The domain is used in more than one table.

- The attribute that uses the value from the domain is rarely null.

Unfortunately, these are more guidelines than rules, because exceptions can be found for each characteristic. The brute-force method for identifying enumerated domains is to look at all possible value sets. We begin by presuming that each column in every table potentially draws its values from a defined domain. For every table, we walk through each column and select all the distinct values. This set is now a candidate domain, and we then apply heuristics to decide whether to call this set a domain. It turns out that sometimes we can make some kind of determination early in the analysis, and sometimes we have to wait until more knowledge has been gained.

Presuming that we have already started to build the domain inventory, we can see whether other data attributes make use of the same domain by analyzing how well the set of values used to populate one attribute matches the values of a known domain. The value-matching process for a specific attribute can be described using the following steps.

1. The attribute's distinct values are collected and counted.

2. The set of unique values is matched against each domain. Fast matching techniques are used for scalability.

3. For each domain, we compute three ratio values. The *agreement* is calculated as the ratio of distinct attribute values that are present in a domain to the total number of distinct values in the attribute. The *overlap* is calculated as the number of domain member values that do not appear in the attribute divided by the number of domain values. Last, we compute the *disagreement* as the number of values that appear in the attribute but are not members of the domain.

4. The domains are sorted by their agreement percentages. The highest agreement percentages are presented as likely identified domains.

When we compare an attributes value set to a known domain, there are four cases.

1. All of the values used in the attribute are members of the known domain, and all of the values in the domain are used in the attribute (agreement = 100%, overlap = 0%, disagreement = 0%). In this case, it is safe to say that the attribute takes its values from the known data domain.

2. All of the values in the attribute are members of the known domain, but there are domain members that are not used in the attribute (agreement = 100%, overlap > 0%, disagreement = 0%). In this case, it is also likely that the attribute takes its values from the domain, but this may also indicate the attribute's use of a subdomain, which should be explored.

3. Some of the attribute values are members of the known domain, but some of the values used in the attribute are not members of the known domain (agreement < 100%, disagreement > 0%). In this case, there are two possibilities: (a) There is no real agreement between the attribute's values and the domain, in which case the search for a match should continue. (b) The known domain may actually be a subdomain of a much larger set of values, which should be explored. The decision will probably depend on the percentages computed.

4. None of the values used in the attribute are taken from the known domain (agreement = 0%, overlap = 100%, disagreement = 100%). In this case it is probably safe to say that the attribute does not take its values from the domain.

Functional Dependency

A functional dependency between two columns, X and Y, means that for any two records $R1$ and $R2$ in the table, if field X of record $R1$ contains value x and field X of record $R2$ contains the same value x, then if field Y of record $R1$ contains the value y, then field Y of record $R2$ must contain the value y. We can say that attribute Y is *determined* by attribute X. Functional dependencies may exist between multiple source columns. In other words, we can indicate that one set of attributes determines a target set of attributes.

A functional dependency establishes a relationship between two sets of attributes. If the relationship is causal (i.e., the dependent attribute's value is filled in as a function of the defining attributes), that is an interesting piece of business knowledge that can be added to the growing knowledge base. A simple example is a "total_amount_charged" field that is computed by multiplying the "qty_ordered" field by the "price" field.

If the relationship is not causal, then that piece of knowledge can be used to infer information about normalization of the data. If a pair of data attribute values is consistently bound together, then those two columns can be extracted from the targeted table and the instance pairs inserted uniquely into a new table and assigned a reference identifier. The dependent attribute pairs (that had been removed) can then be replaced by a reference to the newly created corresponding table entry.

Key Relationships

A table *key* is a set of attributes that can be used to uniquely identify any individual record within the table. For example, people databases might use a Social Security number as a key (although this is ill-advised, considering that many people do not have a Social Security number [see Value Absence on page 118]), because (presumably) no two people share the same one. If we have one table that contains a specified key field, other tables may be structured with references to the first table's key as a way of connecting pairs of records drawn from both tables. When one table's key is used as a reference to another table, that key is called a *foreign key*.

Modern relational databases enforce a constraint known as *referential integrity*, which states that if an attribute's value is used in table A as a foreign key to table B, then that key value must exist in one record in table B. There are two aspects to profiling key relationships: identifying that a key relationship exists, and identifying what are called *orphans* in a violated referential integrity situation.

A foreign key relationship exists between (table A, column x) and (table B, column y) if all the values in (table A, column x) overlap completely with the values in (table B, column y) and the values in (table B, column y) are unique. A data profiling application should be able to apply this assertion algorithmically to find foreign key relationships.

Orphans are foreign key values that do not appear in records in the targeted table. An example might be a reference in a catalog to a product that is no longer being made or sold by the company. The referential integrity constraint asserts that if the product is referenced in the catalog, it must exist in the active products database. If the data profiling tool is told that a foreign key relationship exists, it is simple to check for orphans. Even if the profiling tool has no prior knowledge about foreign keys, it is possible to loosen the rules for identifying the foreign key relationship to find *near-foreign keys* where there are some values that would be orphans if the relationship did really exist. As in other cases, the tool can only propose these discoveries as rules, and it is up to the analyst to determine the value in the proposal.

Management Issues

The most significant management issues involve the relatively steep costs of good data profiling tools and the performance of these tools. We covered the cost justification argument at the beginning of the chapter, but it is worthwhile to explore the questionable performance of these tools. First, some of the algorithms used in data profiling are actually quite computationally intensive, and it is not unusual for some of the analysis to require both large amounts of computational resources (memory, disk space) and time to successfully complete.

Second, because the computations are summaries of frequency analysis and counts, the results presented tend to be almost endless, with long lists of values, each of which may have appeared only once in a column. For small tables this is not really an issue. But if you start looking at large tables (greater than 1 million records, which today is really not unusual), the output can be more than overwhelming. The savvy manager needs to be aware that some expertise is required in absorbing the results of a data profiling application and know how best to use the application.

The Last Word

Data profiling adds significant value to the BI program when it can be used to effectively provide the archeological or forensic evidence of why a specific data is the way it is. Data profiling is also useful in exposing business rules that are embedded in data, and it can help preserve information that may be scrubbed out during the data integration stages. In addition, profiling is actually directly useful in a number of BI applications, such as fraud detection, when the data analyst is familiar with the kinds of results to look for. For more information on data profiling, see *Data Quality: The Accuracy Dimension*, Jack Olson, San Francisco, Morgan Kaufmann, 2002.

CHAPTER 9

Data Quality and Information Compliance

When the quality of your data is suspect, how can you trust the results of any analysis based on that flawed data? In the business intelligence/data warehouse user community, there is a growing confusion as to the difference between *data cleansing* and *data quality*. Although many data cleansing products can help in applying data edits to name and address data or help in transforming data during an extract/transform/load (ETL) process, there is usually no persistence in this cleansing. Each time a data warehouse is populated or updated, the same corrections are applied to the same data.

In reality, improved data quality is the result of a business improvement process that looks to identify and eliminate the root causes of bad data. A critical component of improving data quality is being able to distinguish between "good" (i.e., valid) data and "bad" (i.e., invalid) data. But because data values appear in many contexts, formats, and frameworks, this simple concept devolves into extremely complicated notions as to what constitutes validity. This is because the validity of a data value *must* be defined within the context in which that data value appears. For example, there may be many ways in which customers refer to a corporation, but there is only one legal name under which the corporation is officially registered. In most contexts any of the corporate aliases may be sufficient, whereas in other contexts only the legal name is valid.

This chapter centers on the importance of defining data quality expectations and measuring data quality against those expectations. We will also look at the general perception of data quality and what the savvy manager needs to know to distinguish between data cleansing and data quality.

The Business Case

In Chapter 2, where we discussed the value of information, we determined that a critical aspect of information value is dependent on the quality of data. This is not merely a blanket statement—according to the 2001 Pricewater-houseCoopers Global Data Management Survey, fully 75% of the respondents (senior-level executives) had experienced significant problems as a result of defective data.[1] These problems included:

- Extra costs to prepare reconciliations
- Delays or scrapping of new systems
- Failure to collect receivables
- Inability to deliver orders
- Lost sales

On the other hand, increased levels of data quality accounted for reduced processing costs, reduced reconciliations, and increased sales. According to the Data Warehousing Institute's report *Data Quality and the Bottom Line*, poor-quality customer data costs U.S. businesses $611 billion a year[2] (and this is referring just to *customer* data—consider how much all other kinds of poor quality data can cost).

More Than Just Names and Addresses

What is particularly interesting is that some of these assessments of the commercial costs of poor data quality are based on relatively simple metrics related to incorrect names and addresses. Although I don't want to minimize the value of correct names and addresses, the realm of invalid data spans much more than the question of whether the catalog is being sent to the right person at the right address. In other words, data quality is more than just names and addresses.

In fact, the question of data quality is not one of standardized addresses, but rather of "fitness for use." This relatively simple phrase hides an extremely complicated concept. In practicality, almost everyone has a different understanding of what data quality is; each definition is geared toward the individual's view of what is good and what is not. This leads to the conclusion

---

1. Retrieved May 5, 2003 from *www.pwcglobal.com/extweb/ncsurvres.nsf/DocID/E68F3408A463BD2980256A180064B96A*
2. "Data Quality and the Bottom Line," Wayne Eckerson, Chatsworth, CA, The Data Warehousing Institute, 2002.

that there is no hard and fast definition of data quality. Rather, data quality is defined in terms of how each data consumer desires to use the data, and to this end we must discuss some dimensions across which data quality can be measured.

Data Quality Dimensions

Although there are potentially many dimensions of data quality dealing with data models, data domains, and data presentation, the ones that usually attract the most attention are dimensions that deal with data values, namely:

- Accuracy
- Completeness
- Consistency
- Timeliness

Accuracy

Accuracy refers to the degree to which data values agree with an identified source of correct information. There are different sources of correct information: a database of record; a similar, corroborative set of data values from another table; dynamically computed values; the result of a manual workflow; or irate clients. Inaccurate values don't just cause confusion when examining a database—bad data values can result in increased costs and provide particularly nasty problems when they surface in an analytical environment.

Completeness

Completeness refers to the expectation that data instances contain all the information they are supposed to. Completeness can be prescribed on the basis of a single attribute or can be dependent on the values of other attributes within a record or even be defined with respect to all values within a column. Missing values can wreak havoc on analytical applications, especially when looking at aggregate functions, such as summation, or more complicated analyses.

Consistency

The data quality dimension of consistency can be curiously simple or dangerously complex. In its most basic form, consistency refers to data values in one data set being consistent with values in another data set. Yet what does consistency really mean? If we follow a strict definition, then two data values drawn from separate data sets may be consistent with each other, yet both can be incorrect. Even more complicated is the notion of consistency with a set of predefined constraints. We may declare some data set to be the database of record, although what guarantees that the database of record is of high quality?

More formal consistency constraints can be encapsulated as a set of rules that specify consistency relationships between values of attributes, either across a record or message or along all values of a single attribute. An example for a health-care environment might specify that "if the operation is hysterectomy, the patient may not be male." These consistency rules can be applied to one or more dimensions of a table or even across tables. This becomes particularly important during the data integration and aggregation stages of importing data into a large repository.

Currency/Timeliness

Currency refers to the degree to which information is current with the world that it models. Currency can measure how up to date information is and whether it is correct despite possible time-related changes. *Timeliness* refers to the time expectation for accessibility of information. Timeliness can be measured as the time between when information is expected and when it is readily available for usage.

Data Quality Expectations

In the most general sense, we will use a qualitative definition of data quality and refine that definition on a case-by-case basis. In essence, the level of data quality is determined by the data consumers in terms of meeting or beating their own defined expectations. In practice, this means identifying a set of data quality objectives associated with any data set and then measuring that data set's conformance to those objectives. This is not to say that the tools used for static data cleansing of names and addresses or products that link data records based on specific data fields are not useful, yet the use of these tools does not define a data quality solution. Instead, the best way to get a handle on an organization's data quality is to define a set of expectations about the data, measure against those expectations, and continuously improve until those expectations are met or beaten.

Unfortunately, there are no objective means for defining data quality expectations. That means that it is up to each organization to measure the cost effect of low data quality, to assess the current state of the organization's data, and to develop data quality rules that can be used for ongoing improvement. We will explore a business rules approach to continuous data quality in the section on Business Rule–Based Information Compliance. In that approach, we have objective measures that relate directly to percentage conformance with the defined rules.

Types of Errors

A quick review of some common error paradigms is in order to remind you of the degree to which the quality of information can devolve. In this section we look at some common sources of errors.

Attribute Granularity

The granularity of an attribute refers to how much information is embedded within that attribute. A good example is a customer name attribute whose value incorporates first, middle, and last names all in one field. The inclusion of multiple name components within a single field may be relevant in analyses attempting to resolve multiple instances of individuals that appear throughout a collection of data sets, for example.

Finger Flubs and Transcription Errors

Many data errors can creep in right at the introduction into the processing stream. At a data entry or transcription stage, individuals or systems are likely to introduce variations in spellings, abbreviations, phonetic similarities, transcribed letters inside words, misspelled words, miskeyed letters, etc. In one data environment, where many of the company names used an ampersand (&) character as part of the name (e.g., Johnson & Smith), a frequent error was the appearance of a 7 instead of the ampersand (e.g., Johnson 7 Smith). This is an apparent shift-key problem, because the "&" is the "7" key shifted.

Floating Data

Imprecision in metadata modeling may result in lack of clarity as to whether certain kinds of data go into specific fields. One example I reviewed recently contained columns for "address1" and "address2," referring to the first and second lines of a party's address. Apparently, there was no standard as to what went into the first line and what went into the second line, because suite/apartment/floor information floated into address1 and street number/name/type floated down into address2 (the typical standard prescribes the opposite).

Another common error is data placed in the wrong field. In a similar example, the street address field was insufficiently sized, so the entry person just continued entering street address data that subsequently floated into the city field.

Implicit and Explicit Nullness

The question of nullness is interesting, because the absence of a value may provide more fodder for making inferences than the presence of an incorrect value. The ability of modern relational database systems to impose "not null" constraints on columns may actually create problems that it attempts to solve. The question becomes: If I do not have a value for a specific column that requires a value, what value should be assigned?

The result of this conundrum, as you have probably encountered, is the appearance of a variety of nonstandard values meant to represent different kinds of null values. One example I encountered in a recent data assessment uncovered the frequent use of "X" in many columns. When I discussed this with the subject matter expert, he immediately told me that those fields are not null, and so the data entry person just input the "X" to make sure the transaction would be accepted. Other examples of explicit nulls are shown in Figure 9.1.

Semistructured Formats

Data records in regular databases are formatted in a structured way; information in free text is said to be unstructured. Somewhere in the middle is what we call semistructured data, which is essentially free text with some con-

Telephone number	Names	Dates
000-000-0000	NA	99/99/9999
0000000000	N/A	XX/XX/XXXX
999-999-9999	na	99/99/99
X	n/a	9/9/99
No phone number provided	Unknown	
	UNKNOWN	
	?	
	??	
	???	
	X	

FIGURE 9.1 Different kind of explicit nulls.

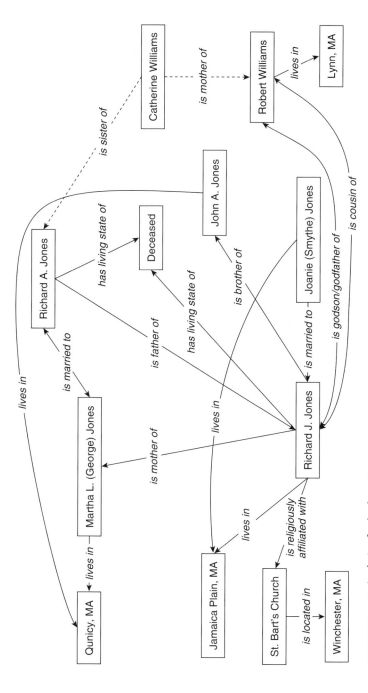

FIGURE 9.2 Analysis of a death notice.

ceptual connectivity. Understanding that connectivity allows for intelligently extracting information embedded within the semistructure. A good example might be a death notice, which typically contains specific information about individuals and their particular roles and relationships.

Here is an example, whose relationships are exposed in Figure 9.2:

> Richard J. Jones, Of Jamaica Plain, Suddenly, Apr 23. Beloved husband of Joanie (Smythe) Jones. Devoted son of Martha L. (George) Jones of Qunicy, and the late Richard A. Jones. Devoted brother of John A. Jones, nephew of Catherine Williams of Lynn, Cousin of Robert Williams of Lynn. Funeral Mass in St. Bart's Church, Winchester, at 10 a.m. Relatives and friends invited.[3]

When the attribute granularity is coarse, what should be a structured piece of data may have morphed into semistructured form. This is particularly visible in data sets containing "comments" fields, where the data provider is able to insert rambling chunks of free text with no hope of automated extraction.

Strict Format Conformance

We naturally tend to view information in patterns, and frequently data modelers will reverse this order and impose a pattern or set of patterns on a set of attributes that may actually prevent those fields from being properly filled in. For example, our expectation that telephone numbers always consist of a three-digit area code, a three-digit exchange number, and a four-digit line number may be generally correct, but it is not correct if we are entering European or Japanese telephone numbers, nor is it necessarily correct if we are viewing U.S. telephone numbers from your office desk in Tokyo. The imposition of strict format compliance may capture correctly formed data a large part of the time and prevent the proper capture the rest of the time!

Transformation Errors

Errors may be introduced during the extraction and transformation process. If the transformation rules are not completely correct or if there is a flaw in the transformation application, errors will be created where none originally existed. For example, in an interesting case, a database of names was found to have an inordinately large number of high-frequency word fragments, such as "INCORP," "ATIONAL," "COMPA." It turned out that the field had been reconstructed from data extracted from a legacy database, which had a limit

---

3. This obituary is adapted, and takes its form, from those that are regularly published in large-city newspapers.

on the size of an attribute, forcing the data modeler to use more than one actual field to make up one virtual field. During the integration process the merging application inserted a space between each of a set of concatenated fields from the source, and because some of the original data spanned two physical fields, the insertion of the space created a collection of fragments that did not appear in the original data.

Overloaded Attributes

Either as a reflection of poor data modeling or as a result of changing business concerns, there is information that is stored in one data field that actually contains more than one data value. Examples of this are prevalent in the financial industries, where companies are moving from an account-oriented view to a customer-oriented view. Typically, account names are the official names associated with a financial account, and they may include many combination forms with many associated context terms. The context terms represent business relationships that may need to be exposed in a customer or party's database. Here are some examples.

1. John Smith and Mary Smith
2. John and Mary Smith
3. John Smith in Trust for Charles Smith
4. John and Mary Smith UGMA Charles Smith
5. John and Mary Smith Foundation, John and Mary Smith Trustees

In each of these examples, we actually see more than just entity names—we may see bound relationships (e.g., the appearance of a male and a female name together, implying a marriage relationship) and business-related attributions (e.g., UGMA = Uniform Gift to Minors Act account) embedded within a single field.

Data Cleansing

A large part of the cleansing process involves identification and elimination of duplicate records; much of this process is simple, because exact duplicates are easy to find in a database using simple queries, or in a flat file by sorting and streaming the data based on a specific key. The difficult part of eliminating duplicates is finding those nonexact duplicates—for example, pairs of records where there are subtle differences in the matching key. The processes used for approximate matching are the same as used for other entity linkage and integration applications (householding is a good example); this is treated in greater detail in Chapter 10 in the section on Record Linkage and Consolidation.

Do not undervalue the importance of data cleansing, because it drives a significant portion of the preloading data preparation. The data cleansing process consists of phases that try to understand what is in the data, transform that into a standard form, identify incorrect data, and then attempt to correct it.

Parsing

The first step in data cleansing is *parsing*, which is the process of identifying meaningful tokens within a data instance and then analyzing token streams for recognizable patterns. A *token* is a conglomeration of a number of single words that have some business meaning; with customer data, these tokens may refer to components of a person or business name, parts of an address, or a part of some other domain-specific data item. For example, we might refer to a "title" token that represents a list of frequently used titles, such as "Mr.," "Mrs.," and "Dr.," and any time we see a word that is in our "titles" list, we can refer to that word as a title for subsequent pattern analysis.

The parsing process segregates each word and then attempts to determine the relationship between the word and previously defined token sets and to form sequences of tokens. Token sequences are submitted to a pattern-matching application that searches for similar patterns. When a pattern is matched, a predefined transformation is applied to the original field value to extract its individual components, which are then reported to the driver applications. Pattern-based tools are flexible, in that they can make use of predefined patterns and absorb newly defined or discovered patterns for ongoing parsing.

Standardization

Standardization is the process of transforming data into a form specified as a standard. That standard may be one defined by some governing body or may just refer to the segregation of subcomponents within a data field that has been successfully parsed. Standardization is a prelude to the record consolidation process and is used as a means of extracting specific entity information (e.g., person, company, telephone number, location) and assigning it semantic value for subsequent manipulation.

Standardization will incorporate information-reduction transformations during a consolidation or summarization application. For example, consider these two customer records:

1.　Elizabeth R. Johnson, 123 Main Street
2.　Beth R. Johnson, 123 Main Street

Our intuition upon eyeballing this pair of records allows us to infer an entity match, because there seems to be enough heuristic data to take that leap: We know that "Beth" is a short version of "Elizabeth," and the street address is a match. Heuristics such as matching a nickname to a full-version name (and others like these) can be collected as business rules (see Chapter 7) as simple transformations that can be generally applied to parsed names.

There are many different data types that fall into a semantic taxonomy that provides some intuitive set of content-related standardization rules. For example, first names in many cultures have variant forms, nicknames, etc., that all can relate any name to at least one standard form. For instance, "Bob," "Rob," "Bobby," and "Robbie" are all different forms of the name "Robert"; "Liz," "Lizzie," and "Beth" may all be forms of the name "Elizabeth."

Once a name is identified that has a number of variants, the standardization process may augment a data value with a chosen standard form to be used during the linkage stage. Note that standardization is not restricted to names or addresses. Other abstract data types that can be standardized include business words, telephone numbers, industry jargon, product codes, and transaction codes. And it doesn't even matter if the standard form is applied in a manner that is not consistent with real life. For example, "Beth Smith" might not be named "Elizabeth," but we can assign the standard "Elizabeth" to the records anyway, because this standardization is being used purely as a means to a different end: linkage and cleansing.

Abbreviation Expansion

An abbreviation is a compact representation of some alternate recognized entity, and finding and standardizing abbreviations is another rule-oriented aspect of data cleansing. There are different kinds of abbreviation. One type shortens each of a set of words to a smaller form, where the abbreviation consists of a prefix of the original data value. Examples include "INC" for incorporated, "CORP" for corporation, and "ST" for street. Another type shortens the word by eliminating vowels or by contracting the letters to phonetics, such as "INTL" or "INTRNTL" for international, "PRGRM" for program, and "MGR" for manager. A third form of abbreviation is the *acronym*, where the first characters of each of a set of words are composed into a string, such as "USA" for "United States of America" and RFP for "request for proposal." Abbreviations must be parsed and recognized, and then a set of transformational business rules can be used to change abbreviations into their expanded form.

Correction

Once components of a string have been identified and standardized, the next stage of the process attempts to correct those data values that are not recognized and to augment correctable records with the corrected information. Obviously, if we can recognize that data is in error, we want to be able to fix that data. There are a few different ways to automatically correct data, and these all rely on some sort of intelligent knowledge base of rules and transformations or some heuristic algorithms for recognizing and linking variations of known data values. It is important to realize that the correction process can only be partially automated; many vendors may give the impression that their tools can completely correct invalid data, but there is no silver bullet.

In general, the correction process is based on maintaining a set of incorrect values and their corrected forms. As an example, if the word *International* is frequently misspelled as "Intrnational," there would be a rule mapping the incorrect form to the correct form. Some tools may incorporate business knowledge accumulated over a long period of time, which accounts for large knowledge bases of rules incorporated into these products; unfortunately, this opens the door for loads of obscure rules that reflect many special cases.

This approach is flawed, because the effect of accumulating correction rules based on analyzing certain kinds of data (usually names and addresses) will bias the corrective process to that kind of information. In addition, a large part of one organization's data is different than any other organization's data, and consequently the business rules that govern the use of that data are also different. Relying on the business rules from other organizations will still add value, especially if the data content is similar, but there will always be some area where humans will need to interact with the system to make decisions about data corrections.

Last, data can be perceived as incorrect only when there are rules indicating correctness. Inaccuracy or imprecise data values may exist within a set, yet there is no way to determine that invalidity without a source of correct values against which to compare. Relying on other sets of correctness rules can lead to a bad problem: What might already be good data may inadvertently be changed to something incorrect. An example of this in address correction is the famous East-West Highway in suburban Washington, D.C. Because the expectation with addresses with the word "East" at the beginning is that the word is being used as a direction prefix and not as part of the street name itself, some applications inappropriately "correct" this to "E. West Highway," which is not the name of the road.

An even worse problem is the perception that the data is correct although it really is not. Sometimes, the only way to identify incorrect data is for an analyst to review the data directly.

Updating Missing Fields

One aspect of data cleansing is being able to fill fields that are missing information. Missing values may carry more information than one might suspect; the absence of a value may be due to one of the following reasons.

1. It is known that there is really no value for this field.

2. It is known that there is a value that should go into a field, but for some reason the value is unknown at this point, and it is not clear if the value will ever be known.

3. It is known that there is a value for this field, and at some point in the future that value will be obtained and filled in.

4. There is no applicable value for this based on some constraint dependent on other attribute values.

5. There is a value for this field, but it does not conform to a predefined set of acceptable values for that field.

This is just a short list of the kinds of null values that exist; I have heard some say there are at least 30 different kinds of nulls! Depending on the null type, there may be ways to impute the missing value, although some approaches are more reliable than others. For example, we might try to fill in a person's sex field based on his or her first name, but this will not necessarily work with a person with a transgender name.

In some other cases, the reason for the missing value may be due to errors in the original data, and after a cleansing process, we may have enough information to properly fill out the missing field. For unavailable fields, if the reason for the omissions has to do with the dearth of data at the time of record instantiation, then the consolidation process may provide enough information leverage to make available data that had been previously unavailable. For unclassified fields, the reason for the inability to classify the value may be that erroneous data in other attributes has prevented the classification. Given the corrected data, the proper value may be filled in. For unknown attributes, the process of cleansing and consolidation may provide the missing value.

It is important to understand, though, that without a well-documented and agreed-to set of rules to determine how to fill in a missing field, it can be (at the least) counterproductive and (at the worst) dangerous to fill in missing values. Maintain strict caution when automating the replacement of absent values.

Business Rule–Based Information Compliance

As described in Chapter 7, a business rules system is designed to capture the knowledge of all the assertions, constraints, guidelines, policies, regulations, etc., that drive a business. In a business rules system, knowledge about a business process is abstracted and separated from its explicit implementation. Rules expressed in a predefined formalism can be integrated with a rules engine to create an application to implement the business process.

Information compliance is a concept that incorporates the definition of business rules for measuring the level of conformance of sets of data with client expectations. Properly articulating data consumer expectations as business rules lays the groundwork for both assessment and ongoing monitoring of levels of data quality.

A Data Quality Rule Framework

Our framework for articulating quality expectations looks at how that data is used and how we can express rules from this holistic approach. This can be decomposed into the definition of metadata-like reference data sets and assertions that relate to values, records, columns, and tables within a collection of data sets.

There are many explicit and implicit rules embedded in the use of reference data, and we capture a lot of these rules through a formal definition of nulls, domains, and mappings. Once we identify known collections of data and assign meaning to them, we begin to get a better understanding of what information is being used in the organization, who is using it, and how that information is being used. Although the values that make up the domains and the mappings may have actually been derived from transactional data, once we categorize the data sets as domains and the relations as mappings, and especially once we ascribe some meaning to the collections, we can move those sets into the reference data arena.

Assertions revolve around specifying some business constraint on the relationship between the abstract data instance and the values bound to individual data attributes. Defining these assertions captures the contextual knowledge that governs true data quality by imposing a semantic metadata layer on top of the data format description.

Domains

By assigning an attribute a data type, we indicate that it draws its values from a specific set of allowed values. Further, we expect that any value is taken from a value set that has some structural (i.e., syntactic) rules and explicit semantic rules governing validity. Either way, these expectations restrict the values that an attribute takes. Whether these rules are syntactic or semantic, we can define an explicit set of restrictions on a set of values within a type and call that a *domain*. Some examples of domains include U.S. states, country currency codes, credit card numbers (they have a predetermined length and there are semantic rules governing validity based on a high-level parity calculation), and colors.

Mappings

We also look at relationships between pairs of values that are taken from different domains. A *mapping* is a relation between domain *A* and domain *B*, defined as a set of pairs of values {*a, b*} such that *a* is a member of domain *A* and *b* is a member of domain *B*. There is an intuitive meaning to this mapping relationship. A familiar example of a mapping is the relationship between ZIP code and city. Every ZIP code belongs to a named area covered by a small post office or postal zone.

Null Conformance

There are different data quality rules regarding nulls. One is whether or not an attribute allows nulls at all. Another kind of rule relates previously defined null representations. If nulls are allowed, the rule specifies that if a data attribute's value is null, then it must use one of a set of defined null representations.

Value Restrictions

A value restriction describes some business knowledge about a range of values, such as "test score is greater than 200 and less than 800." A value restriction rule constrains values to be within the defined range.

Domain and Mapping Membership

Domain membership asserts that an attribute's value is always taken from a previously defined data domain. For example, an online catalog vendor may specify a domain of fabric colors and then assert that all sweaters that can be ordered online must be of one of the named colors. A *mapping membership* rule asserts that the relation between two attributes or fields is restricted based on a named mapping. An example enforces the mapping from U.S. state name to its corresponding two-letter postal abbreviation.

Completeness and Exemption

A completeness rule specifies that when a condition is true, a record is incomplete unless all attributes on a provided list are not null. An example in the financial world would specify that if the security being traded is a stock option, the trade is incomplete unless a strike price and expiration date are provided. An exemption rule says that if a condition is true, then those attributes in a named list should not have values. For example, if the customer's age is less than 16, then the driver's license field should be null.

Consistency

Consistency refers to maintaining a relationship between two (or more) attributes based on the content of the attributes. A consistency rule indicates that if a particular condition holds true, then a following consequent must also be true. An example in a credit analysis application might say that the amount allowed for a monthly mortgage payment must be no more than 35% of the monthly gross income.

Continuous Data Quality Monitoring and Improvement

We iteratively improve data quality by identifying sources of poor data quality, asserting a set of rules about our expectations for the data, and implementing a measurement application using those rules. In operation, a set of rules is instantiated at each point in the information flow where data quality conformance is to be measured. Each data instance is tested against all associated rules; if no nonconformities are detected, the data instance is deemed to be valid; otherwise, it is said to be invalid. Data instances that fail the rules give us clues as to the sources of the nonconformance, which are then isolated and remedied.

Given a set of rules that define fitness for use and a mechanism for determining conformance of data instances to those rules, we have a measurement framework for data quality. Each data instance tested against a rule set can be scored across multiple dimensions. As we define more rules, we build a rule base that defines the basic expectations of data fitness against which each data instance (record, message, etc.) is measured, thereby providing an ongoing process for improved data quality.

Management Issues

Data quality is probably the most critical aspect of the business intelligence (BI) process, and it is a problem that needs to be addressed. Yet the scope of the data quality problem is so large that people frequently do not even know where to begin. But be assured that some investment must be made (preferably at the start of the project) in ensuring high levels of data quality.

Pay Now or Pay (More) Later

The most critical management issue associated with data quality is the lack of true understanding of its importance. No BI program can be successful if the data that feeds that program is faulty. And we have already discussed the claim that 70% or more of the effort associated with implementing a data warehouse project is spent in data integration and addressing data quality problems as the implementation nears completion. Not only that, some projects are completely killed because the data is so bad that the users refuse to allow the system into production.

This would lead the savvy manager to believe that the organization is going to have to pay for data quality eventually, and the cost-efficient way to do this would be to build data quality into the program from the start instead of a panicked attempt at reconciliation moments before the entire project is debudgeted. Spend the time and money on properly capturing and validating data before it enters the BI environment instead of trying to fix it later or during the ETL process.

Personalization of Quality

The distribution of data processing over the past 20 to 30 years has also led to the distribution of the data itself, with the corresponding turf grabs and data fiefdoms. Because team members may psychologically equate their individuality within the organization with their job performance, there is a natural tendency to hide potential problems instead of exposing themselves to job risk, and the management of data is not excluded from this. I refer to this as the "personalization of data quality," where the exposition of data quality problems is viewed by the employee as a personal attack, to be avoided at all costs.

Proper identification of data management roles and responsibilities and performance incentives created for ensuring high-quality data can be coupled with the business rule approach to remove the stigma of "poor quality" from the person entrusted with data management. This depersonalization will lead to smoother transition to an integrated knowledge environment.

Data Ownership and Responsibilities

A similar issue to personalization of quality lies in the organizational delineation of data ownership. The "owner" of data can be defined in many ways, including creator, funder, consumer, business partner, and aggregator, but when the topic of data quality is introduced, it is crucial to determine in whose bailiwick the responsibility for data quality lies. One interesting way to define a data owner is as "the person who can determine just how clean the data needs to be and how to prioritize the cleansing effort." A formal structure for data ownership and a responsibility chain should be defined before the data integration component of implementation.

Correction versus Augmentation

Another important distinction is between the repetitive application of the *same* corrections to the *same* data each time that data set is extracted from its source and brought into the BI environment, and a true data quality improvement process. Correcting bad data is treating the symptom, whereas data quality improvement cures the problem. For this reason we typically don't recommend automatically correcting data immediately; rather, we suggest augmenting invalid records with encoded information about its invalidity and then letting the data consumer determine how to address that issue.

To Learn More

The summary here is pure and simple: Bad data costs money. A BI program that is missing an integrated data quality validation and improvement discipline will at best provide decreased value to the consumer and at worst fail miserably. Integrating ongoing information compliance measurements and improvement processes will lead to a high-value information asset.

To learn more about data quality, see *Enterprise Knowledge Management: The Data Quality Approach*, David Loshin, San Francisco, Morgan Kaufmann, 2001. Another good book is *Improving Data Warehouse and Business Information Quality*, Larry English, New York, John Wiley & Sons, 1999.

CHAPTER 10

Information Integration

The last few chapters have talked about the rules that surround information, the discovery of the metadata through data profiling, and the issues of measuring and maintaining high levels of data quality. Now that you have been introduced to the collection of raw data and its need for both profiling and quality assessment, the next step is to understand how information can be integrated, manipulated, and distributed to information consumers.

There are different aspects to the concept of information integration, because different purposes inspire different kinds of solutions. In this chapter we focus on different aspects of the integration process and the need to link information from multiple data sets.

The Business Case

In Chapter 2 we explored the value of information and identified the fact that the value of information can increase when it can be merged with other information. The business intelligence (BI) process revolves around the ability to collect, aggregate, and, most importantly, leverage the integration of different data sets together; the ability to collect that data and place it in a data warehouse provides the means by which that leverage can be obtained.

The only way to get data into a data warehouse is through an information integration process. The only way to consolidate information for data consumption is through an information integration process. The business case is quite simple: If your organization has committed to building a BI program, you will need to deal with this issue.

ETL: Extract, Transform, Load

A basic premise of constructing a data warehouse is that data sets from multiple sources are collected and then added to a data repository from which analytical applications can source their input data. Of course, this sounds much easier than it really is, because whereas our warehouse data model may have been designed very carefully with the BI clients' needs in mind, the data sets that are being used to source the warehouse typically have their own peculiarities. Yet not only do these data sets need to be migrated into the warehouse, they will need to be integrated with other data sets either before or during the warehouse population process.

This *extract/transform/load* process is the sequence of applications that extract data sets from the various sources, bring them to a data staging area, apply a sequence of processes to prepare the data for migration into the data warehouse, and actually load them. Here is the general theme of an ETL process.

- Get the data from the source location.
- Map the data from its original form into a data model that is suitable for manipulation at the staging area.
- Validate and clean the data.
- Apply any transformations to the data that are required before the data sets are loaded into the repository.
- Map the data from its staging area model to its loading model.
- Move the data set to the repository.
- Load the data into the warehouse.

Staging Architecture

The first part of the ETL process is to assemble the infrastructure needed for aggregating the raw data sets and for the application of the transformation and the subsequent preparation of the data to be forwarded to the data warehouse. This is typically a combination of a hardware platform and appropriate management software that we refer to as the *staging area*. The architecture of a staging process can be seen in Figure 10.1. Note that the staging architecture must take into account the order of execution of the individual ETL stages, including scheduling data extractions, the frequency of repository refresh, the kinds of transformations that are to be applied, the collection of data for forwarding to the warehouse, and the actual warehouse population.

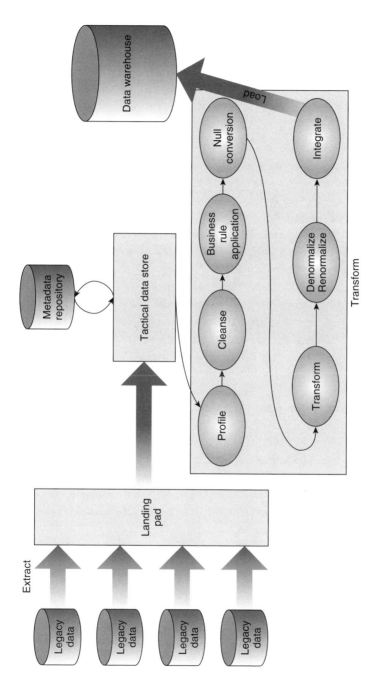

FIGURE 10.1 Architecture of a staging application.

Extraction

Extraction essentially boils down to two questions:

- What data should be extracted?
- How should that data be extracted?

Realize that the first question essentially relies on what the BI clients expect to see ultimately factored into their analytical applications. But it is a deeper question, because the data that we want to flow into the repository is likely to be a subset of some existing set of tables. In other words, for each data set extracted, we may only want to grab particular columns of interest, yet we may want to use the source system's ability to select and join data before it flows into the staging area. A lot of extracted data is formed into flat load files that can be either easily manipulated in process at the staging area or forwarded directly to the warehouse.

How data should be extracted may depend on the scale of the project, the number (and disparity) of data sources, and how far into the implementation the developers are. Extraction can be as simple as a collection of simple SQL queries or as complex as to require ad hoc, specially designed programs written in a proprietary programming language. There are tools available to help automate the process, although their quality (and corresponding price) varies widely.

Automated extraction tools generally provide some kind of definition interface specifying the source of the data to be extracted and a destination for the extract, and they can work in one of two major ways, both of which involve code generation techniques. The first is to generate a program to be executed on the platform where the data is sourced to initiate a transfer of the data to the staging area. The other way is to generate an extraction program that can run on the staging platform that pulls the data from the source down to the staging area.

Transformation

Chapter 8 discussed data profiling and how that can be used as a way to capture the metadata of a data set. What is discovered during the profiling is put to use as part of the ETL process to help in the mapping of source data to a form suitable for the target repository, including the following tasks.

- **Data type conversion**—This includes parsing strings representing integer and numeric values and transforming them into the proper representational form for the target machine, and converting physical value representations from one platform to another (EBCDIC to ASCII being the best example).

- **Data cleansing**—The rules we can uncover through the profiling process can be applied the way discussed in Chapter 9, along with directed actions that can be used to correct data that is known to be incorrect and where the corrections can be automated. This component also covers data-duplicate analysis and elimination and merge/purge (which we cover in more detail later).

- **Integration**—This includes exploiting the discovery of table and foreign keys for representing linkage between different tables, along with the generation of alternate (i.e., artificial) keys that are independent of any systemic business rules, mapping keys from one system to another, archiving data domains and codes that are mapped into those data domains, and maintaining the metadata (including full descriptions of code values and master key-lookup tables).

- **Referential integrity checking**—In relation to the foreign key relationships exposed through profiling or as documented through interaction with subject matter experts, this component checks that any referential integrity constraints are not violated and highlights any non-unique (supposed) key fields and any detected orphan foreign keys.

- **Derivations**—Any transformations based on business rules, new calculations, string manipulations, etc., that need to be applied as the data moves from source to target are applied during the transformation stage. For example, a new "revenue" field might be constructed and populated as a function of "unit price" and "quantity sold."

- **Denormalization and renormalization**—Frequently data that is in normalized form when it comes from the source system needs to be broken out into a denormalized form when dimensions are created in repository data tables. Conversely, data sourced from join extractions may be denormalized and may need to be renormalized before it is forwarded to the warehouse.

- **Aggregation**—Any aggregate information that is used for populating summaries or any cube dimensions can be performed at the staging area.

- **Audit information**—As a matter of reference for integrity checking, it is always useful to calculate some auditing information, such as row counts, table counts, column counts, and other tests, to make sure that what you have is what you wanted. In addition, some data augmentation can be done to attach provenance information, including source, time and date of extraction, and time and date of transformation.

- **Null conversion**—Because nulls can appear in different forms, ranging from system nulls to explicit strings representing different kinds of nulls (see Chapter 9), it is useful to have some kind of null conversion that transforms different nulls from disparate systems.

Loading

The loading component of ETL is centered on moving the transformed data into the data warehouse. The critical issues include the following.

- **Target dependencies,** such as where and on how many machines the repository lives, and the specifics of loading data into that platform
- **Refresh volume and frequency,** such as whether the data warehouse is to be loaded on an incremental basis, whether data is forwarded to the repository as a result of triggered transaction events, or whether all the data is periodically loaded into the warehouse in the form of a full refresh

Scalability

There are two flavors of operations that are addressed during the ETL process. One involves processing that is limited to all data instances within a single data set, and the other involves the resolution of issues involving more than one data set. For example, the merge/purge operation (see later) compares pairs of records taken from different data sets to determine if they represent the same entity and are therefore candidates for merging. In the most naive method, this process requires each instance from one data set to be compared with all the instances from the other set; as more data sets are added to the mix, the complexity of this process increases geometrically.

The story is basically this: The more data sets that are being integrated, the greater the amount of work that needs to be done for the integration to complete. This creates two requirements: (1) More efficient methods must be applied to perform the integration, and (2) the process must be scalable, as both the size and the number of data sets increase.

Enterprise Application Integration and Web Services

Similar to the way that ETL processes extract and transform information from multiple data sources to a target data warehouse, there are processes for integrating and transforming information between active process and applications to essentially make them all work together. This process, called *enterprise application integration* (EAI), which includes a function similar to interacting applications (or, better yet, interacting components) that is provided by ETL.

Enterprise Application Integration

Enterprise application integration (EAI) is meant to convey the perception of multiple applications working together as if they were all a single application. The basic goal is for a business process to be able to be cast as the interaction of a set of available applications and for all applications to be able to properly communicate with each other. This capability is achieved both through a communications connectivity along with the ability of each application to cast its information into a form that can be shared with other applications.

Enterprise application integration is not truly a product or a tool, but rather is framework of ideas comprising different levels of integration, including:

- Business process management, including workflow mapping and management, along with the casting of customer business processes on top of the message and interaction framework

- Communications middleware, which includes a messaging layer that can be adapted to many different hardware architectures, message transport management, ensuring message ordering constraints, and communication security

- Data standardization and transformation, which, similar to the ETL transformation process, translates information messages into a standard form, data field tagging, message packing and unpacking, and application connectors to provide hooks from different applications into the message middleware

- Application of business rules that are critical to the interaction of the different components as a way to implement the expected application

All of these pieces may be better illustrated through a frequently used example. A customer requests a quote for automobile insurance through an interactive Web site; the information is forwarded to different target applications, one that checks the customer's credit rating, one that checks for driving history, and another that queries a database to find insurance products that meet the customer's requests. These applications together provide information that can be configured as a quote that is forwarded back to the customer. If the customer decides to make the purchase, another set of actions are initiated, such as forwarding the policy information to the accounts receivable application to generate a statement and updating a policy database to include the new policy.

Enterprise application integration is important both as a way of incorporating some of the transformation logic required as part of the ETL process into the movement of data and as the integration of analytic process results from multiple sources for convergence within a high-level scorecard or key performance indicator portal.

Web Services

The natural progression of EAI is toward a more Web-centric conceptual implementation of application integration that can mask the implementation details while providing a transparent view to any client who wants to make use of some defined functionality.

Web services are business functions available over the Internet that are constructed according to strict specifications. Conformance to a strict standard enables different, disparate clients to interact. By transforming data into an Extensible Markup Language (XML) format based on predefined schema and providing object access directives that describe how objects (or, more mundanely, how functional applications) are communicated with, Web services provide a higher-level of abstraction than what is assumed by general EAI.

Record Linkage and Consolidation

Consolidation is a catchall term for those processes that make use of collected metadata and knowledge to eliminate duplicate entities and merge data from multiple sources, among other data enhancement operations. That process is powered by the ability to identify some kind of relationship between any arbitrary pair of data instances.

There are different kinds of relationships that we look for. One is *identity*—determining that two data instances refer to the exact same entity. This is what we look for when searching for duplicate entries in one database or searching for multiple instances of the same entity when merging databases. Another is *equivalence classing*, which refers to grouping entities together based on some set of similar attributes. An example of this is finding people from the same family or people who work for the same company.

The key to record linkage is the concept of *similarity*. This is a measure of how close two data instances are to each other, and can be a hard measure (either the two records are the same, or they are not) or a more approximate measure (based on some form of scoring), in which case the similarity is judged based on scores above or below a threshold.

As an example, similarity scoring for names might parse each name into its individual components (first name, last name, title, suffix, etc.) and then compare the individually parsed components to see how many match and how closely they match. Consider comparing "H. David Loshin" with "David Loshin." The first string has a first initial, a middle name, and a last name; the second has a first name and a last name. A naive similarity scoring approach might conclude that this is not a close match, because the first initial of the first string does not match the first name of the second string. A more savvy algorithm would recognize that the match between the middle name of the first string and the first name of the second string represents a close match.

Scoring Precision and Application Context

One of the most significant insights into similarity and difference measurements is the issue of application context and its impact on both measurement precision and the similarity criteria. Depending on the kind of application that makes use of approximate searching and matching, the thresholds will most likely change.

For example, in a simple direct mail sales program, our goal is to find duplicate entries. But if a pair of duplicates is not caught, the worst that can happen is that some household gets more than one catalog. In this case, we might prefer that any borderline matches be assumed to be mismatches so that our coverage is greater (Fig. 10.2).

On the other hand, if we are evaluating potential matches during a criminal investigation, then if a person's name matches one of the names on the list of known criminals, that person can be isolated and a full investigation performed to determine whether there are any reasons for further detention. In this instance, where safety and security are concerned, we all know the worst that can happen if there is a missed match. We might prefer to err on the side of caution and lower the match threshold so that any borderline matches are brought to the attention of the criminal investigators.

Although the basic application in both of these cases is the same (matching names against other names), we can, depending on the expected results, group our applications into those that are *exclusive* searches, which are intended to distinguish as many individuals as possible, and *inclusive* searches, which want to include as many potential matches into a cluster as possible. The direct marketing duplicate elimination would be an exclusive application, whereas the criminal intelligence application is an inclusive application (Fig. 10.3).

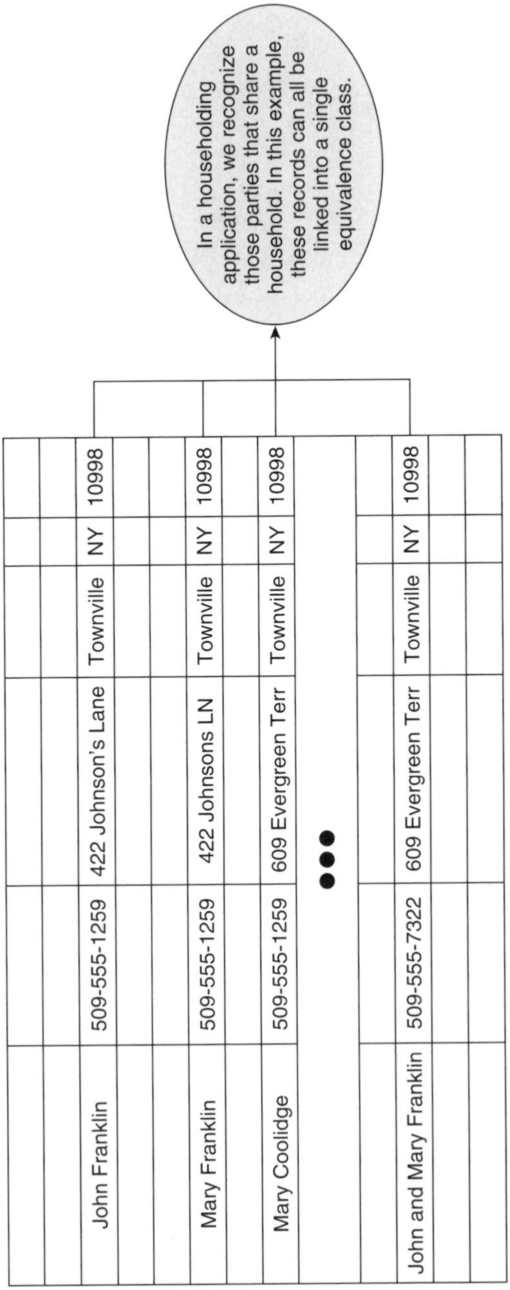

John Franklin		509-555-1259	422 Johnson's Lane	Townville	NY	10998
Mary Franklin		509-555-1259	422 Johnsons LN	Townville	NY	10998
Mary Coolidge		509-555-1259	609 Evergreen Terr	Townville	NY	10998
John and Mary Franklin		509-555-7322	609 Evergreen Terr	Townville	NY	10998

In a householding application, we recognize those parties that share a household. In this example, these records can all be linked into a single equivalence class.

FIGURE 10.2 Different degrees of search precision.

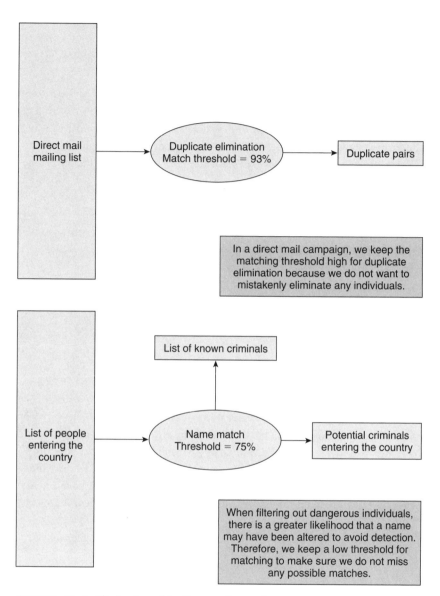

FIGURE 10.3 Elimination of duplicates and merge/purge.

Elimination of Duplicates

The elimination of duplicates is a process of finding multiple representations of the same entity within the data set and eliminating all but one of those representations from the set. In some instances, such as with a primary key in a relational database table, duplicates are not allowed, and so it is imperative that duplicate records be found and reduced to a single entity. When duplicates are exact matches, they can be discovered through the simple process of sorting the records based on the data attributes under investigation. When duplicates exist because of erroneous values, we have to use a more advanced technique, such as approximate searching and matching, to find and eliminate duplicates.

The elimination of duplicates is essentially a process of clustering similar records together and then reviewing the corresponding similarity scores with respect to a pair of thresholds. Any scores above the higher threshold are automatically deemed to be a match; any scores below the lower threshold are automatically deemed not to be a match. Scores between the thresholds are to be pulled for human review.

Merge/Purge

Merge/purge is similar to the elimination of duplicates, except that whereas duplicate elimination is associated with removing doubles from a single data set, merge/purge involves the aggregation of multiple data sets followed by eliminating duplicates (Fig. 10.4). Data from different sources will tend to have inconsistencies and inaccuracies when consolidated, and therefore simple matching is insufficient during an aggregation phase. Again, approximate matching can be used to cluster similar records, which can either have a reduction phase automated or be passed through human review, depending on the application.

Householding

Householding is a process of reducing a number of records into a single set associated with a single household. A *household* could be defined as a single residence, and the householding process is used to determine which individuals live within the same residence.

Householding is more than just finding all people with the same last name living at the same address. Associated with householding is a more advanced set of facts, such as marital status, family structure, and residence type (single-versus multifamily home versus apartment). As in other areas that we have

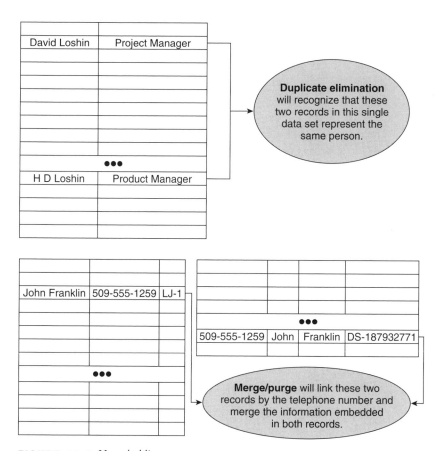

FIGURE 10.4 Householding.

discussed, the goal of the application determines the result of the house-holding process.

For example, a mail-order catalog company might want to ensure that only one catalog was being sent to each residence. In that case, the house-holding process is meant to aggregate records around a particular delivery address, attempting to recognize those names that all belong to the same address, whether or not they belong to the same family. Alternatively, an application that is targeting only the teenagers in a household would want to identify all members of the same family as well as each family member's role. A third application might be to find unmarried individuals living together. In each of these applications, the process is similar, but the details of which attributes are used in the process may differ.

The general approach for householding naturally revolves around the address. All addresses are cleansed and standardized (this is discussed in Chapter 13), and then groups are clustered based on the same address. Addresses are enhanced based on their location status, such as single-family home, two-family home, multifamily dwelling, small apartment, large apartment, storefront, and business address.

The clusters now represent sets of entities residing at the same location. Any distinction based on individual occupancy unit (e.g., apartment number, floor, suite) is done at this time. Within each cluster, each entity is considered as to its relation to other entities within the cluster. Two entities are related if some connection can be established between them using corroborating data. This might include sharing a last name, having the same telephone number, the existence of a third record that contains both names, etc. When two entity records are determine to be related, that relation is documented as a virtual link between them.

Improving Information Currency

There are other applications that make use of a consolidation phase during data cleansing. One application is the analysis of currency and correctness. Given a set of data records collected from multiple sources, the information embedded within each of the records may be either slightly incorrect or out of date. In the consolidation phase, when multiple records associated with a single entity are combined, the information in all the records can be used to infer the best overall set of data attributes. Timestamps, placestamps, and quality of data source are all properties of a record that can be used to condition the value of data's currency and correctness.

Management Issues

Some of the important issues associated with the integration process have been touched on before in this book, but they are important enough to reiterate.

Data Ownership

Who owns data? This seemingly innocuous question has relatively deep ramifications, because the issue of ownership becomes much more relevant when more than one organization wants to exploit a set of information purchased, created, controlled, or managed by a single organization. The question is not really about ownership but, rather, about the limits of data management responsibility, especially if those providing data have no stake in the success of the BI program.

Consider this frequent scenario: A BI group designing and building a data warehouse wants to accumulate and integrate data sets from different groups within an organization, although these group data sets are designed and used with respect to particular (stovepiped or vertical) transactional purposes. The systems that interact with the group data systems have been in production for a long time, and their clients are completely satisfied with their system performance. As soon as many of these data sets are examined and profiled by the BI/data warehouse team, a number of anomalies, errors, and inconsistencies between the different data sets appear as a by-product of the integration process. Essentially, if you were to continue integrating these data sets, you would knowingly have a data warehouse with questionable data.

As the manager of the BI group, you are now faced with a dilemma: How are you to direct your team to maintain a high level of data quality within the warehouse? There are three ways to address this: Correct the data in the warehouse, try to effect some changes to the source data, and leave the errors in the data. I suspect that the third choice is the least desirable, and therefore this is where ownership and responsibility becomes an issue.

Choosing to fix the data in the warehouse means that not only will you be continually correcting the same bad data over and over again as part of the integration process (which will occupy time and computational resources), but the warehouse data will be inconsistent with one or more group's view. Choosing to effect the correction at the data source is also a challenge if there is no positive value added to each group's application by fixing the data (or, better, the process responsible for the flawed data). A savvy manager will arrange for the institutionalization of data management standards, practices, and a responsibility chain that provides for the resolution of problems that are hampered by data ownership issues.

Activity Scheduling

Do you clean the data before you try to merge it? If you do, do you lose information that may have provided a more complete linkage? Do you apply all the transformations to the data right after it is extracted, or do you do this after it has been reformulated for movement to the target repository? These kinds of questions reflect the problem of how to schedule the activities associated with the scheduling process. The answers depend on the available resources, the relative quality of supplied data, and the kind of data sets that are to be propagated to the repository.

Another management issue involves the frequency, scale, and size of the warehouse refresh process. How these questions are answered will direct the sizing, scheduling, and management of the ETL process.

Reliability of Automated Linkage

Although our desire is for automated processes to properly link data instances as part of the integration process, there is always some doubt that the software is actually doing what we want it to do. In the case of record linkage, thresholds are set—a higher one above which we assume there is a match, and a lower one below which there is no match. Two issues arise from this. The first is that similarity scoring attempts to reduce the complexity of assessing the sameness between two objects across multiple dimensions down to a single number; in certain instances, biases creep into the computation to unduly skew that number, which potentially links two records that should not be linked (*false positives*) or misses linking a pair of records that should be linked (*false negatives*). Trying to find these false results is a matter of exhaustive review, which may be approached via sampling, although you may never be sure that the process is doing exactly what is desired.

The second problem is the result of setting too wide a gap between the upper threshold and the lower threshold, which allows a large number of records to fall between those thresholds. Because those records are forwarded to staff members for clerical review, the more records that are shunted into the manual review process, the more work that must be done by people instead of computers.

To Learn More

The crux of the BI process is the ability to efficiently and properly integrate data from multiple sources and prepare that data for loading into the target data repository. This process revolves around ETL, the ability to extract data from multiple data sources and to transform that data in preparation for integration with other data sets, that is, merging and aggregating data, perhaps with some more transformation required for loading the data into a data warehouse.

To learn more about information integration, there are a number of very good articles available at *www.dmreview.com* and *www.intelligententerprise.com*.

CHAPTER 11

The Value of Parallelism

If we were to assess the size of the data sets that are common in any major industry, we would not be surprised at how much data is being created, collected, and stored, even before considering aggregating this data into any sort of data warehouse. It would not be unusual to see large customer databases, accompanied by transaction data sets (e.g., orders, call detail records [CDRs], insurance policies) that are one or two orders of magnitude larger. For example, it would not be unreasonable to expect a telecommunications company to log millions, if not billions, of CDRs each day; a data set containing a year's worth of CDRs can easily exceed a terabyte of data. Add in party reference data, customer service detail records, order transactions, service orders, billing, shipping, etc., and we have the makings of a huge data integration and analysis problem.

When we combine all that information into an analytical framework, we are presented with two major barriers to the timely capture, analysis, and exploitation of information. The first is that the sheer amount of information available overwhelms any individual's ability to understand it, and the second is that the time to complete the amount of processing needed to digest that information is likely to exceed the window of opportunity for exploiting any results.

A successful business intelligence (BI) strategy encompasses more than just the desired analytical functionality. It must also incorporate expectations about the timeliness of the applications. Luckily, there have been significant innovations in the area of *parallel processing* that allow us to decompose a lot of the processing, which can then be farmed out to collections of computers. In this chapter we explore parallel processing—the business case for incorporating parallelism into your enterprise, what conditions must be true to expose parallelism, and the different kinds of parallelism.

The Business Case

Maintaining large amounts of transaction data is one thing, but integrating and subsequently transforming that data into an analytical environment (such as a data warehouse or any multidimensional analytical framework) requires a large amount of both storage space and processing capability. And unfortunately, the kinds of processing needed for BI applications cannot be scaled linearly. In other words, with most BI processing, doubling the amount of data can dramatically increase the amount of processing required.

For example, consider a simple customer name-matching application for duplicate analysis. Given two data sets, each containing 10,000 names, the brute-force approach is to compare each name in the first data set against each name in the second data set, resulting in $10,000 \times 10,000 = 100,000,000$ comparisons. If the two data sets each contain 20,000 names, suddenly we are faced with 400,000,000 comparisons; doubling the size of problem quadruples the amount of work! But let's say we break the first data set into four subsets of 5000 names each and then farm out each subset to one of four identical processing systems to be compared to the 20,000-name second data set. Although the amount of work is the same, each of the four systems performs 100,000,000 comparisons, and because this processing can operate in parallel, the elapsed time for completion is actually one-fourth of the time that a single system would require. By scaling our resources to meet the size of the problem, we have achieved a scalability that could not have been made explicit in the application.

This then poses another issue—as BI projects succeed, the demand for more analytical services increases, which in turn increases the size of the project. Whether the size of the input grows or the number of applications grows, the demands on the system may potentially be met by making use of parallel processing.

Within certain constraints, there is an appeal to exploiting multiple processor execution, for a few reasons, among them the following.

- Loosely coupled parallel systems can be configured using commodity parts; for example, large numbers of homogeneous workstations can easily be networked using high-speed switches.

- Software frameworks can be instituted on top of already available resources to make use of underused computer capability (*cycle-stealing*), thereby increasing return on hardware investment.

- Small-scale multiple processor systems (4–16 processors) are readily available at reasonable prices in configurations that can be expanded by incrementally adding processors and memory.

- Programming languages and libraries (such as in C++ and Java) have embedded support for thread- or task-level parallelization, which eases the way for implementation and use.

Parallelism and Granularity

Whenever we talk about parallelism, we need to assess the size of the problem as well as the way the problem can be decomposed into parallelizable units. The metric of unit size with respect to concurrency is called *granularity*. Large problems that decompose into a relatively small number of large tasks would have *coarse granularity*, whereas a decomposition into a large number of very small tasks would have *fine granularity*. In this section we look at different kinds of parallelism ranging from coarse-grained to fine-grained parallelism. Ultimately, our goal is to be able to achieve a speedup that correlates to the resources we have allocated to the problem.

A sequence of operations that are collected together is called a *unit of work*. Each concurrent unit of work can be allocated as a job to be performed by a computational executor, but these executors have different characteristics, depending on the granularity of the unit of work. The decision boils down to the amount of overhead required for each kind of executor. For example, coarsely grained work may be allocated to a high-overhead process, a medium-grained unit of work may be allocated to a lightweight process, or *task*, and finely grained units may be integrated directly into function calls to a parallel runtime system.

Scalability

When we decompose a problem into smaller units of work, we expect to gain speedup when concurrently executing those units of work allocated to multiple-execution resources. *Scalability* refers to the situation when the speedup linearly increases as the number of resources is increased. For example, if the time for a program halves each time the number of processors increases, that program exhibits linear scalability.

Task Parallelism

Imagine that you are preparing a three-course dinner, with an appetizer, a main course, and a dessert. Although our cultural bias constrains the order of *eating* those courses, there are no rules about the order of *preparing* the courses. In other words, you can make the dessert before cooking the main course, because there is nothing inherent in dessert preparation that depends on main course preparation.

How long does it take to prepare this meal? If there is only one chef, then the total time to prepare the meal is the sum of the times to prepare each course. But if we assume that there are three competent chefs in the kitchen, then each one can take on the task of preparing one of the courses. If all the participants start at the same time, then the total time to prepare the meal is bounded by the longest preparation time of each of the three courses. By delegating each independent task to an available resource, we reduce the overall preparation time, possibly by two-thirds of the original time requirement (Fig. 11.1).

This is an example of task parallelism, which is a coarsely grained parallelism. In this case, a high-level process is decomposed into a collection of discrete tasks, each of which performs some set of operations and results in some output or side effect.

Pipeline Parallelism

Let's consider a different example that can inherently benefit from a different kind of parallelism. In an automobile assembly line, a car is incrementally built in a sequence of stages. At each stage, another set of parts is added to the developing product, until the final stage, when a working car rolls off the line. What is nice about this process is that it forms what we call a pipeline,

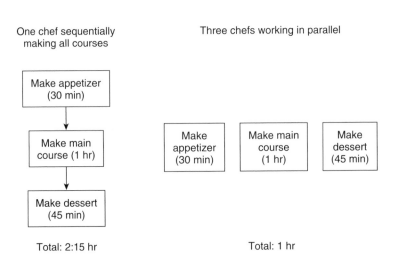

FIGURE 11.1 Task parallelism in the kitchen.

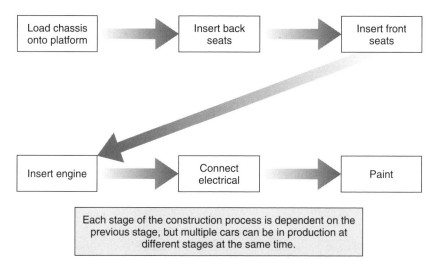

FIGURE 11.2 A simplified automobile construction line.

and it is appealing because the different teams can execute their stages of the pipeline on many partially completed cars all at the same time. In other words, while one group is fitting the chassis for one car, another group is inserting the engine on another car. In fact, the beauty of the assembly line is its inherent parallelizability, because many partial tasks can be in process simultaneously.

This kind of parallelism is called *pipeline parallelism* (or *pipelining*); any process that can be broken up into a discrete sequence of stages can benefit from pipelining. Pipelining is an example of medium-grained parallelism, because the tasks are not fully separable (i.e., the completion of a single stage does not result in a finished product); however, the amount of work is large enough that it can be cordoned off and assigned as operational tasks (Fig. 11.2).

Data Parallelism

Data parallelism is a different kind of parallelism. Here, instead of identifying a collection of operational steps to be allocated to a process or task, the parallelism is related to both the flow and the structure of the information. An analogy might revisit the automobile factory from our example in the previous section. There we looked at how the construction of an automobile could be transformed into a pipelined process. Here, because the construction of cars along one assembly has no relation to the construction of the same kinds of cars along any other assembly line, there is no reason why we can't duplicate the same assembly line multiple times; two assembly lines will result in twice as many cars being produced in the same amount of time as a single assembly line.

For data parallelism, the goal is to scale the throughput of processing based on the ability to decompose the data set into concurrent processing streams, all performing the same set of operations. For example, a customer address standardization process iteratively grabs an address and attempts to transform it into a standard form. This task is adaptable to data parallelism and can be sped up by a factor of 4 by instantiating four address standardization processes and streaming one-fourth of the address records through each instantiation (Fig. 11.3). Data parallelism is a more finely grained parallelism in that we achieve our performance improvement by applying the same small set of tasks iteratively over multiple streams of data.

Vector Parallelism

Vector parallelism refers to an execution framework where a collection of objects is treated as an array, or vector, and the same set of operations is applied to all elements of the set. A vector parallel platform can be used to implement both pipeline and data parallel applications.

Combinations

Note that these forms of parallelism are not mutually exclusive. For example, the data parallel address standardization process discussed earlier may be one stage of a pipelined process propagating data from a set of sources to a final target. We can embed pipelined processing within coarsely grained tasks or even decompose a pipe stage into a set of concurrent processes. The value of each of these kinds of parallelism is bounded by the system's ability to support the overhead for managing those different levels.

Parallel Processing Systems

In this section we look at some popular parallel processing architectures. Systems employing these architectures either are configured by system manufacturers (such as symmetric multiprocessor [SMP] or massively parallel processing [MPP] systems) or can be homebrewed by savvy technical personnel (such as by use of a network of workstations).

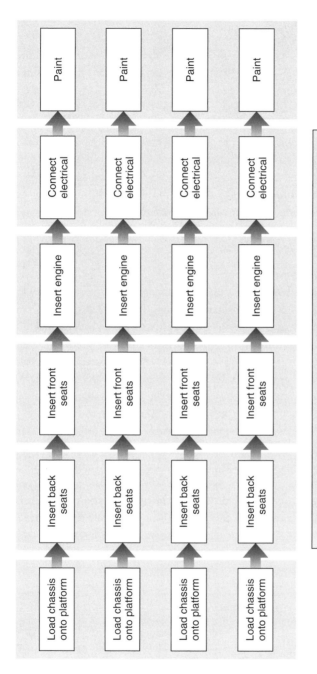

FIGURE 11.3 Duplicating the assembly provides linear scalability—a feature of data parallelism.

Duplicating the assembly shows how the same operations can be executed on different cars in production, even in the same stage. If the cars correspond to partially completed data processing stages, this can be compared to data parallelism.

Symmetric Multiprocessing

An SMP system is a hardware configuration that combines multiple processors within a single architecture. All processors in an SMP machine share a single operating system, input/output (I/O) devices, and memory, and each processor (or CPU) maintains its own cache related to the shared memory. In an SMP system, multiple processes can be allocated to different CPUs within the system, which makes an SMP machine a good platform for coarse-grained parallelism.

An SMP machine can also be formulated for pipelined execution by allocating each CPU a different stage of an application and propagating partial results through communication via the shared memory system.

Massively Parallel Processing

An MPP system consists of a large number of small homogeneous processors interconnected via a high-speed network. The processors in an MPP machine are independent—they do not share memory, and typically each processor may run its own instance of an operating system, although there may be systemic controller applications hosted on a leader processor that instruct the individual processors in the MPP configuration on what tasks to perform.

Nodes on MPP machines may also be connected directly to their own I/O devices, or I/O may be channeled into the entire system via high-speed interconnects. Communication between nodes is likely to occur in a *coordinated* fashion, where all nodes stop processing and participate in an exchange of data across the network, or in an *uncoordinated* fashion, with messages targeted for specific recipients being injected into the network independently.

Because data can be streamed through the network and targeted for specific nodes, an MPP machine is nicely suited for data parallel applications. In this case, all processors execute the same program on different data streams. In addition, because individual processors can execute different programs, an MPP machine is nicely suited to coarse-grained parallelism and can be configured for pipelined execution as well.

Networks of Workstations

A network of workstations is a more loosely coupled version of an MPP system; the workstations are likely to be configured as individual machines that are connected via network. The *communication latencies* (i.e., delays in exchanging data) are likely to be an order of magnitude greater in this kind of configuration, and it is also possible for the machines in the network to be heterogeneous (i.e., involving different kinds of systems).

Because of the configuration, a network of workstations is better suited to coarse-grained parallelism, although any data parallel application without a lot of communication could be nicely adapted to this configuration.

Hybrid Architectures

A hybrid architecture is one that combines or adapts one of the previously discussed systems. For example, system manufacturers will connect multiple SMP machines using a high-speed interconnect to create a hybrid system with a communications model involving two different levels of service. *On-node* communication (where a node is a single SMP machine) is significantly faster than *cross-node* communication. Another configuration might connect small MPP (i.e., 16-node) machines, each of which shares some memory with other small MPP machines within a single box. The use of a hybrid architecture may be very dependent on the specific application, because some systems may be better suited to the concurrency specifics associated with each application.

Dependence

The key to exploiting parallelism is the ability to analyze dependence constraints within any process. Basically, if there are two tasks that exhibit any kind of dependence relationship, they cannot be executed concurrently. In this section we explore both control dependence and data dependence, as well as issues associated with analyzing the dependence constraints within a system that prevent an organization from exploiting parallelism.

Control Dependence

Control refers to the logic that determines whether a particular task is performed. For example, a system may check the date to determine whether the payroll processing should be run. Most control logic relates to some aspect of a particular state of the environment, which may have been altered as a side effect of some processing task.

Frequently, one task may not start because it is waiting for a condition that is to be set by another task. Process control cannot be initiated at that first task until (at best) the condition is set by the other task or (at worst) the other task completes. In this case, the first task is *control dependent* on the second task.

Input/Output Data Dependence

A *data dependence* between two processing stages represents a situation where some information that is "touched" (i.e., either read or written) by one process is read or written by a subsequent process, and the order of execution of these processes requires that the first process execute before the second process. For example, during and extract/transform/load (ETL) process, the data extraction from multiple source databases must execute before an integration process can start.

There are potentially four kinds of data dependencies.

- **Read after read (RAR),** in which the second process's read of data occurs after the first process's read. In reality, this is not a critical dependence with respect to application correctness as long as there are no intervening writes, but identifying RAR dependencies may expose some optimization opportunities. An example of this kind of dependence would include a pair of processing stages, each of which refers to the same set of reference data (such as a customer entity database).

- **Read after write (RAW),** in which the second process's read of data must occur after the first process's write of that data. This kind of dependence implies a true ordering constraint in which the second processing stage's use of the data item essentially relies on the value that is written by the first process. A customer database duplicate analysis application that executes after an address standardization process is an example of this kind of dependence.

- **Write after read (WAR),** in which the second process's write of data must occur after the first process's read of that data item. This is also a true ordering constraint: The second process's write cannot take place until after the first process reads the data, because the second process may overwrite the value expected by the first process. In some reporting applications that execute on a periodic (e.g., nightly) fashion, daily transactional processing may overwrite data that is used in the reporting process, and in this example all reporting must be completed before the transactions may commence.

- **Write after write (WAW),** in which the second process's write of data must occur after the first process's write of that data item. This represents a true ordering constraint as well, because the effect of executing both processes is that the write of the second process is expected to be the one seen by any subsequent processing stages.

Dependence Analysis

Dependence analysis is the process of examining an application's use of data and control structure to identify true dependencies within the application. The goal is first to identify the dependence chain within the system and then to look for opportunities where independent tasks can be executed in parallel. We use the information flow model discussed in Chapter 5 as the basis for our initial assessment. For a quick analysis, we can use these guidelines.

- Any processing stage that is the target of an information channel is data dependent on the data that moves along that channel.

- Any processing stage that is the target of an information channel is control dependent on the processing stage from which that channel is sourced.

At each processing stage, data dependence should be analyzed by evaluating the tasks applied to the data. If there is a series of tasks, each of which needs to be completed before the next can continue, then there may be a data dependence between tasks, although that may allow for pipelining. If each task is applied to a discrete data instance or record and there is no relevance to the order in which those data instances are processed, then this indicates no data dependence. In this case, the task may be decomposed into a data parallel operation.

Parallelism and Business Intelligence

At this point it makes sense to review the value of parallelism with respect to a number of the BI-related applications we have discussed so far. In each of these applications, a significant speedup can be achieved by exploiting parallelism. First we look at one example of query processing, which is integral to most analytical data functions. In this example, the right kind of parallelism can provide linear scalability. Our second example shows how the column analysis of data profiling can be sped up through task parallelism, and our third example discusses coarse-grained parallelism and the ETL process.

Query Processing

Although the complexity of query optimizations may be beyond the scope of this book, a very simple query example can demonstrate the scale of the problem. Consider a database system with a customer table and an orders table. To make things simple, each order entry refers to a specific quantity order of a single product by the referenced customer, along with the total for that order. Assume that there are 100,000 entries in the customer table, that each customer has some dollar rating indicating the minimum order total for which an order is profitable, and that there are 2 million entries in the orders table. We want to identify those customers who have made at least one order whose total is greater than that customer's dollar rating. This request can be configured as a query joining the customer table to the orders table, by selecting any customers from the customer table where there exists an order placed by that customer in the orders table and that order's total is greater than the customer's dollar rating.

The brute-force approach to implementing this join requires examining each of the orders for every customer, which results in $100,000 \times 2,000,000 = 200,000,000,000,000$ comparisons. If we can execute 1 million comparisons per second on a single processor, it would still take more than 2 days to finish this query.

In this case, each comparison between the customer table and the orders table is not related to any other comparison—in other words, no comparison is data dependent on any other comparison. If we had eight processors, we can replicate the customer table at each processor and distribute equal-sized chunks of the orders table to each processor. Then each processor is executing $100,000 \times 250,000 = 25,000,000,000$ comparisons. At the same execution speed, this cuts the overall time down to just under 7 hours to complete the entire task. Doubling the number of processors decreases the time by one-half again; in fact we could achieve a linear speedup that is proportional to the number of processors participating.

Of course, relational database management systems (RDBMS) will most likely have taken advantage of internal query optimization as well as user-defined indexes to speed up this kind of query. But even in that situation there are different ways that the query can be parallelized, and this will still result in a speedup.

Data Profiling

The column analysis component of data profiling is another good example of an application that can benefit from parallelism. Every column in a table is subject to a collection of analyses: frequency of values, value cardinality, distribution of value ranges, etc. But because the analysis of one column is distinct from that applied to all other columns, we can exploit parallelism by treating the set of analyses applied to each column as a separate task and then instantiating separate tasks to analyze a collection of columns simultaneously.

As each task completes, its results are reported, and then the resources used by that task can be allocated to a new task operating on the next available column.

Extract, Transform, Load

The extract, transform, load (ETL) component of data warehouse population is actually well suited to all the kinds of parallelism we have discussed in this chapter. Because we are collecting data from multiple independent sources, the extraction of data from each data source can be configured as a separate task, yielding coarse-grained parallelism as a result of all those extractions that are being performed concurrently. The ETL process itself consists of a sequence of stages that can be configured as a pipeline, propagating the results of each stage to its successor, yielding some medium-grained parallelism. Last, many of the stages performed during the ETL process exhibit data parallel characteristics (i.e., record-by-record transformations are data independent), which can then take advantage of fine-grained parallelism.

Management Issues

In this section we discuss some of the management issues associated with the use of parallelism in a BI environment.

Training and Technical Management Requirements

Although advances in hardware manufacturer configurations of parallel systems have eased the transition in integrating higher-end parallel systems, significant technical training is required to understand both system management and how best to take advantage of parallel systems.

Minimal Software Support

Not many off-the-shelf application software packages take advantage of parallel systems, although a number of RDBMS systems do, and there is an increasing number of high-end ETL tools that exploit parallelism. Many packages commonly used as part of the BI application environment were not architected to dynamically make use of any kind of parallel resources other than at the most coarse-grained level. Although there are effective subsystems that act as a barrier level between applications and the hardware to exploit parallel resources, these systems require applications to make use of defined application program interfaces (APIs) to interact with the subsystem. This trend is likely to change as more programmers become trained in programming for parallel systems.

Scalability Issues

Scalability is not just a function of the size of the data. Any use of parallelism in an analytical environment should be evaluated in the context of data size, the amount of query processing expected, the number of concurrent users, and the kinds and complexity of the analytical processing.

Need for Expertise

Ultimately, control and data dependence analysis are tasks that need to be incorporated into the systems analysis role when migrating to a parallel infrastructure, because the absence of valid dependence analysis will prevent proper exploitation of concurrent resources. Reliance on hardware and software vendor solutions will not necessarily lead to success, and a capital investment in parallel infrastructure will not provide a return on investment without demonstrating scalability.

To Learn More

In an environment where the physical demands for storing and managing terabyte and even petabyte data collections, the need for performance optimization within the analytical environment will drive increased reliance on high-performance and parallel computer systems. Operational performance will be driven both by the physical demands of the raw data requirements and by the increased computation demanded by many complex queries. In the BI environment, success breeds success, so a positive analytical experience will drive greater usage demands on the system.

Most of the increase in performance can be addressed by leveraging multiple resources to attain high scalability. Parallel computing can serve that need, and an investment in training staff in understanding how parallel computing can improve analytical performance will pay off in the long run.

To learn more about parallelism, consider the Web sites of the major hardware manufacturers, who are likely to provide white papers and other collateral material describing the benefits of parallel high-performance computing.

CHAPTER 12

Alternate Information Contexts

An interesting aspect of the business intelligence (BI) process is that although to a large degree it relies on relatively well-defined methods, architectures, and techniques, much of the success of a BI program stems from insight and intuition related to the use of data. Sometimes it is valuable to take a step back from the traditional data collections that we see on a regular basis, such as customer data, product data, and sales transactions, to evaluate the integration of information from a completely different context.

For example, by itself geographical data may not be of great interest, but merging customer transactions with rolled-up psychographic profiles associated with geographic data may provide insight into the how's and why's of your customers' behavior. In this chapter we examine alternate information contexts—what kind of data is available, what its value is, and how to plan to integrate that information into your enterprise.

In this chapter, we discuss some of the more interesting issues and applications associated with the BI program: the use of demographics (i.e., nonqualitative descriptions, such as age and marital status) and psychographics (i.e., qualitative descriptions of lifestyle characteristics) for enhancement, the use of geographic information systems, and Web activity and behavior monitoring.

The Business Case

A lot of the bits of knowledge we can uncover through a BI application are not actionable unless we have some idea of what to do once we have discovered them. Making use of other data to tell us what to do with our knowledge not only provides insight into how to convert knowledge into dollars—it also continues to leverage our use of data in the first place. The kinds of data uses described in this chapter (and to some extent in the following two chapters) focus on the processes that can result in improving a business.

Psychographics and Demographics

As an augmentation to a customer relationship management application, the business client may be interested not just in who the company's customers are, but what kind of people they are—how old are they, what kinds of foods they like, how they like to have fun. Knowing this kind of information can enhance the way that products and services are marketed, especially when customers are grouped into market segments.

By analyzing the demographics and psychographics of those people who populate each market segment, the business analyst can try to formulate a profile of characteristics that model or represent each segment. Although Chapter 14, Knowledge Discovery and Data Mining, discusses how this segmentation is performed, as well as how new individuals are mapped into the previously defined segments, in this section we look at those characteristic details that can help describe people as a prelude to segmentation.

Demographics

Demographics represent a quantitative statistical representation of the non-qualitative aspects characteristics of a human population. Demographics include a person's age, marital status, gender, race, religion, ethnicity, income level, etc. Demographics incorporate that information about a person that is not necessarily a result of a lifestyle choice, but rather is more likely to be some attribution related to some external set of variables. For example, people do not choose their age; age is related to the difference between the date they were born and today's date. Similarly, people do not (except in extreme cases) choose their gender.

Typically, demographics are used to demonstrate the similarity between people. For example, a population is grouped by membership within a certain characteristics (e.g., ages 18–34, 35–49, 50–75).

Psychographics

Psychographics refer to the quantitative representation of the lifestyle characteristics of a segmented population. Whereas demographics measure those attributes that are not chosen, psychographics measure chosen attributes related to lifestyle, such as what television programs one watches, what kind of beer one drinks, and where one likes to vacation.

Psychographics are often used to differentiate people within a population. For example, psychographic information can be used to segment the population by component lifestyles based on individual behavior.

Representational Profiles

The value of demographics and psychographics lies in the ability to combine the two to form profiles. Demographic and psychographic data frequently are presented in a summarized, comparative form. An example is "75% of males between the age of 18 and 34 have sampled at least four kinds of French wine." A statement like this relates a demographic population (males between the age of 18 and 34) with a lifestyle characteristic (wine drinking) through some metric (75%).

The psychographic data is collected from a variety of sources, such as surveys, contest forms, customer service activity, registration cards, specialized lists and even magazine subscriptions. In the Internet age, even more information can be accumulated through Web site interaction and subscription to various online services and alerts. As is discussed in Chapter 15, there is a wealth of this kind of information available, ranging from the aggregated level, such as the example just given, down to the personal level.

Linking personalized psychographics relies on the kind of data enhancement capabilities discussed in Chapter 13, but having done so can provide fuel for the automated clustering and segmentation that can be provided by data mining software. Groups can be evaluated based on fixing a number of attributes (such as having purchased one of your company's products) and then looking at the comparative statistics associated with each discovered segment. For example, someone in the travel business might discover that those customers who purchased travel to Central America tend to be between the ages of 18 and 34, have a yearly income greater than $76,000, belong to a private golf club, and live either in the Northeast or the Southwest.

This kind of information can then be used for proactive marketing: Focus your advertising dollars on print ads in golf magazines largely distributed in the Northeast and Southwest. Or even better, seek out those prospects who match the segment profile and market directly to them.

Geographic Data

There is a lot of value to incorporating the analysis of BI in the context of location—where your customers live, where they shop, what are the closest warehouses to your retail locations, etc. Geographic data is largely available, and geographical information system (GIS) tools will provide creative visualization methods for extracting actionable knowledge from your data when it is enhanced with geographical data.

Geographic Information Systems

A geographic information system is capable of assembling, storing, manipulating, and displaying geographically referenced data. At the lowest level, a GIS presents geographical information as a map, but the power of a GIS lies in the ability to analyze data based on specific location information. For example, GIS software can help:

- Analyze where a company's customers live.

- Figure out the best place to open a new retail location.

- Determine where and how to allocate maintenance and emergency planning resources.

- Map customers by demographics for the purposes of determining segmented trade areas.

Geographic data represented as those components that compose a map—points, lines, and polygons—is used as the base layer of any GIS presentation. That data to be fed into the system must be enhanced with geographic attribution data, which is a cross between specific location information and attribution based on that location information. That data is then merged with standard GIS mapping data. Business information that contains location information can be enhanced to be compatible with a GIS. Initially, address standardization (see Chapter 13) should be performed, which will ease the assignment of point data. A geographic point is expressed as a (latitude, longitude) pair, frequently referred to as a *LatLong*. Once LatLongs have been assigned, each individual point can be merged with the data composing the base map, which can then be materialized in visual form.

Geographic attribution data provides additional information associated with any point or collection of points or regions within a map. For example, a fast-food chain may be interested in the location of their restaurants. Each location is attributed with information regarding the amount of foot traffic that passes by that location, the number of cars that pass by during different time periods of the day, the amount of office space and residential space that is within certain distances of that location, and the fast-food psychographics associated with the population within that area. All of this information can help determine the best places to open a new restaurant.

Using Geographic Data

Other applications might require demographic or psychographic attribution. Certainly, a large source of geographic attribution data is the U.S. Census Bureau, which publishes the results of each ten-year census. This data details all sorts of demographic information about geographic regions as small as a *census tract* (on the order of a few thousand people).

For example, consider the information displayed in Table 12.1, which is derived from U.S. Census data. If we were provided with a customer record whose address was located within census tract 4060.02, we could infer with some degree of certainty that the customer is white (86.4% are white), is married (69.2% of homes are occupied by married couples), lives in a house with one or two children (average family size is 3.52), and lives in an owner-occupied home (82.3% homes are owner occupied). The more information we have to enhance the customer record, the better position we are in to make these inferences.

Geographical Clusters

Census data can be used for more than the kind of attribution just described. Enhancing the census data itself with data from other sources can provide significant information about the kinds of people that live within a specific area. For example, let's enhance our previous example and see what else we can learn about our customer.

- We know that 82.3% of the households are owner occupied. By integrating average home sale prices over the last 5 years along with the average mortgage interest rates for the same time period, we can determine the average monthly mortgage payment a homeowner makes. Because mortgage brokers typically lend money as a function of a set of ratios of monthly debt to monthly salary, we can calculate an educated guess as to the average monthly salary of homeowners within the geographic area, which in turn can contribute to a geographic clustering profile.

- If our customer record contains a business or daytime telephone number, we can locate where the customer works and then determine the distance between home and work.

- By integrating this data with GIS data about transportation options between the two locations, we can also infer how the customer travels to work. By enhancing that with details of transportation schedules (which may also be available electronically), we can infer the length of time of the customer's commute to work.

GEOGRAPHIC AREA: CENSUS TRACT 4060.02, NASSAU COUNTY, NEW YORK[1]

Subject	Number	Percent
Total population	**3130**	**100.0**
Sex and Age		
Male	1536	49.1
Female	1594	50.9
Less than 5 years	246	7.9
5–9 years	284	9.1
10–14 years	241	7.7
15–19 years	224	7.2
20–24 years	155	5.0
25–34 years	393	12.6
35–44 years	487	15.6
45–54 years	428	13.7
55–59 years	159	5.1
60–64 years	119	3.8
65–74 years	205	6.5
75–84 years	144	4.6
85 years and older	45	1.4
Median age (years)	35.4	(X)
18 years and older	2213	70.7
Male	1051	33.6
Female	1162	37.1
21 years and older	2095	66.9
62 years and older	461	14.7
65 years and older	394	12.6
Male	166	5.3
Female	228	7.3
Race		
One race	3055	97.6
White	2705	86.4
Black or African American	143	4.6
American Indian and Alaska Native	2	0.1
Asian	107	3.4
Asian Indian	36	1.2
Chinese	34	1.1
Filipino	12	0.4
Japanese	1	0.0
Korean	12	0.4
Vietnamese	0	0.0
Other Asian	12	0.4
Native Hawaiian and Other Pacific Islander	0	0.0
Native Hawaiian	0	0.0
Guamanian or Chamorro	0	0.0

GEOGRAPHIC AREA: CENSUS TRACT 4060.02,
NASSAU COUNTY, NEW YORK[1] (Continued)

Subject	Number	Percent
Race		
Samoan	0	0.0
Other Pacific Islander	0	0.0
Some other race	98	3.1
Two or more races	75	2.4
Households by Type		
Total households	980	100.0
Family households (families)	813	83.0
With own children less than 18 years	419	42.8
Married-couple family	678	69.2
With own children less than 18 years	368	37.6
Female householder, no husband present	108	11.0
With own children less than 18 years	47	4.8
Nonfamily households	167	17.0
Householder living alone	135	13.8
Householder 65 years and older	63	6.4
Households with individuals less than 18 years	441	45.0
Households with individuals 65 years and older	275	28.1
Average household size	3.19	(X)
Average family size	3.52	(X)
Housing Occupancy		
Total housing units	988	100.0
Occupied housing units	980	99.2
Vacant housing units	8	0.8
For seasonal, recreational, or occasional use	1	0.1
Homeowner vacancy rate (percent)	0.1	(X)
Rental vacancy rate (percent)	0.0	(X)
Housing Tenure		
Occupied housing units	980	100.0
Owner-occupied housing units	807	82.3
Renter-occupied housing units	173	17.7
Average household size of owner-occupied unit	3.27	(X)
Average household size of renter-occupied unit	2.80	(X)

1. Modified from the United States 2000 census. For more information please see *www.census.gov*. For information on confidentiality protection, nonsampling error, and definitions, see *factfinder.census.gov/home/en/datanotes/expsf1u.htm*.

For the most part, similar people tend to aggregate in the same areas (e.g., rich people live among other rich people); we can take advantage of this by purchasing additional demographic and psychographic data and performing these kinds of enhancements to specially attribute geographic regions to much greater detail. Fortunately, there are a number of companies that package and sell this kind of geographic detail, which is ready for importation into a GIS as well as generic databases. These data sets will provide not only detail but also essentially a reverse mapping between profile characterization and the places in which people live.

Web Behavior Intelligence

Web statistics, page visit logs, time stamps, etc., are all examples of data created and collected at Web sites. E-commerce vendors who can track the movements of every visitor to their Web sites have an opportunity to approach one-to-one marketing strategies through the combination of traditional demographic and psychographic information with online behavioral (click-stream) data. This information can be used in the creation of rich customer profiles, and the mining of these profiles for useful behavioral patterns and the application of the knowledge inherent in those patterns can help solve numerous business problems. Particularly exciting is the potential to convert Web visitors from browsers to purchasers. Profiling customers in the context of an e-business intelligence strategy can assist in providing microsegmentation for targeting value-added products and services for cross-sell and up-sell opportunities.

User Actions

Whereas customer profiles describe what kind of people your users *are*, customer behavior describes what those users *do*. *Behavior* is defined as a recognizable pattern of actions, exhibited either by an individual user or by a set of users interacting within the system. *Actions* are those activities that a user can perform while navigating a Web site (of course, tailored by specific business goals).

Tracking user behavior involves more than just collecting server log files. Instead of relying on the traditional server log data, we can incorporate a more meaningful characterization of user activity. First, it is necessary to specify the kinds of actions that a user may perform while browsing at your site. This is more than just page views; rather, we want to superimpose business meaning on top of appropriate page views and to ignore meaningless ones. Behavior modeling then becomes a process of analyzing the sequence of actions that users perform, within what context those actions are performed, and whether any particular behaviors can be generalized for later predictive purposes.

Although each e-business's list of user actions may vary, here is a short list of some user actions that are interesting to log.

1. Content impression, when a Web page containing specific content is served

2. Content read, when served content is read

3. Hyperlink click-through

4. Advertisement impression, when an advertisement is served

5. Advertisement click-through

6. Initial registration, when a user registers

7. Subsequent registration, when a user reregisters

8. User login

9. User logout

10. Password change

11. Password request, when a user forgets a password

12. Input of new profile information (any time a user voluntarily enters new profile information)

13. Forced data input accepted (when a user is asked to input new information and that request is followed)

14. Forced data input rejected (when a user is asked to input new information and does not follow through)

15. Information query (the user searches for information)

16. Select product for purchase, such as when using a shopping basket and a product is selected for purchase

17. Purchase sequence initiated, when purchase information is requested

18. Purchase sequence completed, when enough information has been collected to complete a purchase

19. Purchase sequence aborted, when a user does not complete the purchase sequence

A specific data mart can be constructed to capture this kind of activity for later analysis.

Customer Behavior Patterns

Now, after having captured customer actions for a period of time, the information in the user activity table will represent a collection of times series of the ways that all the e-commerce business visitors browse the site. We can analyze this time series data to look for particular user behavior patterns. If these patterns represent desired business activity, we have discovered actionable BI!

One analysis framework presumes a desired outcome, and it looks for patterns that lead to that outcome. For example, we might want to explore how viewing a specific content item correlates to making an online sale. Or we may want to see how well the placement of advertising affects click-through rates associates with browsing sequences. This is actionable knowledge, because it gives us information about how well our expectations are converting into good business practices.

A different analysis framework looks for behaviors that are not known a priori. For example, we might extract activity sequences that lead to a completed purchase and then look for patterns in those sequences. We might discover that a purchase-completed action takes place 25% of the time that a specific order sequence of content views take place. This becomes actionable knowledge, because it suggests different ways to configure the browsing experience to accelerate a customer's purchase.

Management Issues

Privacy

The most significant issues associated with the use of personal demographics and psychographics revolve around the privacy question, which is discussed in greater detail in Chapter 15.

Application Expertise and Training

Especially when it comes to augmenting tools like GISs, there are limited numbers of engineers with the necessary expertise to best exploit these tools. If there is a belief that something like a GIS is going to be an ongoing component of your BI strategy, it is a good idea either to hire someone who already has expertise in the area or, even better, to provide significant training in the use of GIS software.

The Suitability of Web Data

To best make use of Web log data, it may be necessary either to transform the data after it has been captured or, better yet, to devise a more creative logging scheme. Unfortunately, the latter is probably not easy to do and may affect Web site performance. There are tools on the market for clickstream analysis, and these may be suitable for the task of data preparation, as a prelude to a data mining activity, such as sequence analysis or market basket analysis (see Chapter 14).

To Learn More

The use of different kinds of information contexts can add breadth and dimensionality to the kinds of data that may be created internally. By making use of creative data analysis tools that augment the traditional BI framework, you may exploit out-of-the-box thinking to achieve better actionable results.

A good book that can provide valuable insight into geographic and psychographic clustering is *The Clustered World*, Michael J. Weiss, Boston, Little, Brown, 2000.

CHAPTER 13

Data Enhancement

Data enhancement is a process to add value to information by accumulating additional information about a base set of entities and then merging all the sets of information to provide a focused view of the data. To understand the value of data enhancement, consider this scenario. You are a sales manager, and your entire compensation is based on commissions on the sales that you and your team can make. Imagine that the director of sales handed each member of your staff a list of leads containing names, addresses, and telephone numbers. The chances that any particular representative will close a sale with any random lead are relatively slim, and therefore the strategy is to hire many untrained sales representatives to make the calls, hoping that the volume will make up for the indeterminate probability of making a sale.

Now imagine that each marketer was handed a list containing each sales lead's annual salary, the amount of money each has spent on similar products over the last 5 years, where the sales lead lives, a list of the last five purchases the lead has made, his age, marital status, and number of children, along with a set of scores describing that individual's purchasing profile. Which of these lists would you rather have?

That second list, containing enhanced data, is basically the original list improved by adding the extra personal and demographic information. The marketers can use these enhancements to increase their effectiveness by prioritizing the sales leads in the order of propensity to buy. In addition, as the sales team makes sales, they annotate each sales lead with the details of how the sale was made, what product was sold, how long it took to make the sale, as well as other details about the process. These notes are also enhancements, which in turn can increase the effectiveness not only of the sales team but also of other groups within the same company.

Through the accumulation of data from different sources, we can improve the overall quality of data, standardize it, and prepare it for further business intelligence (BI) applications, such as data mining. In this chapter, we examine different ways to enhance data and provide some examples of the business process of data enhancement.

The Business Case

There are two aspects to the business value of data enhancement. The first is that as organizational data environments mature and data managers want to exploit the corporate data asset, there is an increased necessity for sharing data from different groups; frequently, the disparate data sets represent different aspects of the same entities. The second aspect emerges from the actionable knowledge that can be discovered only by analyzing the results of composing multiple data sets. Enhancement can be used to learn more about entities such as customers and vendors, to create a value-added information product, to investigate fraudulent behavior, or even to increase the quality of a given data set.

As an example in marketing, assume that the definition of a *preferred* customer is one who engages the customer service department for less than 15 minutes a month, purchases more than $100 worth of products every quarter, and never makes a late payment on the revolving charge card. We can enhance the customer profile using sales, customer service, and credit data to build a data mart that can be used to identify and offer incentives to these preferred customers. Another example involves fraud detection: Suppose there are many duplicate types of claims or that exceptional charges appear on claims paid to members of a professional organization. This may arouse suspicion of insurance fraud. Merging health insurance claim information with professional billing data can be used to form an enhanced data set through which this kind of behavior can be discovered.

Data enhancement is a critical component to the BI program, especially as a value-adding process to the following.

- **Competition in knowledge industries**—Businesses that traditionally rely on the leverage of timely information (e.g., retail securities sales, market data providers, analytical market analysis) suddenly have competition from players whose barrier to entry is low. For example, in the retail securities investment business, the combination of low-cost electronic securities trading combined with the widespread availability of financial and investment recommendations demonstrates that margins on securities transactions can be lowered but businesses can still profit.

- **Customer relationship management**—Through internal consolidation of different data sets that reside across the enterprise, an organization can develop a much more sophisticated view of its customer base. This is evidenced by an increasing number of organizations changing a view of databases of "accounts," "policies," "agreements," etc., to a database of "parties" or "customers," each of which is associated with an account or a policy in the context of some operational role.

- **Micromarketing and personalization**—Businesses that rely on marketing analysis will find that data enhancement based on multiple-source aggregation will provide opportunities for micromarket penetration. For example, businesses that have not traditionally relied on marketing analysis are beginning to use information gleaned from multiple operational sources, such as telephone transactions, online transactions, customer email interactions, written letters, as well as geographic and demographic and psychographic clustering.

- **Cooperative marketing**—Increasingly, companies in different industries join in cooperative marketing programs, such as offering frequent-flyer miles coupled with mobile phone service, and affinity credit cards that accumulate credit with a particular vendor. Because of the potential disparity between different organizations' data models and the currency of their stored data, these arrangements provide strong opportunities for data enhancement and improvement.

- **Industry deregulation**—This frequently leads to increased merger and acquisition activity, as is occurring in the telecommunications industry, insurance and brokerage industries, and the energy industry. In addition, as companies perform poorly during an economic downturn, they may also drift toward mergers as a means for staying afloat. The merger of two (or more) independent organizations prompts an eventual merging of both their operations as well as their combined data resources as a way of streamlining operations and increasing customer response and customer satisfaction.

In any situation where there is an opportunity for enhancement, the goal is to produce a data set whose added value can help optimize a business process. In the customer relationship world, the goal is to produce a set of customer profiles that can provide both a framework for more efficient sales efficiency and a streamlined mechanism for customer service. In the sales analysis world, this may imply enhancing point-of-sale data to understand purchase patterns across the organization's sales sites. In the health/pharmaceuticals industry, a goal could be to understand the interactions between different drugs and to suggest the best possible treatments for different diseases.

Types of Data Enhancement

There are two approaches to data enhancement. One focuses on incrementally improving or adding information as data is viewed or processed. Incremental enhancements are useful as a component of a later analysis stage, such as sequence pattern analysis and behavior modeling. The other approach is batch enhancement, where data collections are aggregated and methods are applied to the collection to create value-added information. Here are some examples.

Auditing Enhancement

In business processes that require some degree of tracing capability (such as supply-chain processing), a frequent data enhancement is the addition of auditing data. Creating a tracking system associated with a sequence of related events provides a framework for evaluating efficiency within a business process. For example, in a customer support database, each time a customer has a discussion with a customer support representative, not only is the conversation noted, but also the name of the representative with whom the customer spoke, along with a timestamp.

Temporal Enhancement

Historical data provides critical insight to a BI program. Whereas in some cases the history is embedded in the collected data, other instances require that activity (i.e., events or transactions) be enhanced by incrementally adding timestamps noting the time at which some event occurred. With data, this can refer to the time at which a transaction took place, the time at which a message was sent or received, the time at which a customer requested information, or the like.

Contextual Enhancement

Sometimes it is not the *time* that is interesting, but rather the *place* where some action was performed that is critical. The place, or context, of data manipulation is an enhancement as well. A physical location, a path of access, the login account through which a series of transactions were performed, etc., are examples of context that can augment data. Here are some other examples.

- Logging the IP address from which a user's account is accessed
- Tracking the stores in which credit cards are used
- Keeping track of the companies from which specific products are purchased
- Identifying and logging the locations from which calling-card calls are made

Contextual enhancement also includes tagging data records in a way to be correlated with other pieces of data. An interesting example can be seen on a number of retail Web sites, where source location information regarding the sales popularity of particular products is displayed under the heading "This item is popular with these groups." In terms of personal marketing, using contextual popularity provides both an internal direct marketing directive ("If the user's domain is one of the popularity groups, then display the product on the home page") and an information-driven influence technique ("Be like the others in your peer group and buy this product").

Geographic Enhancement

As discussed in Chapter 12, data enhanced with geographic information allows for analysis based on regional clustering and data inference based on predefined geodemographics. The first kind of geographic enhancement is the process of address standardization, where addresses are cleansed and then modified to fit a predefined postal standard, such as the United States Postal Standard. Once the addresses have been standardized, other geographic information can be added, such as locality coding, neighborhood mapping, latitude/longitude pairs, and other kinds of regional codes.

Demographic Enhancement

Demographics describe the similarities that exist within an entity cluster, such as customer age, marital status, gender, income, and ethnic coding. For business entities, demographics can include annual revenues, number of employees, size of occupied space, number of parking spaces, years in business, etc. Demographic enhancements can be added as a by-product of geographic enhancements or through direct information merging.

Psychographic Enhancement

Psychographics describe what distinguishes individual entities within a cluster. For example, psychographic information can be used to segment the population by component lifestyles, based on individual behavior. This includes product and brand use, product and brand preferences, organization memberships, leisure activities, vacation preferences, commuting transportation style, shopping time preferences, etc. Psychographic information is frequently collected via surveys, contest forms, customer service activity, registration cards, as well as specialized lists. The trick to using psychographic data is in being able to make the linkage between the entity within the organization database and the supplied psychographic data set.

Inference Enhancement

Analysts are constantly asked to draw conclusions from supplied data, and in fact a large component of the BI process is interpreting the patterns that emerge through analysis, and applying some business value to that interpretation. Information inference is a BI technique that allows the user to draw conclusions about the examined entity based on supporting evidence and business rules. Inferred knowledge can be used to augment data to reflect what we have learned, and this in turn provides greater insight into solving the business problem at hand.

Incremental Enhancements

Incremental enhancements are those that can be attached to data in process. For example, enhancements that can be tagged to a record as it passes through a processing point, such as time- or placestamping are incremental.

Provenance

The provenance of an item is its source. This idea generalizes the temporal and auditing enhancements described earlier. An interesting enhancement is the operation of associating a provenance with a data record, which would consist of a location code and a timestamp (i.e., marking the time at which the data was updated). A provenance can be as simple as a single string data field describing the source or as complex as a separate table containing a timestamp and a location code each time the record is updated, related through a foreign key. Because there is a complete audit trail for all tagged data records, this second approach allows for a more complete itinerary to be compiled.

Audit Trails

Whereas the time and place of an event may be sufficient for some analytical purposes, an advanced form of audit data allows for enhancing data with source, creation, update to, as well as activity and action-owner information. For example, let's look at a customer service interaction. The transaction can be tagged with the date, the time, the location from which the customer called, the activity that was performed, and the name of the customer service agent that performed the action. The combination of location, time, and activity information associated with a series of manipulations of a data record allows us to trace back all occasions at which that information was touched, giving us the audit data allowing us to see how activities cause data to flow through a system.

Context

In the Internet environment there are numerous ways to track all sorts of context information, such as when a user is touching a data set and where the user is sitting when the activity occurs. This information is an enhancement as well, including the virtual location from which the activity takes place (e.g., visiting a particular Web domain name), a physical location (e.g., from a home computer versus an office computer), as well as other data that can be collected directly from the user through direct interaction. This kind of enhanced data provides significant marketing benefit, because this context information can be fed into a statistical framework for reporting on the behavior of users based on their locations or times of activity.

For example, a business can determine that many of its customers browse online catalogs during the daytime while at work but peruse the content for a subselection of entries at home in the evening. This kind of enhancement can drive the respinning of the Web site to provide different kinds of presentations during work hours or leisure hours as a way to influence customers to purchase products.

Batch Enhancements

Batch enhancements are applied to a large set of data instances as an offline process. They typically involve the merging of data from multiple instances within a single data set or multiple data instances drawn from multiple data sets. Many of the example batch enhancements described in this section rely on information linkage, used to link two distinct records together.

Householding

Householding is a process that attempts to reduce a set of individuals to a single grouped housing unit based on the database record attribution. A household consists of all people living as an entity within the same residence. The simplest example is that of consolidating husband records and wife records into a single household. Households can be differentiated by demographics as well as geographics. And in one household there may be different subsidiary roles, such as primary earner and primary decision maker (these two may be different individuals). More complex examples include the identification of dependents, categorizing dependents by class, as well as separating out boarders or transient residents. Householding can be used to improve demographic analysis, to optimize marketing, as well as to target particular defined roles in the household.

Organizational Merging

When organizations merge, they will eventually want (or sometimes, based on regulations, need) to merge their vendor, customer, and employee databases as well as their base reference data. Consolidating customer records prevents potentially embarrassing marketing mistakes, such as having more than one sales representative contacting the same customer on the same day (or even worse—having the *same* sales rep contact the same customer on the same day!).

Other Batch Enhancements

Other batch enhancements include data scrubbing, data cleansing, and health care diagnosis assistance, as well as building affinity programs and constructing relational associations, among others.

Standardization

According to *Webster's New Collegiate Dictionary*, a *standard* is "something set up and established by authority, custom, or general consent as a model or example."[1] In the data world, we can say that a standard is a model to which all objects of the same class must conform. Bringing data into a standard form is a significant enhancement, because it enables other BI applications to exploit the data, especially in an environment where a large amount of data that is easily accessible is in what is called *semistructured* form, which implies some (loose) degree of structure imposed on the presentation of information. Harvesting semistructured data and bringing it into a standard form is an extremely challenging process.

---

1. *Webster's New Collegiate Dictionary*, Springfield, MA, G. & C. Merriam Co., 1975.

Standardization refers to ensuring that a data instance conforms to a pre-defined expected format. A *data standard* is a format representation for data values that can be described using a series of rules. In addition, in order for a format representation to be a standard, there should be an agreement among all interacting parties that their data values will conform to that standard. Because a standard is a distinct model to which all items in a set must conform, this means we can try to automate two components of any standardization process:

- Determination of conformance to the standard
- Bringing a nonstandard data instance into conformance with the standard

There is usually a well-defined rule set describing both how to determine if an item conforms to the standard and what actions need to be taken to bring the offending item into conformance.

Data Standards and Standardization

The value of data standardization lies in the notion that given the right base of reference information and a well-defined rule set, additional data can be added to a record in a purely automated way (with some exceptions). Probably the most important benefit of standardization is that through the process of defining standards, organizations create a streamlined means for the transference and sharing of information. The introduction of information structure definition frameworks that can be embodied with Extensible Markup Language (XML) descriptions is evidence of the growing popularity of this idea.

As companies agree on how to exchange information, they also create a means for increasing the volume of exchanged information. With formal standards, more organizations can subscribe to the standard and participate. This is not to say that automated standardization is simple; in fact, transforming into standard form can be relatively complex. Although it is easy to determine whether a piece of data conforms to a standard, when it does not conform it may be a challenge to determine how to parse the data so that it can be transformed into a standard form.

For example, consider people names: A business client may want to represent all people names in some standard form, including title (e.g., MR or MRS), first name, middle name, last name, generational (e.g., JR or III), and suffix (such as PHD or OD). Yet the desire to project anyone's name into this structure is hampered by the fact that humans can

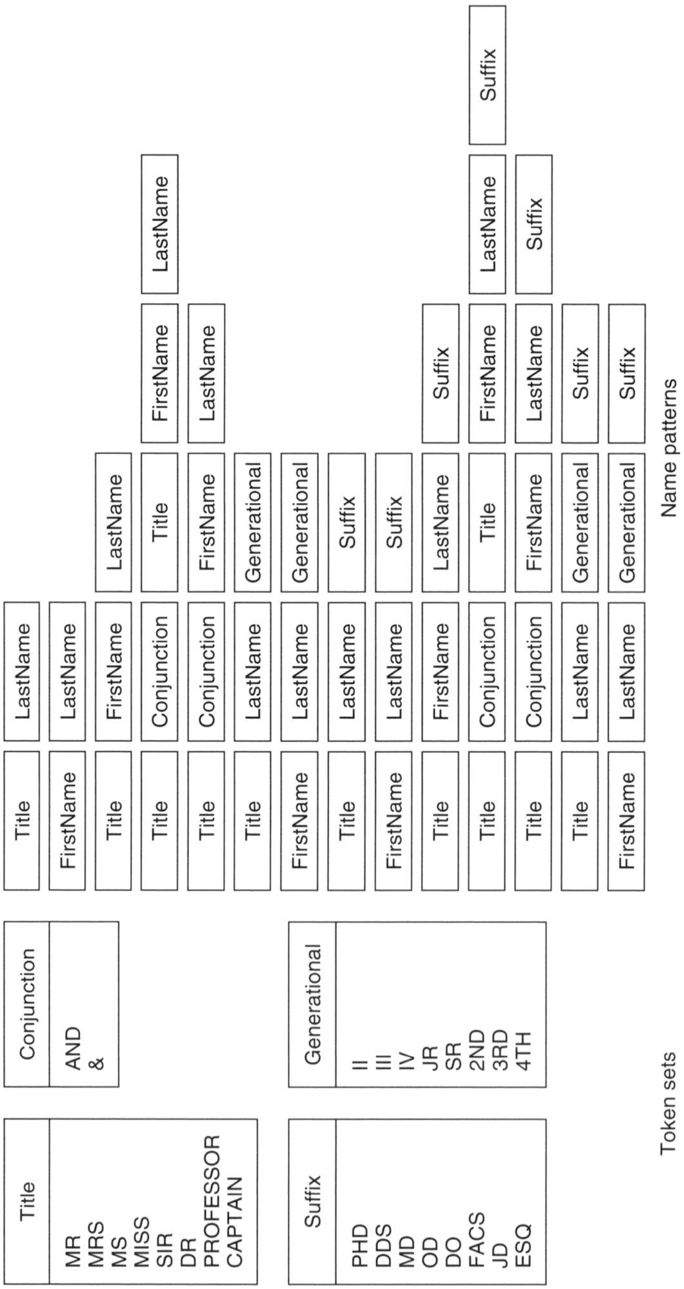

Token sets

Title
MR
MRS
MS
MISS
SIR
DR
PROFESSOR
CAPTAIN

Conjunction
AND
&

Suffix
PHD
DDS
MD
OD
DO
FACS
JD
ESQ

Generational
II
III
IV
JR
SR
2ND
3RD
4TH

Name patterns

Title	LastName

FirstName	LastName

Title	FirstName	LastName

Title	Conjunction	Title	FirstName	LastName

Title	Conjunction	FirstName	LastName

Title	LastName	Generational

FirstName	LastName	Generational

Title	LastName	Suffix

FirstName	LastName	Suffix

Title	FirstName	LastName	Suffix

Title	Conjunction	Title	FirstName	LastName	Suffix

Title	Conjunction	FirstName	LastName	Suffix

Title	LastName	Generational	Suffix

FirstName	LastName	Generational	Suffix

FIGURE 13.1 Different kinds of name patterns.

recognize many different forms that a name (or set of names) can take (Figure 13.1).

Kinds of Standards

Most standards either are dictated by some authority (such as the government), are developed through cooperation (such as an industry-defined standard), or are derived from common use (such as geographical biases toward representing dates). Many standards already exist, such as the following.

- The USPS Postal Standard is defined by a (quasi-) governmental agency.
- Telephone numbering and allocation of area codes and exchange codes are defined by an industry collective.
- Format standards, such as dates, are biased by location and use.

As organizations rely more on standardized data exchange definitions described using XML, we will see more format and content standards. Sometimes the standardization information is explicit, such as definitions associated with structure (as in an XML DTD or Schema), and sometimes the standard information is embedded within a document as a comment or sidebar. For example, I noticed an implied standard in a definition document for a supply-chain EDI application in comments for particular data fields, such as "The value of the SHIPPING field must be either AIR, GROUND-TRUCKING, or RAIL."

Example: Address Standardization

To get a good understanding of the complexity involved in standardization, it is worthwhile to look at the U.S. Postal Service addressing standard, which is comprehensively documented in USPS Publication 28. Here we explore the degree of detail expressed in this standard by reviewing some aspects of Publication 28. In this section, we look at the different components of an address.

The Address Standard

1. **Recipient line**—The recipient line indicates the person or entity to which the mail is to be delivered. The recipient line is usually the first line of a standard address block, which contains a recipient line, a delivery address line, and the last line. If there is an "attention" line, the standard specifies that it should be placed above the recipient line.

2. **Delivery address line**—The delivery address line is the line that contains the specific location associated with the recipient. Typically, this line contains the street address and should contain at least some of these components:

   a. **Primary address number**—This is the number associated with the street address.

   b. **Predirectional and postdirectional**—A *directional* is the term the Postal Service uses to refer to the address component indicating compass-based direction data, such as NORTH, NW, W. A predirectional appears before the street name, whereas the postdirectional appears after the street name. Spelled out directionals are accepted, but the preferred form is the abbreviated one. When two directionals appear consecutively as one or two words before or after the street name or suffix, the two words become the directional, except when the directional is part of the street's primary name. When the directional is part of the street name, the preferred form is not to abbreviate the directional.

   c. **Street name**—This is the name of the street, which precedes the suffix. The Postal Service provides a data file that contains all the valid street names for any ZIP code area.

   d. **Suffix**—The suffix is the address component indicating the type of street, such as AVENUE, STREET, or CAUSEWAY. When the suffix is a real suffix and not part of a street name, the preferred form is the abbreviated form, for which a list of transformations is enumerated within the publication's appendix.

   e. **Secondary address designator**—The secondary address unit designator provides additional address precision, narrowing the delivery point to an apartment, a suite, or a floor. Examples of secondary unit designators include APARTMENT, FLOOR, and SUITE. The preferred form is to use the approved abbreviations, which are also enumerated in Publication 28.

3. **Last line**—The last line of the address includes the city name, state, and ZIP code. The format of the last line is a city name, followed by a state abbreviation, followed by a ZIP + 4 code, each of which should be separated by at least one space. Other than the dash in the ZIP + 4 code, punctuation is acceptable, but it is preferred that punctuation be removed. The standard recommends that only city names that are provided by the Postal Service in its City State file be used (this addresses the issue of vanity city names). The standard also prefers that full city names be spelled out. But if there are labeling constraints as a result

of space, the city name can be abbreviated using the approved 13-character abbreviations provided in the City State file.

Additionally, there are other rules associated with the delivery address line. Numeric street names should appear the way they are specified in the Postal Service's ZIP + 4 file and should be spelled out only when there are other streets with the same name in the same delivery area and spelling the numeric is the only way to distinguish between the two streets. Corner addresses are acceptable, but use of the physical numeric street address is preferred. There are also rules associated with rural route delivery addresses, military addresses, post office boxes, Puerto Rican addresses, and highway contract route addresses.

Standard Abbreviations

The Postal Service provides, in the appendices to Publication 28, a set of enumerations of standard abbreviations, including U.S. State and Possession abbreviations, street abbreviations, as well as common business word abbreviations. Other standard abbreviations, such as for city names, are included in the City State file, which can be purchased from the Postal Service.

ZIP + 4

ZIP codes are postal codes assigned to delivery areas to improve the precision of sorting and delivering mail. ZIP codes are five-digit numbers, assigned state-by-state and based on geography, narrowed down by the first three digits coupled with the last two digits. ZIP + 4 codes are a further refinement, narrowing down a delivery location within a subsection of a building or a street.

Address Standardization Software

Luckily, because the USPS addressing standard is so well documented, it is relatively straightforward to build automated address standardization software, which eases the way in which this enhancement can be performed.

Enhancement Methodologies

There are many issues involved in data enhancement, but because a large number of them revolve around information record linkage, it is worthwhile to explore this in greater detail.

Record Linkage

Any two records that can be connected based on a set of chosen attributes are candidates to be linked together. For example, if the last name, first name, street address, city, and Social Security number match between two records, they likely refer to the same entity.

Usually record linkage is performed only when the chosen attributes match exactly, but simple record linkage is limited, for the following reasons.

- **Information is missing**—When a characterization attribute's value is missing, all other attributes may match and still prevent two records from linking.

- **Information sources are in different formats**—It is easy to say that two records match when they come from the same table, with the same attributes (with the same column names, etc.). But when the records come from different data sets, it may not be clear which are the right attributes to match. For example, the customer's name may be in a column called CUST_NM and in a second data set in the column called CUSTOMER_NAME.

- **Record linkage is imprecise**—Whereas two records might actually represent the same entity, a slight difference in one or more attribute values will prevent those records from being linked.

- **Information is out of synchronization**—Customer information in a database can stay relatively static, even if the customer herself is not. People move, get married, divorced. The data that may be sitting in one database may be completely out of synch with information in another database, making positive matching difficult.

- **Information is lost**—The actual database joins may be constructed in such a way that important information originally contained in one of the data sets is lost during the merge. For example, when my baby daughter receives a letter asking her to switch her long-distance service in return for an extra 5000 frequent-flyer miles, the information that my wife and I purchased a child's seat for her is apparently lost.

When the limitations of standard linkage are combined, it eventually causes inefficiencies and increased costs. Here are some real examples.

- A large frequent-traveler program had fielded many complaints because patrons who had visited member hotels were not credited with the points corresponding to their purchases. It turns out that the company providing the frequent-traveler program had recently merged with a few other hotel chains, and the number of different data formats had ballooned to more than 70, all out of synchronization with each other.

- A bid/ask product pricing system inherited its prices from multiple market data providers, the information for which was collected and filtered through a mainframe system. When the mainframe did not forward new daily prices for a particular product, the last received price was used instead. There was significant embarrassment when customers determined that the provided prices were out of synchronization with other markets!

- Very frequently with direct mail campaigns, multiple mailings are sent to the same household, multiple mailings are sent to the same person, and a large number of items are sent to incorrect addresses.

- Current customers are pitched items they have already purchased.

Improper record linkage leads to errors in judgment when it comes to exploiting the results. It is appropriate to review the algorithms used for the linkage process before relying on the results of that process.

Semistructured Data

Only a very small percentage of the data managed today is in a structured (e.g., database) form. *Semistructured data* refers to information that is partially formatted, such as data elements on a Web page or the comments field in a customer service database. Although database records and electronic data interchange messages are highly structured, information presented on Web pages conforms to the barest of standards. For example, business home pages most often contain links to other sections of a Web site, with a contact page, an information page, a products page, a services page, a privacy policy page, a "terms of service" page, etc. In another example, regulatory forms (such as those required by the SEC) may contain corporate data with a list of the top managers in a company, followed by a short biography. We can even drill down to finer detail in our expectations—in the corporate biographies, we can expect to see some reference to college and graduate school degrees, a listing of prior work experiences (with durations), and professional affiliations. Although the format of these biographies is not standardized at all, in general we learn the same kind of stuff about each manager in each company.

Semistructured data may be a good source for both association and relation information, but the problem of extracting information out of the data is particularly difficult. There are certain text arenas for which a notional taxonomy has been defined, but for the most part the ability to extract useful information from semistructured data is limited to human intervention.

Inference

An inference is an application of a heuristic rule that essentially creates a piece of information where it didn't exist before. Even though inferencing represents the application of intuition, it is done so in a way that can be automated. In effect, one of the goals of a BI program is to construct the machinery to be able both to identify the heuristics representing inferencing rules and to automatically evoke a notification when the inference can be made.

Inference rules usually reflect some understood business analysis that can be boiled down to a set of business rules. These are rules that specify how certain attribute values are determined by operations applied to other attributes. Combining inference rules with data merging yields a powerful process for enhancement. An example of an inference for credit card databases might be if there are two names associated with the account number; if more than 70% of the dollar amount of purchases is made by one of the two account holders, that account holder is the primary decision maker for that account. Using this rule, we can populate an attribute for the primary decision maker with either a definitive value or an indeterminate null value.

Types of Inference

Enhancements based on inferencing are usually very focused bits of information relevant within a particular analytical context. Inferences are likely to center on demographic or psychographic details that can be derived as a direct result of data merging and analysis. For example, by combining U.S. Census data with a customer database, a series of educated guesses about any particular customer could be made based on the general demographics from the census. The next step is to incorporate the next data set (home sales and interest rate data) to help derive an educated guess about salary, followed by transportation information to derive a guess about commuting patterns.

This kind of inferencing is a business operation that is being done on a constant basis, which spurs the existence of the market research industry. Market research organizations attempt to perform focused surveys by engaging individuals as part of a population sample. Although the information gleaned from this approach has been used with relative success over a long period of time, there are flaws in this system, due, among other reasons, to the following.

- The samples may not always be statistically valid as a result of unexpected biases that creep into the process.
- The employees assigned with performing the survey have no stake in the proper execution of the survey, which allows errors to creep into the results.
- The structure of the survey imposes a bias on the result based on the presentation of the question.

We are always making inferences about entities (people, places, things) based on the information presented to us. There is no reason why we can operationalize the same inference logic as an automated application, by expressing our inference intuition as a collection of business rules that specify the derivation of inferred enhancement attributes.

Management Issues

Buy versus Build

In the software and services market, the term *data enhancement* is overloaded and can be used to refer to anything from data cleansing and address standardization all the way to services-based record linkage as a means to add data fields to submitted data, such as credit ratings. If your organization is small or you do not have access to many sets of data that can be used for aggregation, it may be worthwhile to consider external data enhancement services, although this may require you to continue using these services as you accumulate new data. Taking this path should not preclude the incremental enhancements discussed earlier.

Performance Issues

If there are many data sets available or if it important to maintain control over the data enhancement process, establishing a data enhancement capability in-house is suggested. Some data enhancement applications are likely to be of high computational complexity, and therefore members of the team should be aware of (if not experts in) high-performance computing as well as database manipulation, ETL, and pattern matching.

To Learn More

Essentially, data enhancement is a process of improving the value of a data set by augmenting selected data instances with more interesting bits of data.

By supplementing a data set with additional information, the possibility of exposing revealing knowledge about your business process could provide insight into solving specific business problems. There are different kinds of enhancements, some of which are of greater value for operational intelligence, while others are for marketing or strategic intelligence.

Some enhancements can be added incrementally, whereas others are performed as part of a batch process. Many important BI enhancements are related directly to record linkage and data merging, and any successful BI strategy will require some degree of enhancement. To learn more, consider *www.dmreview.com* and *www.intelligententerprise.com* for articles an data enhancement.

CHAPTER 14

Knowledge Discovery and Data Mining

The term *data mining* evokes an image of the old-time panner for gold—sifting through mounds of dirt trying to find those elusive valuable nuggets that make the whole process worthwhile. The translation into the information world is the data analyst sifting through terabytes of data looking for the corresponding knowledge nugget. This image is so powerful that the original meaning of data mining has been lost in the media hype that surrounds information exploitation. Now any information worker with a query tool connected to a database running ad hoc queries is called a "data miner," and the concepts that I discuss in this chapter are lost in that translation.

As an alternative to proactive business intelligence (BI) operations, the knowledge discovery process is a means for finding new intelligence from collections of data. Although the methods discussed in this chapter have traditionally been referred to as *data mining*, that term has become overloaded and so we will use the more correct term, *knowledge discovery*. Knowledge discovery refers to the process of discovering patterns that lead to actionable knowledge from large data sets through one or more traditional data mining techniques, such as market basket analysis and clustering. A lot of the knowledge discovery methodology has evolved from the combination of the worlds of statistics and computer science.

In this chapter, a lot of which is adapted from the very fine writings of Michael Berry and Gordon Linoff, we will look at the business use of knowledge discovery techniques and the kinds of methods used. In addition, we will look at some of the management issues associated with this process, as well as how to properly set expectations for the results of an iterative proactive process whose results may not be measurable right away.

The Business Case

Of the analytical processes we have discussed in this book, most have been focused on specific a priori drivers, such as the manifestation of visualization of key performance indicators appearing on a business executive's desktop browser and building reports via an online analytical processing (OLAP) tool to allow a data client to examine and drill down through cross-dimensional metrics. Essentially, the resulting analytical frameworks have always been to allow the data consumer either to verify that things are going the way they should or to look for situations where they are not so that the process and, correspondingly, the business can be improved.

Data mining fills a niche in the BI arena where the data consumer is not necessarily sure what to be looking for. The kinds of knowledge that are discovered may be directed toward a specific goal (e.g., finding out why you are losing customers) or not (e.g., finding some interesting patterns), but the methods of data mining are driven by finding patterns in the data that reflect more meaningful bits of knowledge. And those discovered bits of knowledge can then be fed into the more general areas of BI. For example, you may discover some new business rules that predict a business situation requiring an action. Those rules can then be integrated into a business rule system as well as the intelligence portal that notifies the proper person when some condition suddenly becomes true.

Data mining algorithms used to be relegated to the supercomputers attached to the large-scale data systems because of the computational complexity and storage requirements of the data mining process. But as high-performance computing and large-scale storage work their way into the mainstream, the availability of production-quality data mining software applications has essentially brought what was once a relatively boutique operation into the mainstream. It would be unwise to engage in building a BI program and ignore the promise of a data mining component.

Data Mining and the Data Warehouse

Knowledge discovery is a process that requires a lot of data, and that data needs to be in a reliable state before it can be subjected to the data mining process. The accumulation of enterprise data within a data warehouse that has been properly validated, cleaned, and integrated provides the best source of data that can be subjected to knowledge discovery. Not only is the warehouse likely to incorporate the breadth of data needed for this component of the BI process, it probably contains the historical data needed. Because a lot of data mining relies on using one set of data for training a process that can then be tested on another set of data, having the historical information available for testing and evaluating hypotheses makes the warehouse even more valuable.

The Virtuous Cycle

As Berry and Linoff state in their book *Data Mining Techniques*, the process of mining data can be described as a virtuous cycle. The virtue is based on the continuous improvement of a business process that is driven by the discovery of actionable knowledge and taking the actions prescribed by these discoveries.

Identify the Business Problem

One of the more difficult tasks is identifying the business problem that needs to be solved. Very often, other aspects of the BI program can feed into this process. For example, an OLAP report may indicate that sales of one class of product in the Northeast region may lag behind sales in other regions or that the average wait time at the inbound call centers peaks at certain times of the day. Given these facts, it would be useful to understand why they are true; this is the basis for formulating the business problem to be examined.

Other kinds of business problems are actually part of the general business cycle. For example, planning a new marketing campaign and understanding customer attrition are frequent business problems that can be attacked through data mining. Once the problem has been identified and a goal set (e.g., lower the attrition rate by 50% or relieve the issues that are causing sales to lag in particular areas), you must assemble the right data needed for analysis and then move onto the next stage.

Mine the Data for Actionable Information

Depending on the problem, there are a number of different data mining techniques that can be used to look for actionable knowledge (see Directed versus Undirected Knowledge Discovery on page 208). But no matter what techniques are used, the process is to assemble the right set of information, prepare that information for mining, apply the algorithms, and analyze the results to find some knowledge that is actionable. For example, it may be discovered that, with some degree of frequency, bank customers tend to close their checking accounts once they have been assessed bank fees more than three times in a single year. The embedded suggestion is that bank customers of high value who have been assessed a fee more than three times in a year are at risk, and if the bank wants to keep them as customers, some action must be taken.

Take the Action

The next logical step is to take the actions suggested by the discoveries during the data mining process. To continue our example from the previous section, the attrition of a high-value customer may be prevented by taking some action when that customer is assessed his or her third fee for the year. There may be a number of different actions to take, and it is useful to try more than one. Here are a few possible actions.

- Remove the assessed fee.
- Offer a different checking account plan.
- Provide some alternate benefit on another product (such as a decreased interest rate on a home equity loan).

Keep track of which actions were taken, because that leads into the next stage.

Measure Results

The importance of measuring the results of the actions taken is that it refines the process of addressing the original business problem. The goal here is to look at what the expected response was to the specific actions and to determine the quality of each action. To finish our attrition example, three different actions were suggested in the previous section. The goal was to reduce attrition among the high-value customers. Here we would measure the decrease in attrition associated with those customers offered each of the three suggested actions and see which provided the largest decrease in attrition. Perhaps another round of testing and measurement might be in order, but the ultimate result is to identify the precursor to attrition and offer the most effective promotion in attrition reduction to those high-value customers at risk.

Directed versus Undirected Knowledge Discovery

There are two different approaches to knowledge discovery. The first is when we already have the problem we want to solve and are applying the data mining methods to discover the relationship between the variables under scrutiny in terms of the other available variables. This is called *directed* knowledge discovery, as opposed to *undirected* knowledge discovery.

Undirected knowledge discovery is the process of using data mining techniques to find interesting patterns within a data set as a way to highlight some potentially interesting issue. This approach is more likely to be used to recognize behavior or relationships, whereas directed knowledge discovery is used primarily to explain or describe those relationships once they have been found.

Six Basic Tasks of Data Mining

So what is data mining? We can essentially boil the most significant methods down to a set of six tasks, some of which we have already briefly introduced in other chapters.

Classification

The world is divided into two groups of people: those who classify the world into two groups, and those who do not. But seriously, our natural tendency is to assign things into groups based on some set of similar characteristics. For example, we break up groups of customers by demographic and psychographic profiles (e.g., marketing to the lucrative 18- to 34-year-olds) or divide products into product classes, etc.

A frequent data mining task is classification, which involves examining the attributes of a particular object and assigning it to a defined class. Classification can be used to divide a customer base into best, mediocre, and low-value customers, to distinguish suspicious characters at an airport security check, to identify a fraudulent transaction, or to identify prospects for a new service.

Estimation

Estimation is a process of assigning some continuously valued numeric value to an object. For example, credit risk assessment is not necessarily a yes/no question; it is more likely to be some kind of scoring that assesses a propensity to default on a loan. Estimation can be used as part of the classification process (such as using an estimation model to guess a person's annual salary as part of a market segmentation process).

A value of estimation is that because a value is being assigned to some continuous variable, the resulting assignments can be ranked by score. So, for example, an estimation process may assign some value to the variable "probability of purchasing a time-share vacation package" and then rank the candidates by that estimated score, making those candidates the best prospects.

Estimation is used frequently to infer some propensity to take some action or as a way to establish some reasonable guess at an indeterminable value. An example is customer lifetime value, which can never be completely accurately stated.

Prediction

The subtle difference between prediction and the previous two tasks is that prediction is the attempt to classify objects according to some expected future behavior. Classification and estimation can be used for the purposes of prediction by using historical data, where the classification is already known, to build a model (this is called *training*). That model can then be applied to new data to predict future behavior.

Affinity Grouping

Affinity grouping is a process of evaluating relationships or associations between data elements that demonstrate some kind of affinity between objects. For example, affinity grouping might be used to determine the likelihood that people who buy one product will be willing to try a different product. This kind of analysis is useful for marketing campaigns when trying to cross-sell or up-sell a customer on additional or better products. This can also be used as a way to create product packages that have appeal to large market segments. For example, fast-food restaurants may select certain product components to go into a meal packaged for a particular group of people (e.g., the "kid's meal") and targeted at the population who is most likely to purchase that package (e.g., children between the ages of 9 and 14).

Clustering

Clustering is the task of taking a large collection of objects and dividing them into smaller groups of objects that exhibit some similarity. The difference between clustering and classification is that during the clustering task, the classes are not defined beforehand. Rather, it is the process of evaluating the classes after the clustering has completed that drives the determination or definition of that class.

Clustering is useful when you are not really sure what you are looking for but want to perform some kind of segmentation. For example, you might want to evaluate health data based on particular diseases along with other variables to see if there are any correlations that can be inferred through the clustering process. Clustering can be used in concert with other data mining tasks as a way of identifying a business problem area to be further explored. An example is performing a market segmentation based on product sales as a prelude for looking at why sales are low within a particular market segment.

Description

The last of the size tasks is description, which is the process of trying to characterize what has been discovered or trying to explain the results of the data mining process. Being able to describe a behavior or a business rule is another step toward an effective intelligence program that can identify knowledge, articulate it, and then evaluate actions that can be taken. In fact, we might say that the description of discovered knowledge can be incorporated into the metadata associated with that data set.

Data Mining Techniques

Although there are a number of techniques used for data mining, this section enumerates some techniques that are frequently used as well as some examples of how each technique is used.

Market Basket Analysis

When you go to the supermarket, usually the first thing you do is grab a shopping cart. As you move up and down the aisles, you will pick up certain items and place them in your shopping cart. Most of these items may correspond to a shopping list that was prepared ahead of time, but other items may have been selected spontaneously. Let's presume that when you check out at the cashier, the contents of your (and every other shopper's) cart are logged, because the supermarket wants to see if there are any patterns in selection that occur from one shopper to another. This is called *market basket analysis.*

More formally, market basket analysis is the process of clustering objects to look for groups of objects that frequently appear together. There is the famous (and probably apocryphal) data mining anecdote about the discovery that on Friday nights, males who buy diapers are also likely to buy beer. This is an example of a result of market basket analysis.

Market basket analysis is a good way to look for items that appear together or a set of discrete events that take place in a particular sequence. As an example, a store may want to modify the placement of objects on the shelves based on what customers tend to buy together as a way to force customers to scan more shelf space to encourage impulse buying. We have already seen another example—the sequence of events that take place before a customer closes his or her checking account.

Memory-Based Reasoning

Memory-based reasoning (MBR) is a process of using one data set to create a model from which predictions or assumptions can be made about newly introduced objects. The main component of the technique revolves the concept of measuring similarity between pairs of objects, both during the training process and later, trying to match the new object to its closest neighbor within the classified set. There are two basic components to an MBR method. The first is the *similarity* (sometimes called *distance*) *function*, which measures how similar the members of any pair of objects are to each other. The second is the *combination function*, which is used to combine the results from the set of neighbors to arrive at a decision.

Memory-based reasoning is a technique that can be used for classification, presuming that an existing data set is used as the basis for determining classes (perhaps by clustering) and then using the results to classify new objects. It can also be used for prediction, via the same method as the matching process to find the closest match. The resulting behavior of that matching object can be used to predict the outcome of the new object.

As an example, consider a database that tracks cancer symptoms, diagnoses, and treatments. Having already performed a clustering of the cases based on symptoms, MBR can be used to find the cases closest to a newly introduced one to guess at the diagnosis as well as propose a treatment protocol.

Cluster Detection

Given a large set of heterogeneous objects, a common data mining task is to divide that set into a number of smaller, more homogeneous groups. Automated clustering applications are used to perform this grouping. Again, as in memory-based reasoning, we must have a concept of a function that measures the distance between any two points based on an element's attributes. An example where clustering is useful would be segmenting visitors to an e-commerce Web site to understand what kinds of people are visiting the site.

There are two approaches to clustering. The first approach is to assume that a certain number of clusters are already embedded in the data; the goal is to break the data up into that number of clusters. A frequently used approach is the K-Means clustering technique, which initially designates clusters and then iteratively applies these steps: Identify the exact middle of the clusters, measure the distance of each object to that exact middle, assign each object to the cluster owning that exact middle, then redraw the cluster boundaries. This is repeated until the cluster boundaries no longer change.

In the other approach, called *agglomerative clustering*, instead of assuming the existence of any specific predetermined number of clusters, every item starts out in its own cluster, and an iterative process attempts to merge clusters, again through a process of computing similarity. In this case, though, we will need a way to compare similarity between clusters (as opposed to points within an *n*-dimensional space), which is a bit more complicated. The result of the agglomerative method is ultimately to have composed all clusters into a single cluster. But as each iteration takes place the history is recorded, so the data analyst can choose the level of clustering that is most appropriate for the particular business need.

Link Analysis

Link analysis is the process of looking for and establishing links between objects within a data set as well as characterizing the weight associated with any link between two objects. For example, we can look at telephone call detail records to examine links established when a connection is initiated at one telephone number to a different telephone number. Not only does this form a link between the two numbers, but other variables or attributes can be used to characterize that link, such as the frequency of the calls, the duration of the calls, or the times at which those calls are made.

Link analysis is useful for analytical applications that rely on graph theory for drawing conclusions. One example is looking for closely connected groups of people. In other words, are there collections of people that are linked together where the linkage between any pair within that set is as strong as the link between any other pair? Answering this question might uncover information about the existence of illegal drug rings or perhaps about a collection of people who can exert strong influence on one another.

Another analytical area for which link analysis is useful is process optimization. An example might be evaluating the allocation of airplanes and pilots (who are trained for flying specific kinds of airplanes) to the many routes that an airline travels. Every flight represents a link within a large graph, and the assignment of pilots to airplanes is guided by the goal of reducing both lag time and extra travel time required for a flight crew, as well as any external regulations associated with the time a crew may be in the air.

Rule Induction

Chapter 7 discussed business rules and how those rules can be used as part of the BI program. Part of the knowledge discovery process is the identification of business (or other kinds of) rules that are embedded within data. The methods associated with rule induction are used for this discovery process.

One approach to rule discovery is the use of decision trees (Fig. 14.1). A completed decision tree is a tree where each node represents a question and the decision as to which path to take from that node is dependent on the answer to the question. For example, we can have a binary decision tree where one internal node asks whether the employee's salary is greater than $50,000. If the answer is yes, the left-hand path is taken, but if the answer is no, the right-hand path is taken.

At each step along the path from the root of the tree to the leaves, the set of records that conform to the answers along the way continues to grow smaller. At each node in the tree, we have a representative set of records that conform to the answers to the questions along that path. Each node in the tree represents a segmenting question, which subdivides the current representative set into two smaller segments. Every path from the root node to any other node is unique. Each node in the tree also represents the expression of a rule, and at each point in the tree we can evaluate the set of records that conform to that rule as well as the size of that record set.

Another approach to rule induction is the discovery of association rules. *Association rules* specify a relation between attributes that appears more frequently than expected if the attributes were independent. Basically, an association rule states that the values of a set of attributes determine the values of another set of attributes, with some degree of *confidence* and some measure of *support*.

An association rule is specified as {source attribute value set} → {target attribute value set}. The source attribute set is also referred to as the *left-hand side* (for obvious reasons) and the target attribute set as the *right-hand side*. The confidence of the association rule is the percentage of the time that the rule applies. For example, if 85% of the time that a customer buys a network hub she will also buy a network interface card (NIC), the confidence of the rule {item1: Buys network hub} → {item2: Buys NIC} is 85%. The support of a rule is the percentage of all the records where the left-hand side and right-hand side attributes have the assigned values. In this case, if 6% of all the records have the values set {item1: Buys network hub} and {item2: Buys NIC}, then the support for the rule is 6%.

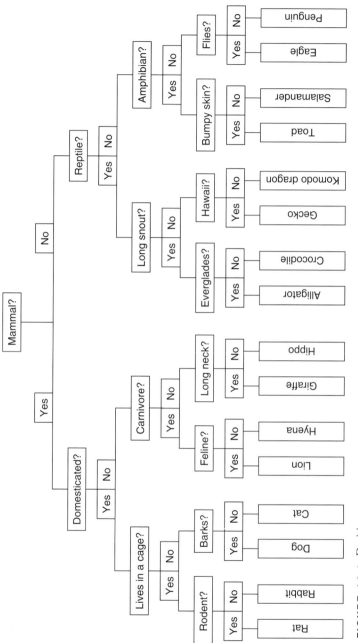

FIGURE 14.1 Decision trees.

Neural Networks

A neural network is an attempt to represent the model of a human brain as a collection of individual neurons connected within a network. A neural network essentially captures a set of statistical operations embodied as the application of a weighted combination function applied to all inputs to a neuron to compute a single output value that is then propagated to other neurons within the network. Ultimately, the input values are connected as the initial inputs, and the resulting output(s) represent some decision generated by the neural network. This approach is good for classification, estimation, and prediction.

The connections and weights assigned to those connections within a neural network are determined through a training process, where a data set with known conclusions is used to configure the network to "get the right answers." Sometimes the representation of data needs to be modified to get the kinds of values required for proper value calculation. For example, historical data represented as dates may need to be transformed into elapsed days, and continuous value results may need to be rounded to 0 or 1 when looking for a discrete yes/no answer.

Management Issues

Knowledge discovery and data mining are very valuable components of the BI program. It is through the data mining process that a lot of the questions business partners raise can be examined and answered. To maintain the high value of the knowledge discovery process, keep the following management issues in mind.

Buy versus Build

A number of years ago, when data mining started to be recognized as a valuable process, there were not many usable data mining tools available on the market, and so the leading-edge companies adopting data mining needed to hire engineers to build their own data mining tools. Today, there are a large number of data mining tool products that are as good as or better than what is likely to produced in-house. My suggestion is to determine what kinds of data mining techniques are most appropriate for the business problems that arise within your organization and then to buy the tools that support those techniques and hire experienced engineers to work with those tools.

Data Preparation

One issue that can destroy the effectiveness of any data mining activity is using data that has not been properly prepared for the task at hand. At the lowest level, the cleanliness of the data should not be questioned (see Chapter 9 for more discussion); at the highest level, individual data idiosyncrasies need to be addressed and managed.

A good example is the existence of null values in any process involving aggregation, similarity, or distance computations. When computing averages, how are nulls to be treated? And when trying to compare two objects that both have assigned nulls to a specific attribute, what is the weight that this match of nonvalues carries? Another issue involves normalization and quantization of continuous values into discrete groups, because relying on continuous values can make the cluster resolution process much more complicated.

Understanding the Results

Some of the techniques described in this chapter are better suited for understanding results than others. For example, market basket analysis through association rule discovery not only provides the rule, it also opens the door for understanding whether the association is causal and what the meaning of the rule is. On the other hand, neural networks are notorious for providing results without any means of explaining how those conclusions were reached. If it is important to be able to explain results, be careful in the methods and tools you select. Remember: To successfully draw conclusions from the results of data mining, you should have a good understanding of the data.

Managing Business Client Expectations

Remember that data mining is an exploratory process and that sometimes what we discover during an exploration is that there is nothing to discover. It is the manager's responsibility to remind the business partner that although data mining can be a powerful value-adding technology, it does not always provide the expected magic bullet solution to all the problems.

Remember the Virtuous Cycle

Last, recall what we said earlier: The data mining and knowledge discovery process is a virtuous cycle, and the process will not have as much value if you do not identify actions to take, actually take those actions, and then measure the results. Determining which techniques provide the best insight into a business problem and figuring out the best ways to exploit discovered knowledge are the critical components to data mining success.

To Learn More

Data mining is not magic. It is, rather, a disciplined approach to exploring patterns within data, determining actionable knowledge from those patterns, and putting that knowledge to use. Data mining techniques make use of data in the data warehouse in a way that augments the other analytical techniques, such as business reporting and OLAP analysis.

The basic tasks of data mining are to use existing models either for classifying objects within a data set, for predicting future behavior, or for exposing relationships between objects. In addition, data mining can be used to help identify classes as a prelude to future classification by automatically clustering heterogeneous data into more homogeneous groups.

To learn more about data mining, read anything written by Berry and Linoff, and also consider *Data Preparation for Data Mining*, Dorian Pyle, San Francisco, Morgan Kaufmann, 1999.

CHAPTER 15

Using Publicly Available Data

Throughout this book I have tried to emphasize the ultimate extraction of actionable value from aggregated sets of data. So what would you say if you were told there was a huge data resource that was widely available, easily accessible, and essentially free? I am referring to public data, which comes in a variety of sizes, shapes and forms, as well as what we might call "publicly available" data sets that are packaged and sold by value-added information resellers.

For the most part, a public data set is a collection of data that is collected as a by-product of some legal or regulatory mandate that requires registration of some event or transaction. In some cases, personal data supplied directly by individuals is made available in both individual and aggregated forms. In addition, there are public data sets made available by government bodies as a convenience to their constituents, specifically for public use. In either of these cases, depending on the context or source, significant value can be added to internal data sets by acquiring and integrating publicly available data.

In this last chapter, we look at publicly available data sets so that we can consider their value in terms of information integration and exploitation and hopefully show the value of acquiring and managing this kind of data. In addition, we will briefly discuss the political aspects of collecting and manipulating public data in a way that poses the perception of an invasion of privacy.

I have to admit that I was surprised when I performed a Web search looking for details of the use of public data as part of a business intelligence (BI) strategy and did not find a lot of relevant matches. Whether it is using individual entity detail, aggregate demographics, or historical trends, there is great value in linking internal data with publicly available data.

The Business Case

On a recent plane trip, I struck up a conversation with the man sitting next to me, who told me that he was in the business of buying and selling large construction equipment to different companies around the world. He described to me how he built his business by cleverly creating a database to track construction companies and equipment and the corresponding ownership relationship. When he saw that one company might be starting a new project, he would contact them and see what kind of equipment they might need, and he was then able to search the database for those companies that owned that particular piece of machinery.

The interesting part is that he built this database by scanning through publicly available documents, such as corporate asset listings, and Uniform Commercial Code (UCC) lien filings, looking for references to an ownership relationship between a machine and a company. Every time he brokered a transaction, he also updated his own database. By doing this, not only was he able to keep track of who owned what, but he could also track the history of the machine, from its original construction (via serial number) through each subsequent owner. With this knowledge at his fingertips, he had successfully created a niche business in machinery exchange, enabling faster convergence on brokered deals. This is a good example of the exploitation of public data for business value.

We have also already seen another good example of the use of public data as part of a BI program in Chapter 13 when we looked at merging geographic and demographic data made available by the Census Bureau. It is very simple to make the case for using public data. Data that has been collected and made available by government resources is available at a low cost, and the only costs involve storage, management, and integration with other BI data. In any company that has set up a BI environment, the processes associated with importing, managing, and integrating data have already been streamlined for internal data set aggregation. And so the only increase is in those variable costs associated with executing those processes. On the other hand, in the right circumstances there can be significant value through data enhancement using publicly available data.

Management Issues

There are three major management issues associated with the use of publicly available data: integration, privacy, and its lack of structure. The integration issue is similar to the general data integration problems discussed in other chapters, except that because data sets may be provided by some agency that has no vested interest in its use, the structure and the quality of the data may be called into question. In fact, there are a number of companies whose business is to enhance and improve public data sets and then resell them based on their added value.

The second major issue revolves around personal privacy. There is a perception that any organization that collects data about individuals and then tries to exploit that information is invading a person's privacy. In fact, companies are now required to state their privacy policies explicitly to their customers, and much BI work can be done within the constraints described therein; we discuss this in greater detail in the later section on The Myth of Privacy.

The third major issue is that a lot of publicly available data is not always in a nicely structured form that is easily adaptable. Frequently, this data is semistructured, which means that the data requires some manipulation before it can be successfully and properly integrated. We discuss this kind of data in the upcoming section on Semistructured Data.

Public Data

There is a large amount of public data that is easily accessible, and how to explore all of that data could fill an entire book. What is important is to explore the process of locating the data resources that are available and how to determine the usage possibilities for that data. In this section, we will look at different kinds of public data as examples of the exploitation process.

There are many ways that data sets can be categorized, but we will break the realm of public data into these areas:

- **Personal information,** which attributes individuals
- **Business information,** which provides information about business entities
- **Legal information,** which documents legal cases
- **Factual information,** which provides facts that may not be directly linked to individuals

All of these data sets may contain bits of data that, when linked to internal records, provide the catalyst for new knowledge inferences. For example, if we know the price a person paid for a house and whether that is the first house that person has bought, then based on the assumption that the person obtained a mortgage for 80% of the purchase price and knowing the current interest rates and the local tax rates, we can take a reasonable guess at his monthly mortgage and tax payments. This piece of information, along with the assumption that the lender would allow the buyer to pay 38% of his gross monthly income, allows us to infer his monthly salary!

Personal Information

Any data that attributes the information about a person could be called personal information. For example, in most, if not all, of the United States, life events require some kind of registration with the state government. Public certificates are issued and the details registered when a child is born, before people are married, when people get divorced, and not long after they die. Other personal information that is recorded includes:

- Driver's licenses (although this information may be limited in release by many states)
- Immigration records (which may be accessible from the government or through alternate genealogy Web sites)
- Real property sales (which may contain purchase price and mortgage information)

Although in many cases there is no bulk electronic versions of this data, there are some localities that will provide this data for a small fee. For example, according to the Maryland State Department of Assessments and Taxation, the "Real Property Sales File" (which contains, on a cumulative basis, all real property accounts in Maryland that were transferred during the preceding 12 months) is available for $75 per tape.

Business Information

Aside from personal information, there is a lot of data that can be used to attribute business entities. These public records are frequently related to rules and regulations imposed on business operations by federal or state government jurisdictions. This kind of data includes the following.

- **Incorporations**—Company incorporations fall under state jurisdiction, and the incorporation is registered with the state. Typical information that is in a statement of incorporation includes the name of the incorporated entity and the names of the principals involved.
- **Uniform Commercial Code (UCC)**—A UCC filing is meant to document a security interest incurred by a debtor and to document liens held on consumer goods or personal property. A UCC filing may show

that one person or company is using personal property as collateral for a loan. Perusing UCC filings allows one to accumulate information about the types and values of an individual entity's assets, as well as loan amounts.

- **Bankruptcy filings**—Bankruptcy filings contain information about the entity's assets, creditors, and the amount of money owed to each creditor, the trustee that was assigned to the case, among other things. This kind of information allows for enhancement of relationship data by establishing a link between the individuals associated with the bankruptcy and all other named parties (creditors and trustees).

- **Professional licensing**—The establishment of a connection between a specific individual and a profession that requires licensing (of which there are many) provides multiple enhancement opportunities, such as adding to the psychographic profile, as well as possibly establishing a connection with other individuals with the same profession in the same geographic area.

- **Securities filings**—The Securities and Exchange Commission is a governmental body that enforces and manages federal securities regulations, which mandate the filing of significant statements and events associated with public companies. There are many different kinds of filings, ranging from quarterly statements, to statements regarding percentage of beneficial ownership an individual or an organization holds in a different company. Although the bulk of the information contained in these filings is in a non-structured (i.e., free text) form (from which it is difficult to extract interesting data), a lot of the text may be in a structured or semistructured form, which may be amenable to entity extraction.

- **Regulatory licensing**—In areas of business that are regulated by government bodies, there may be requirements for individuals or companies to acquire a license to do certain kinds of business, and these license applications (and notification of license grant) are public data. An example is the many uses associated with the radio spectrum that must be licensed through the Federal Communications Commission (FCC), such as radio and television stations, mobile telephone services, mobile telephone antenna construction and management, etc.

- **Patents and trademarks**—The Patent and Trademark office (PTO) provides access to the text of a large number of granted patents, which provide a source of business and psychographic data, as well as linkage between individuals and sponsoring institutions.

Legal Information

A large number of legal cases are accessible online, providing the names of the parties involved in the cases as well as free text describing the case. These documents, many of which having been indexed and made available for search, contain embedded psychographic and geographic enhancement potential, along with opportunities for entity extraction and entity linkage. Those linkages may represent either personal (such as family relationships) or business relationships.

Factual Information

There is an abundance of factual information embedded in available data sets. Although there may be some restrictions on specific uses of some of this data, there is still much business value that can be derived from data sets such as the following.

- **Census summary**—Every ten years, the Census Bureau counts all of the people living in the United States. For the years following the annual census, a number of data products are generated and made available both interactively through the Census Bureau's Web site and in raw form that can be downloaded via FTP. For example, the first data set, called "Summary File 1" (SF1) contains rolled-up demographic information by geographic unit; it is this information that we used as an example in Chapter 13 to demonstrate the use of geographic data.

- **TIGER**—Another data product made available by the Census Bureau is a set of extracts from the Topologically Integrated Geographic Encoding and Referencing database, also known as TIGER. The TIGER/Line files contain selected geographic and cartographic information, including details of line features (e.g., roads, railroads) and landmarks (e.g., schools, cemeteries) as well as geographic entity codes for areas that link to the Census statistical data. These tables provide details of geographic attributes, such as the latitude and longitude of street segments. This kind of data can be used to identify the nearest physical neighbors to a particular street address or to provide geographic enhancement to the summary data referenced in SF1.

- **Federal Election Commission**—There are many laws that constrain political donations, and regulations require that most campaign contributions be reported to the Federal Election Commission (FEC). These contributions are logged in a database that details who made the contribution, from which address, to which candidate or political action committee, and the amount given. The data in this table can be used to track support of individual candidates over time, as well as review rolled-up aggregate views of political spending. This in turn can be used to infer geographical political preferences and trends.

- **Bureau of Labor Statistics (BLS)**—The BLS provides summary historical information about many different product prices over long periods of time.

- **Pharmaceutical data**—Information about individual drugs, devices, delivery methods, and narcotic ingredients is available from both the Food and Drug Administration (FDA) and the Drug Enforcement Agency (DEA). This kind of data maybe useful in the insurance industry as well as in individual criminal jurisdictions.

Data Resources

Having determined that we want to make use of publicly available data, how do we get it? There are basically two approaches: gather data from the original source, and pay a data aggregator for a value-added data set.

Original Source

As mentioned in the previous sections, the government is a very good source of publicly available data. On the other hand, I refer to the government in quotes because there are so many agencies and divisions of international, U.S. federal, and state governments that source/supplier management becomes an additional management risk. Although the price may be right, there may be added costs associated with the process of internalizing the multiple external data models as well as creating the processes to exploit that data in the right way. In addition, because these data sets are being provided for general use for a low or no price, there is little leverage that a data consumer can use to enforce any levels of data quality or timeliness expectations.

Another source of publicly available information may be provided by third parties in a form that is not meant for exploitation. A good example is a Web site, which may have some data but not in a directly usable form. Another example is semistructured data instances that reflect some knowledge taxonomy, such as birth notices, wedding announcements, obituaries, death notices, legal notices, biographies, job descriptions, and resumes. We will discuss this in greater detail shortly.

Surprisingly, another interesting source of publicly available data is the subject of that data itself. Frequently, individuals and even representatives of organizations are willing to provide very detailed information about themselves or their organization for little or no incentive. Telephone or online surveys, product registration cards, free magazine subscription applications, preferred customer programs, etc., are all sources for information that can be used to enhance an entity profile. I include this as publicly available data, although it is not necessarily public, because most frequently those providing the data are not aware of how the provided information is going to be used, making it effectively public data.

Data Aggregators

I use the term *data aggregator* to refer to any organization that collects data from one or more sources, provides some value-added processing, and repackages the result in a usable form. Sometimes the data comes directly to the client through a sales or licensing agreement, although frequently data aggregators will act as an agent to enhance the clients' data. This is typically done by giving a data set to the data supplier, who then enhances the data and returns it to the client.

Another method for providing aggregated data is through a query-and-delivery process. For example, an interface allows the client to request all data instances that relate to a particular party or entity. The aggregator will provide a list of matched records, and then the user can purchase any or all of the matched data instances.

Semistructured Data

Consider the following text extracted from my personal bio.

> David is a veteran of the financial industry, having worked for Morgan Stanley Dean Witter in their IT Division in Options Pricing and Securities Processing. At MSDW, David worked on automating the generation of code for creating options pricing objects, and later assisted in the accounts renovation project, creating inline data validation routines for preventing duplicate customer account creation. Prior to MSDW, David was a senior compiler designer for Thinking Machines Corporation.

We can immediately recognize certain facts and relationships that exist within this text; unfortunately, it is not so easy for a computer program to do the same thing. The reason is that we are accustomed to identifying patterns of information in text based on the context in which the critical facts lie. But software has not evolved to the point where context-sensitive facts can always be inferred from free text.

On the other hand, when the content is limited to a vocabulary or a format that can be reasonably modeled, it is possible, with some degree of certainty, to extract bits and pieces of information from semistructured data. The point is that although the data has not been broken down into a distinct set of attributes and their assigned values, there is some predictable context that appears frequently enough that allows an application to extract information. So, in our bio example, the following facts might be inferred with reasonable success.

- David worked for Morgan Stanley Dean Witter.
- David worked on options pricing.
- David was a senior compiler designer.

These are really just extracted chunks of text that exhibit more clearly parsable structure (i.e., it is easy to extract object references and a relationship between them).

The Myth of Privacy

As mentioned earlier, one of the major issues in using publicly available data is the fear of invasion of privacy. To explore this, let's perform a small thought experiment.

A friend of mine, Brian, recently moved to my neighborhood. Very excitedly, he told me all about his experience—how he was able to get a great deal on a mortgage because he borrowed the money from the bank holding his checking accounts. Brian had saved enough money to apply some of the proceeds of the sale of his previous home toward a vacation in Europe—the tickets were free because he applied frequent-flyer miles accumulated from using an affinity card associated with his favorite airline.

Brian loves living in my area, because he and his wife can manage the cost of living much better than in his previous neighborhood, especially because all the supermarkets have bonus cards that provide additional discounts off many food item purchases. They also love shopping at the local warehouse club, because there are a lot of rebate offers on the products they buy there. By using his credit card to buy groceries, he has quickly accumulated additional frequent-flyer miles.

Yet Brian is subject to the marketing tsunami that affects us all. He is inundated with junk mail offers of new credit cards. His family's dinner is interrupted by telemarketing phone calls. His morning at work is taken up with sifting through a flood of spam e-mails peddling discount life insurance and human growth hormone. "Where is my privacy protection?" Brian asks.

Fear of Invasion

Brian is not a real person, but his behavior strongly resembles reasonable behavior for a large percentage of the population. And, as reflected by Brian's question, there is a growing fear that some monolithic organizations sneak around collecting our deepest, darkest secrets and are using computers to invade our privacy.

According to the Federal Trade Commission (FTC), "Advances in computer technology have made it possible for detailed information about people to be compiled and shared more easily and cheaply than ever." At the FTC's Privacy Initiatives Web site (*www.ftc.gov/privacy/*), there is a warning about allowing the misuse of personal information. The truth is, as BI professionals, we are somewhat responsible for collecting customer information and manipulating that information for marketing purposes, but are we really guilty of invasion of privacy?

Let's take a second look at Brian's behavior.

- The purchase of his home must be registered with the public agencies, because real estate transactions are recorded in public records.

- Publicly available information from the Census Bureau describes fine details about the area into which Brian has moved.

- The widely available regional cluster databases can accurately describe the demographics and psychographics of people that live in his neighborhood.

- His use of cross-marketed products from his financial institution provides a lot of information about his finances and lifestyle to his bank—information that is likely to be shared with all bank subsidiaries as well as affiliated third parties.

- Brian's use of an affinity credit card, along with his selection of destination for his vacation (as well as his choice of how and when to apply his frequent-flyer miles) also is registered as personal preference entries in some database.

- Their choice to use a supermarket bonus card not only registers the kinds of foods that he and his wife buy, but also allows someone to infer their preferred shopping time, their weekly food budget, the number of children they have, when they have company, etc.

- Each time they fill out a rebate slip, they provide feedback to the vendor regarding the purchase patterns of their products and specific information about who buys what products and when.

Any of the activities in which Brian is engaged potentially generates *usable* information that could be construed as personal information. In reality, the data that feeds the marketing machine the consumers fear so much is most likely supplied by those very same consumers.

The Value and Cost of Privacy

This demonstrates an interesting model of information valuation, in that the consumer is being compensated in some way in return for providing information. For example, in return for the supermarket's ability to track every food item purchase, the consumer is rewarded with incremental coupon savings. In return for supplying information about the purchase of a product, the company will pay you a $5 rebate. In return for providing information about flight preferences and transactions, the airlines provide free air travel. There are second-order consumer benefits that are rarely articulated well, such as a better ability to provide products targeted only to those consumers who might be interested in those products and more efficient placement of products on supermarket shelves.

On the other hand, most organizations that collect data allow the consumer to prevent any misuse of that data by opting out. But opting out is an active process, requiring the consumer to take the action, which in turn generates some cost, perhaps in terms of time and energy spent (which can be lengthy, if waiting on hold). In other words, there is an incurred cost associated with managing personal information.

The public relations problem stems from the *perception* that because of the availability of fast computational resources along with knowledge discovery applications, companies are sifting through mounds of data eking out the smallest bits of private information. In reality, under the right circumstances (i.e., we all are obeying the law), companies are using provided personal information in a way that is consistent with the consumers' directives. Unfortunately, the onus for directing the prevention of the use personal information is placed on the consumer through the opt-out process.

The "Privacy" Statement

So what about all those privacy statements that we get in the mail each year? Under the Gramm–Leach–Bliley Act, any financial institution that collects nonpublic personal information must provide, both at the time of establishing a relationship and on an annual basis, a "clear and conspicuous disclosure to such consumer, in writing or in electronic form, . . . of that financial institution's policies and practices" with respect to disclosing nonpublic personal information to affiliates and nonaffiliated third parties.

But the issuing of a privacy statement does not imply that your data is being treated as private data. These statements actually are the opposite—they tell the consumer how the information is *not* being kept private. For example, one bank's privacy statement says, "We may share any of the personal information that we collect about you among companies within the ⟨omitted⟩ family." Later in the statement's text is an enumeration of 30 different companies within the family, including auto leasing, insurance, investment advisors, credit card, and real estate advisors.

Not only that, this privacy statement also says that the bank "may disclose any of the personal information that we have collected about you to:

- other financial institutions with whom we have joint marketing agreements; and

- companies that perform services, including marketing services, for us or for us and the financial institutions with whom we have joint marketing agreements."

This pretty much opens the door for sharing a consumer's personal data with just about anyone. So as long as the consumer does not actively opt out of participation, it is likely that personal information is being widely broadcast!

The Good News for Business Intelligence

There are a lot of benefits in society to the (limited) dissemination of personal information, such as the ability to track down criminals, detect fraud, provide channels for improved customer relationship management, and even track down terrorists. As BI professionals, we have a twofold opportunity with respect to the privacy issue. The first is to raise awareness regarding the consumer's value proposition with respect to data provision, leading to raised awareness about both the legality and the propriety of BI analysis and information use. The second is to build better BI applications. For example, if these darn computers are so smart, why are companies trying to sell long-distance service to my 2 year old? And why do representatives of the company we use for our home alarm system keep calling us and asking if we want an introductory system?

All joking aside, junk mail and marketing calls are viewed as annoyances and invasions only because companies are *not* able to analyze that information as well as the populace thinks. When we can build better BI applications and use them properly, the perception of invasion will likely change.

To Learn More

There is a large body of publicly available information that is either free or inexpensive and that can add a lot of value to your data. Much of this data deals with either demographic or behavioral attribution associated with personal or organizational entities. Whether this data is provided by government resources or by separate data aggregator/packagers, there may be some issues with the quality of the data that will need to be addressed from within the organization.

The best places to start to learn more about public data are government Web sites. There is a lot of public data available from the U.S. government as well as from state governments. There are numerous public data vendors who can be found via a search with your favorite search engine.

CHAPTER 16

Quick Reference Guide

This Quick Reference Guide encapsulates some of the more important topics covered in the book. The treatment here sometimes mimics and sometimes summarizes the material. Each section gives an overview and a pointer to where in the book you should look for more detail.

Business Analytics

Business analytics refers to the front-end applications that are used within a business intelligence (BI) environment. As opposed to standard reporting applications, which report about the mechanics of the running of a business, business analytics provide insight into how to improve a business.

Business analytics can incorporate applications associated with analyzing the following.

- **Customers and their behaviors,** including customer profiling, call center effectiveness, targeted marketing, personalization of presentation (such as for a Web site), customer lifetime value estimations, and customer loyalty. Customer relationship management (CRM) covers a large number of these topics and is the process of understanding who your customers are, what they like and don't like, and how to manage your relationship with them.

- **Human productivity analytics,** such as call center utilization, process optimization, and productivity effectiveness metrics. This can be applied in trying to understand when and where the best productivity is achieved within an organization and perhaps why this is true.

- **Business productivity analytics,** such as defect analysis, capacity planning, financial reporting, risk management, credit management, resource planning, asset management, and inventory risk assessment. What is usually referred to as financial reporting can be grouped into this category.

- **Sales channel analytics,** including the creation and analysis of marketing campaigns, evaluating sales performance, and looking at sales channel effectiveness.

- **Supply chain analytics,** used to characterize and benchmark a company's supply channels from various vendors and suppliers, including supplier management, shipping effectiveness, inventory control, and the analysis of the distribution network.

- **Behavior analysis,** which deals with evaluating activity trends as a way to identify interesting or predictive behavior, relating to purchasing trends, Web activity, fraud detection, customer attrition analysis, and social network analysis.

Business analytic applications use or extract data from the central data warehouse and either formulate an interactive analytical process by providing access to different focused aspects of the data (as separated into individual subject area data marts) or manage their own views of the data internally.

Business Intelligence

The Data Warehousing Institute, a provider of education and training in the data warehouse and BI industry defines BI as:

> The processes, technologies, and tools needed to turn data into information, information into knowledge, and knowledge into plans that drive profitable business action. Business intelligence encompasses data warehousing, business analytic tools, and content/knowledge management.[1]

This is a great working definition, especially because it completely captures the idea that there is a hierarchy imposed on the different scopes of intelligence. In addition, this definition also exposes two critical notions:

- A BI practice is more than just a collection of tools. This means that without the processes and the right people, the tools are of little value.
- The value of BI is defined in the context of profitable business action.

---

1. The Data Warehousing Institute Faculty Newsletter, Fall 2002.

This means that if knowledge that can be used for profitable action is ignored, the practice is of little value.

Unfortunately, the words *data* and *information* are frequently used interchangeably. At the risk of clashing with any individual's understanding of the terms *data*, *information*, and *knowledge*, let's use the following conceptual definitions.

- *Data* is a collection of raw value elements or facts used for calculating, reasoning, or measuring. Data may be collected, stored, or processed but not put into a context from which any meaning can be inferred.

- *Information* is the result of collecting and organizing data in a way that establishes relationships between data items, which thereby provides context and meaning.

- *Knowledge* is the concept of understanding information based on recognized patterns in a way that provides insight to information.

The process of turning data into information can be summarized as determining what data is to be collected and managed and in what context. Turning information into knowledge involves the analytical components, such as data warehousing, online analytical processing (OLAP), data quality, data profiling, business rule analysis, and data mining. Being able to take action based on the intelligence that we have learned is the key point of any BI strategy. It is through these actions that a senior management sponsor can see the true return on investment for his or her information technology (IT) spending. For more information see Chapter 1.

Business Rules

A business rule is a directive that is intended to influence or guide business behavior, in support of business policy that is formulated in response to an opportunity or threat. From the information system perspective, a business rule is a statement that defines or constrains some aspect of the business. It is intended to assert business structure or to control or influence the behavior of the business.[2]

From a practical standpoint, a business rule asserts a statement about the state of a business process or a directive describing changes in the state of a business process. More simply, a business rule dictates what happens when a sequence of inputs is applied to one or more well-described scenarios.

A rule is a statement that asserts some truth about the system, along with

---

2. Retrieved May 5, 2003 from *www.businessrulesgroup.org/brgdefn.htm*

optional actions to be performed, depending on the assertion's truth value. Rules can be classified as falling into one of the following areas:

- **Definitions and specifications,** which provides a well-defined vocabulary for more complex rule specification. Rules in this class should enumerate the descriptive figures of speech used in describing business processes.

- **Assertions,** which are statements about entities within the system that express sensible observations about the business. Assertions describe relationships between entities and activities within the framework. Together, the definitions and assertions drive the construction of the logical data model within which the business rules operate.

- **Constraints,** which express unconditional conformance to a business statement; compared to a constraint, a data instance either conforms to that constraint or violates it. An event that violates a constraint will be rejected by the system; therefore, by definition, no action can be taken that will violate a constraint.

- **Guidelines,** which express a desire about the state of the system or a warning about a potential change in the system.

- **Actions,** which are operations that change the system state, typically as a result of the violation of some constraint or guideline.

- **Triggers,** which specify a collection of conditions and the initiation of an action contingent upon the conditions' values.

- **Inferences,** which specify a collection of conditions establishing a fact that becomes true as a by-product of changes within the states of the system.

A business rule system encapsulates sets of states, variables, and rules that reflect business processes and policies and provides a means for defining and managing business rules while creating an environment in which a rules engine will execute those rules. For more information see Chapter 7.

Data Cleansing

Data cleansing is the process of finding errors in data and either automatically or manually correcting the errors. A large part of the cleansing process involves the identification and elimination of duplicate records; a large part of this process is easy, because exact duplicates are easy to find in a database using simple queries or in a flat file by sorting and streaming the data based on a specific key. The difficult part of duplicates elimination is finding those nonexact duplicates—for example, pairs of records where there are subtle differences in the matching key. Data cleansing, which we discuss in Chapter 9, focuses mostly on the following.

- **Parsing,** which is the process of identifying tokens within a data instance and looking for recognizable patterns. The parsing process segregates each word, attempts to determine the relationship between the word and previously defined token sets, and then forms patterns from sequences of tokens. When a pattern is matched, there is a predefined transformation applied to the original field value to extract its individual components, which are then reported to the driver applications.

- **Standardization,** which transforms data into a standard form. Standardization, a prelude to the record consolidation process, is used to extract entity information (e.g., person, company, telephone number, location) and to assign some semantic value for subsequent manipulation. Standardization will incorporate information reduction transformations during a consolidation or summarization application.

- **Abbreviation expansion,** which transforms abbreviations into their full form. There are different kinds of abbreviation. One type shortens each of a set of words to a smaller form, where the abbreviation consists of a prefix of the original data value. Examples include "INC" for incorporated and "CORP" for corporation. Another type shortens the word by eliminating vowels or by contracting the letters to phonetics, such as "INTL" or "INTRNTL" for international. A third form of abbreviation is the acronym, where the first characters of each of a set of words are composed into a string, such as "USA" for "United States of America."

- **Correction,** which attempts to correct those data values that are not recognized and to augment correctable records with the correction. Realize that the correction process can only be partially automated; many vendors may give the impression that their tools can completely correct invalid data, but there is no silver bullet. In general, the correction process is based on maintaining a set of incorrect values as well as their corrected forms. As an example, if the word *International* is frequently misspelled as "Intrnational," there would be a rule mapping the incorrect form to the correct form. Some tools may incorporate business knowledge accumulated over a long period of time, which accounts for large knowledge bases of rules incorporated into these products; unfortunately, this opens the door for loads of obscure rules that reflect many special cases.

Data Enhancement

Data enhancement is a process to add value to information by accumulating additional information about a base set of entities and then merging all the sets of information to provide a focused view of the data.

There are two approaches to data enhancement. One focuses on incrementally improving or adding information as data is viewed or processed. *Incremental* enhancements are useful as a component of a later analysis stage, such as sequence pattern analysis or behavior modeling. The other approach is *batch* enhancement, where data collections are aggregated and methods are applied to the collection to create value-added information.

Data can be enhanced with different kinds of information, including the following.

- **Auditing information,** which provides some kind of historical tracking information through which the sequence of business processes applied to data can be traced.

- **Temporal information,** where data is enhanced by incrementally adding timestamps noting the time at which some event occurred. With data, this can refer to the time at which a transaction took place, the time at which a message was sent or received, the time at which a customer requested information, etc.

- **Contextual information,** which describes the place where some action was performed.

- **Geographic information,** which provides location information, such as locality coding, neighborhood mapping, latitude/longitude pairs, and other kinds of regional codes.

- **Demographic information,** such as customer age, marital status, gender, ethnic coding (for people), annual revenues, number of employees, and size of office space (for companies).

- **Psychographic information,** which describes lifestyle preference information for people, such as product and brand use and preferences, leisure activities, and vacation preferences.

Data enhancement is a value-adding component of a BI program, especially in the areas of increasing competitive intelligence, improved CRM, micro-marketing and focused targeting, personalization, and cooperative marketing, among other areas. Data enhancement frequently makes use of publicly available data sets that provide additional rolled-up demographics or psychographics. We discuss data enhancement in greater detail in Chapter 13, and we look at publicly available data in Chapter 15.

Data Integration

Data integration refers to the process of accumulating data sets from disparate locations and combining those data sets together. Data integration incorporates the extract/transform/load (ETL) process, enterprise application integration (EAI), and the record linkage and consolidation process.

The ETL process comprises the sequence of applications that extract data sets from the various sources, bring them to a data staging area, apply a sequence of processes to prepare the data for migration into the data warehouse, and the actual loading process. Extraction focuses on selecting the right data to be extracted and determining how that data should be extracted. Frequently ETL tools provide system adapters that automatically generate code to perform the extraction, either on the source system or across the enterprise. After data is extracted, a number of transformations may be applied, in preparation for the data consolidation.

Enterprise application integration is encapsulated as intelligent middleware that provides the glue allowing multiple applications to interoperate. Enterprise application integration is not truly a product or a tool, but rather a framework of ideas comprising different levels of integration, including business process management, communications middleware, data standardization and transformation, and the application of business rules in process.

Consolidation is a catchall term for those processes that make use of collected metadata and knowledge to eliminate duplicate entities, merge data from multiple sources, and other data enhancement operations. That process is powered by the ability to identify some kind of relationship between any arbitrary pair of data instances, based on the ability to link data instances together.

There are two kinds of relationships we look for. The first is *identity*— determining that two data instances refer to the exact same entity. This is what we look for when searching for duplicate entries in one database or when merging multiple instances of the same entity when merging databases. The other kind of relationship is *equivalence classing*—grouping entities together based on some set of similar attributes. The key to record linkage is the concept of *similarity*, which is a measure of how close two data instances are to each other. Similarity can be measured using a hard measure ("either the two records are the same, or they are not") or a more approximate measure (based on some form of scoring), in which case the similarity is judged based on scores above or below a threshold.

Data Mart

A data mart is a subject-oriented data repository, similar in structure to the enterprise data warehouse, but holding the data required for the decision support and BI needs of a specific department or group within the organization. A data mart could be constructed solely for the analytical purposes of the specific group, or it could be derived from an existing data warehouse. Data marts are built using a dimensional data model.

There are differences between a data mart and a data warehouse, mostly because of the different natures of the desired results. There is a school of thought that believes that data warehouses are meant for more loosely structured, exploratory analysis whereas data marts are for more formalized reporting and for directed drill-down. Because data marts are centered on the specific goals and decision support needs of a specific department within the company, the amount of data is much smaller, but the concentration is focused on data relevant to that department's operation. This implies that different departments with different analytical or reporting needs may need different kinds of data mart structures (which may account for the diverse set of data mart products on the market).

A data mart is likely to be configured for more generalized reporting for the specific business users within the department. Standard reports are more likely to be generated off of the data mart, which will be much smaller than the data warehouse and will provide better performance.

Data Mining

Data mining, or knowledge discovery, is a process of discovering patterns that lead to actionable knowledge from large data sets through one or more traditional data mining techniques, such as market basket analysis and clustering. A lot of the knowledge discovery methodology has evolved from the combination of the worlds of statistics and computer science. Data mining focuses mostly on discovering knowledge in association with six basic tasks.

- **Classification,** which involves examining the attributes of a particular object and assigning it to a defined class. Classification can be used to divide a customer base into best, mediocre, and low-value customers, for instance, to distinguish suspicious characters at an airport security check, identify a fraudulent transaction, or identify prospects for a new service.

- ***Estimation,*** which is a process of assigning some continuously valued numeric value to an object. For example, credit risk assessment is not necessarily a yes/no question; it could be some kind of scoring that assesses a propensity to default on a loan. Estimation can be used as part of the classification process (such as using an estimation model to guess a person's annual salary as part of a market segmentation process).

- **Prediction,** which is an attempt to classify objects according to some expected future behavior. Classification and estimation can be used for prediction by applying historical data where the classification is already known to build a model (this is called *training*). That model can then be applied to new data to predict future behavior.

- **Affinity grouping,** which is a process of evaluating relationships or associations between data elements that demonstrate some kind of affinity between objects.

- **Clustering,** which is the task of dividing a large collection of objects into smaller groups of objects that exhibit some similarity. The difference between clustering and classification is that during the clustering task, the classes are not defined beforehand. Rather, the process of evaluating the classes after the clustering has completed drives the determination or definition of that class.

- **Description,** which is the process of trying to describe what has been discovered, or trying to explain the results of the data mining process.

There are a number of techniques that are used to perform these tasks: market basket analysis, memory-based reasoning, cluster detection, link analysis, rule induction, neural networks, etc. For more information see Chapter 14.

Data Model

A data model is a discrete structured data representation of a real-world set of entities related to one another. Over time, our understanding of the best way to represent our perceived model has changed to reflect the ways we understand information along with the ways that we want to process that information. There is a significant difference between how we use data in an operational/tactical manner (i.e., to run the business) and the ways we use data in a strategic manner (i.e., to improve the business).

The traditional modeling technique for operational systems revolves around the entity-relationship model. Unfortunately, analytical applications that are relevant to BI are less able to take advantage of data when it is structured in the entity-relational form; alternatively, casting the same information into a dimensional structure greatly simplifies the use of data for strategic purposes.

In the early 1980s, a number of practitioners and researchers (most notably Chris Date) explored the concept of a relational database, in which the way that information was modeled was viewed in the context of representing entities within separate tables and relating those entities within a business process context between tables using some form of cross-table linkage. This is referred to as *entity-relationship modeling*.

The apparent failure of the relational model to efficiently provide data to knowledge workers is due mostly to the complexity of the data models and the difficulty in reconstructing a natural view of information that can be used in an analytical context. In contrast, an alternate technique to model data has evolved that allows for information to be represented in a way that is more suitable to high-performance access. This technique, called *dimensional modeling*, captures the basic unit of representation as a single multikeyed entry in a slender *fact* table, with each key exploiting the relational model to refer to the different *dimensions* associated with those facts. A maintained table of facts, each of which is related to a set of dimensions, is a much more efficient representation for data in a data warehouse. This is due to the ability to quickly and efficiently create aggregations and extractions of data specific to particular dimensional constraints while aggregating information.

Data Profiling

The goal of profiling data is to discover metadata when it is not available and to validate metadata when it is available. Data profiling is a process of analyzing raw data for the purpose of characterizing the information embedded within a data set. Data profiling incorporates column analysis, data type determination, and intercolumn association discovery. The result is a constructive process of information inference to prepare a data set for later integration.

Data profiling is a hierarchical process that attempts to build an assessment of the metadata associated with a collection of data sets. The bottom level of the hierarchy characterizes the values associated with individual attributes. At the next level, the assessment looks at relationships between multiple columns within a single table. At the highest level, the profile describes relationships that exist between data attributes across different tables.

Data profiling includes (among others) the following activities.

- **Data model inference,** which attempts to derive the data model from undocumented data.

- **Type inference,** a process to determine the data types associated with the data in each column of a table.

- **Value range analysis,** which explores the possibility that the values within a column fall within a defined value range (such as 0 to 100).

- **Cardinality and uniqueness**—*Cardinality* refers to the number of discrete values that appear within a column; *uniqueness* tests to see that each row in a table has a unique value for any particular set of attributes.

- **Frequency distribution,** which yields the number of times each distinct value appears in a value set.

- **Nullness,** which evaluates the existence of null values, whether they be explicit system nulls or represented null values (such as 999-99-9999 for a Social Security number) extant in the data.

- **Domain analysis,** which is a process of identifying and isolating collections of data values that have some specific business value.

- **Functional dependency analysis,** which looks for relationships between columns within the same table and across different tables.

- **Key discovery,** which looks for candidate keys within a single table, and foreign keys that link different tables.

Data Quality

Data quality differs from data cleansing in that whereas many data cleansing products can help in applying data edits to name and address data or in transforming data during an ETL process, there is usually no persistence in this cleansing. Each time a data warehouse is populated or updated, the same corrections are applied to the same data.

Data cleansing is an action, whereas data quality describes the state of the data. A data cleansing process can contribute to improving the quality of data. Improved data quality is the result of a business improvement process that looks to identify and eliminate the root causes of bad data. A critical component of improving data quality is being able to distinguish between "good" (i.e., valid) data and "bad" (i.e., invalid) data. But because data values appear in many contexts, formats, and frameworks, this simple concept devolves into extremely complicated notions as to what constitutes validity. This is because the validity of a data value *must* be defined within the context in which that data value appears.

There are many dimensions of data quality. The ones that usually attract the most attention are dimensions that deal with data values:

- **Accuracy,** which refers to the degree with which data values agree with an identified source of correct information.

- **Completeness,** which refers to the expectation that data instances contain all the information they are supposed to. Completeness can be prescribed on a single attribute, can be dependent on the values of other attributes within a record, or can even be defined with respect to all values within a column.

- **Consistency,** which refers to data values in one data set being consistent with values in another data set; formal consistency constraints can be encapsulated as a set of rules that specify consistency relationships between values of attributes, either across a record or message or along all values of a single attribute.

- **Currency and timeliness,** which refers to the degree to which information is current with the world that it models. *Currency* can measure how up-to-date information is and whether it is correct despite possible time-related changes. *Timeliness* refers to the time expectation for accessibility of information.

In essence, the level of data quality is determined by the data consumers in terms of meeting or beating their own defined expectations. In practice, this means identifying a set of data quality objectives associated with any data set and then measuring that data set's conformance to those objectives. Business rule systems (see Chapter 7) can be used to encapsulate data quality expectations as abstract rules that can be used to validate data as it moves from one location to another. For more information on data quality, see Chapter 9.

Data Warehouse

A data warehouse is the primary source of information that feeds the analytical processing within an organization. In Chapter 2 we discussed a number of different analytic applications that are driven by business needs, yet most, if not all, of these applications are driven by the data that has been migrated into a data warehouse.

It is interesting that there is a general consensus as to what constitutes a data warehouse. If you ask a number of experts, you will probably get a variety of answers, but they will focus on the following concepts.

- A data warehouse is a centralized repository of information.

- A data warehouse is arranged around the relevant subject areas important to the corporation as a whole.

- A data warehouse is a queryable source of data for an enterprise.

- A data warehouse is used for analysis and not for transaction processing.

- The data in a data warehouse is nonvolatile.

- A data warehouse is the target location for integrating data from multiple sources, both internal and external to an enterprise.

A data warehouse is constructed using a dimensional model. Information is loaded into the data warehouse after a number of preprocessing steps, including extracting data from the various data sources, data profiling (see Chapter 8), data cleansing (Chapter 9), and a series of transformations (see Chapter 10) that may incorporate the application of business rules (Chapter 7). That data is subsequently reformulated into dimensional form and loaded into the target warehouse. These processes comprise what is referred to as the data warehouse's *backend.*

Once the data is in the warehouse, it may be extracted for canned reporting purposes, be subject to ad hoc querying, or be subject to subsetting for the construction of data marts, (or, conversely, could be virtually constructed as the union of a set of data marts!). Certain OLAP tools may draw their input directly from the data warehouse or from the extracted data marts. The data warehouse is discussed in its appropriate context in Chapter 6.

Dimensional Modeling

An alternate technique to entity relationship modeling of data has evolved that allows for information to be represented in a way that is more suitable to high-performance access. This technique, called *dimensional modeling,* captures the basic unit of representation as a single, multikeyed entry in a slender *fact* table, with each key exploiting the relational model to refer to the different *dimensions* associated with those facts. A maintained table of facts, each of which is related to a set of dimensions, is a much more efficient representation for data in a data warehouse. This is due to the ability to quickly and efficiently create aggregations and extractions of data specific to particular dimensional constraints while aggregating information.

A fact table contains records that refer to observable objects, usually within a business context, and each record contains a key whose components are keys into individual dimension tables along with some specific pieces of information relevant to the fact. By imagining the way that each dimension is linked to facts in the fact table, you can see how the relationships between the fact table and the dimensions resemble a star, which is why this model layout is referred to as a *star join layout* or a *star schema.* Each entry in a dimension represents a description of the individual entities within that dimension.

Using a dimensional model for managing data in a data warehouse has a number of benefits.

- The framework is simple and predictable, which simplifies the process of extracting data, whether through client query tools, user interfaces, or general reporting tools. In fact, there is a generic process for extracting information that relies on the star schema: Create a join between the fact table and the desired dimensions and then group by dimension, which usually requires only a single pass.

- There is no inherent bias toward any individual dimension, which means that as data consumers change their activity or behavior associated with the kinds of analyses or reports they desire, no specific action needs to be taken to "re-balance" the data to improve performance.

- Changes to the model can be handled gracefully without disrupting the operation of the data warehouse. For example, adding new values to a dimension is simply adding new rows to that dimension; adding a new dimension is done by creating the new dimension table and modifying the key values in the fact table to incorporate the references back to the new dimension. Adding new attributes to dimension values is done by altering the tables and adding the new attribute values.

There are variations on the star schema that involve breaking out additional dimension information associated with a preexisting dimension (called *snowflaking*), but the general star schema is a powerful representational abstraction that is ubiquitous in building data warehouses. We discuss dimensional modeling as the structure for data warehouses and data marts in Chapter 6.

Extract/Transform/Load

A basic premise of constructing a data warehouse is that data sets from multiple sources are collected and then added to a data repository from which analytical applications can source their input data. Of course, this sounds much easier than it really is, because although our data warehouse data model may have been designed very carefully with the BI clients' needs in mind, the data sets that are being used to source the warehouse typically have their own peculiarities. Yet not only do these data sets need to be migrated into the warehouse, they will need to be integrated with other data sets either before or during the warehouse population process.

This is usually referred to as the extract/transform/load process, the sequence of applications that extract data sets from the various sources, bring them to a data staging area, apply a sequence of processes to prepare the data for migration into the data warehouse, and then actual loading the data. Here is the general scheme of an ETL process.

- Get the data from the source location.

- Map the data from its original form into a data model that is suitable for manipulation at the staging area.

- Apply any transformations to the data that are required before the data sets are loaded into the repository.

- (*Optional*) Map the data from its staging area model to its loading model.

- Move the data set to the repository and load it.

How data should be extracted may depend on the scale of the project, the number (and disparity) of data sources, and how far into the implementation the developers are. Extraction can be as simple as a collection of simple SQL queries and as complex as to require ad hoc, specially designed programs written in a proprietary programming language. There are tools available to help automate the process, although their quality (and corresponding prices) varies widely.

The transformation process incorporates all the conversions and computations that need to be applied as data moves from its source to its ultimate destination. This includes data type conversion, cleansing, integration, referential integrity checking, derived values, denormalization and renormalization, data aggregation, adding audit trail data, and null conversion.

The loading process is centered on moving the transformed data into the data warehouse, including evaluating target dependencies, actually moving the data into the data warehouse, and deciding on the refresh volume and frequency.

Geographical Information System

A geographical information system is capable of assembling, storing, manipulating, and displaying geographically referenced data. At the lowest level, a GIS presents geographical information as a map, but the power of a GIS lies in the ability to analyze data based on specific location information. For example, a GIS system can help:

- Analyze where a company's customers live.

- Figure out the best place to open a new retail location.

- Determine where and how to allocate maintenance and emergency planning resources.

• Map customers by demographics for the purposes of determining segmented trade areas.

Geographic data represented as those components that compose a map—points, lines, and polygons—is used as the base layer of any GIS presentation. That data to be fed into the system must be enhanced with geographic attribution data, which is a cross between specific location information and attribution based on that location information. That data is then merged with standard GIS mapping data. Business information that contains location information can be enhanced to be compatible with a GIS. Initially, address standardization (see Chapter 13) should be performed, which will ease the assignment of point data. A geographic point is expressed as a (latitude, longitude) pair, frequently referred to as a *LatLong*. Once LatLongs have been assigned, each individual point can be merged with the data composing the base map, which can then be materialized in visual form.

Geographic attribution data provides additional information associated with any point or collection of points or regions within a map. For example, a fast-food chain may be interested in the location of their restaurants. Locations are attributed with information regarding the amount of foot traffic that passes by a location, the number of cars that pass by during different time periods of the day, the amount of office space and residential space that is within certain distances of that location, and the fast-food psychographics associated with the population within that area. All of this information can help determine the best places to open a new restaurant.

Metadata

The standard definition of *metadata* is "data about the data," which unfortunately is not a particularly enlightening description. It is useful to think of metadata as a catalog of the intellectual capital that surrounds the creation, management, and use of a collection of information. That can range from simple observations about the number of columns in a database table to complex descriptions about the way that data flowed from multiple sources into the target database.

The management of metadata is probably one of the most critical tasks associated with a successful BI program, for a number of reasons.

• Metadata encapsulates both the logical and physical business knowledge required to transform disparate data sets into a coherent warehouse.

• Metadata captures the structure and meaning of the data that is being fed into the warehouse

- The recording of operational metadata provides a road map for deriving an information audit trail.

- You can capture differences associated with how data is manipulated over time (as well as the corresponding business rules), which is critical with data warehouses whose historical data spans large periods of time.

- Metadata provides the means for tracing the evolution of information as a way to validate and verify results derived from an analytical process.

Metadata is divided into two areas: technical metadata, which describes the data mechanics, and business metadata, which describes the business perception of that same information.

Technical metadata describes the structure of information, whether it is the data that is sourcing the warehouse or the data in the warehouse. Technical metadata characterizes the structure of data, the way that data moves, and how it is transformed as it moves from one location to another.

Business metadata incorporates much of the same information as the technical metadata, as well as information about how business clients perceive the data, business rules and meanings associated with the data, and reporting directives, among other things. For more information on metadata, see Chapter 6.

Online Analytical Processing

Online analytical processing is distinguished from operational online transaction processing (OLTP). The most frequently used terms to describe OLAP are "multidimensional" and "slice and dice." OLAP tools provide a means for presenting data sourced from a data warehouse or a data mart in a way that allows the data consumer to view comparative metrics across multiple dimensions. In addition, these metrics are summarized in a way that allows the data consumer to *drill down* (which means "to expose greater detail") on any particular value or dimension.

The dimensions of data to be analyzed in an OLAP environment are arranged in a cube (actually, a hypercube) structure, where summaries of any dimension can be seen in the context of other dimensions Typically, values are aggregated up and down each dimension's natural hierarchy. For example, consider a database of sales information that records every sales transaction, including date, time, location, customer, product, quantity, price per product, and total sales. We might configure an OLAP cube with these dimensions:

- Customer
- Sales Location
- Product
- Time

Within these dimensions is a hierarchical structure, such as time periods (hour, day, week, month, quarter, year), sales locations (point of sale, store, city, county, state, region), and product classes (including specialized products such as shampoo, which is contained within the hair-care product class, which is contained within the beauty aids product class). The OLAP environment provides an aggregate view of data variables across the dimensions across each dimension's hierarchy. This might mean an aggregate function applied to any individual column across all the data related to each dimension (such as "total dollar sales by time period" or "average price by region").

Because of the cube structure, there is an ability to "rotate" the perception of the data to provide different views into the data using alternate base dimensions. This conceptual ability to pivot or rotate the data provides the "slice" part; the ability to drill down on any particular aggregation provides the "dice" part.

The value of an OLAP tool is derived from the ability to quickly analyze the data from multiple points of view, and so OLAP tools are designed to precalculate the aggregations and store them directly in the OLAP databases. Although this design enables fast access, it means there must be a significant amount of preparation of the data for the OLAP presentation, as well as a potentially large storage space, because the number of cells within the cube is determined by both the number of dimensions and the size of each dimension. The value of OLAP in the context of a BI environment is discussed in Chapters 4 and 6.

Parallelism

Maintaining large amounts of transaction data is one thing, but integrating and subsequently transforming that data into an analytical environment (such as a data warehouse or any multidimensional analytical framework) requires both a large amount of storage space and processing capability. And unfortunately the kinds of processing needed for BI applications cannot be scaled linearly. In other words, with most BI processing, doubling the amount of data results in dramatically increasing the amount of processing required.

A successful BI strategy encompasses more than just the desired analytical functionality. It must also incorporate expectations about the timeliness of the applications. Luckily, there have been significant innovations in the area of *parallel processing* that allow us to decompose a lot of the processing that can then be farmed out to collections of computers. Whether the size of the input grows or the number of applications grows, the demands on the system may potentially be met by making use of parallel processing.

Within certain constraints, there is an appeal to exploiting multiple processor execution frameworks for a few reasons, among them are the following.

- Loosely coupled parallel systems can be configured using commodity parts; for example, large numbers of homogeneous workstations can easily be networked using high-speed switches.

- Software frameworks can be instituted on top of already available resources to make use of underused computer capability (*cycle stealing*), thereby increasing return on hardware investment.

- Small-scale multiple-processor systems (4–16 processors) are readily available at reasonable prices in configurations that can be expanded by incrementally adding processors and memory.

- Programming languages and libraries (such as C++ and Java) have embedded support for thread- or task-level parallelization, which eases the way for implementation and use.

Parallel computer systems make use of replicated computational and I/O resources to provide scalable improvement in the time required for many of the processes associated with BI: query processing, data profiling, extraction and transformation, data cleansing, and data mining. For more detail on parallelism, see Chapter 11.

Query and Reporting

It is useful to distinguish the packaging and delivery of information from the information that is expected to be inside these delivered reports. Typically, these are the kinds of reporting that would be expected in a BI environment.

- **Standard reporting,** which are meant to convey the status of the business in operation, such as P&L reports, budget versus actual spending, expense reports, and production reports.

- **Structured queries,** which result in exposing specific routine queries such as sales per region. These can be parameterized to allow different clients to modify aspects of the queries for their own personalized use.

- **Ad hoc query systems** that allow the client to formulate his or her own queries directly into the data. Some systems will provide query builders to help those who are not familiar with the query language syntax-assemble proper ad hoc queries.

- **Exception-based reporting,** which alerts individuals to events that have taken place within the environment.

A query and reporting tool is a visual interface that allows the data client to formulate the queries required for a particular business report and then to assemble the report presentation. The tool will mask out the technical details of the data access and configuration and can be used to manage and reuse canned queries or sequences of ad hoc queries.

Index

Enterprise Knowledge Management

The Data Quality Approach

By David Loshin

President, Knowledge Integrity Inc., Silver Springs, Maryland

ENTERPRISE KNOWLEDGE MANAGEMENT

The Data Quality Approach

David Loshin

Your company captures and stores tremendous amounts of information about every aspect of its business. But with this rise in the quantity of information has come a corresponding decrease in its quality. Now more than ever, reversing this trend may spell the difference between success and failure. How can you and your organization respond to this challenge?

Enterprise Knowledge Management gives you just what you need: a precise yet adaptable methodology for defining, measuring, and improving data quality and managing business intelligence. This one-of-a-kind book begins by laying out an economic framework for understanding the real business value of data quality. It then outlines rules for measuring data quality and determining where it can and should be improved. Finally, it teaches proven techniques through which you can achieve meaningful advances in the quality of your business data, including domain- and mapping-based consolidation of enterprise knowledge.

FEATURES

- Expert advice from a highly successful data quality consultant.

- Rigorously methodical in its approach to the problem and the detailed solution it presents.

- Teaches you to measure quality in real business terms and to achieve meaningful, demonstrable improvement.

- Uniquely combines business acumen and technical expertise — an indispensable resource for managers and IT professionals alike.

- Documents the high costs of bad data and details the options available to any company that wants to transform mere data into true enterprise knowledge.

ISBN 0-12-455840-2 • Paperback • 512 pages

Email: custserv.mkp@elsevier.com
Phone: 800.545.2522 / 314.453.7010
Fax: 800.535.9935 / 314.453.7095

MORGAN KAUFMANN PUBLISHERS
AN IMPRINT OF ELSEVIER

WWW.MKP.COM